Developing Web Services with Apache CXF and Axis2

By

Kent Ka Iok Tong

TipTec Development

Publisher:	TipTec Development
Author's email:	freemant2000@yahoo.com
Book website:	http://www.agileskills2.org
Notice:	All rights reserved. No part of this publication may be reproduced, stored in a retrieval system or transmitted, in any form or by any means, electronic, mechanical, photocopying, recording, or otherwise, without the prior written permission of the publisher.
ISBN:	978-0-557-25432-3
Edition:	Third edition Jan 2010

Foreword

Learn web services and Apache CXF and Axis2 easily

If you'd like to learn how to create web services (in particular, using Apache CXF or Axis2) and make some sense of various standards like JAX-WS, JAX-RS, JAXB, SOAP, WSDL, REST, MTOM, WS-Security, WS-Policy, XML Encryption and XML Signature, then this book is for you. Why?

- It has a tutorial style that walks you through in a step-by-step manner.
- It is concise. There is no lengthy, abstract description.
- Many diagrams are used to show the flow of processing and high level concepts so that you get a whole picture of what's happening.
- It contains working code.
- The first two chapters are freely available on http://www.agileskills2.org. You can judge it yourself.

Content highlights in this book

This book covers the following topics not commonly found in other books on Java web services:

- How to work with both Apache CXF 2.2.x and Axis2 1.5.x using standard API (JAX-WS, JAX-RS) as much as possible.
- How to use caching to create scalable RESTful web services.
- How to encrypt and sign SOAP messages using Rampart.
- How to send user authentication information using Rampart.
- How to send and receive binary files using MTOM.
- How to unit test web services.

Target audience and prerequisites

This book is suitable for those who would like to learn how to develop web services in Java.

In order to understand what's in the book, you need to know Java and to have edited XML files. However, you do NOT need to know the more advanced XML concepts (e.g., XML schema, XML namespace), servlet, Tomcat or PKI.

Acknowledgments

I'd like to thank:

- The CXF developers for creating CXF.
- The Axis2 developers for creating Axis2.
- The WSS4J developers for creating WSS4J.
- Anne Thomas Manes, an expert in web services, for reviewing the book (first edition).
- Helena Lei for proofreading this book.
- Eugenia Chan Peng U for doing book cover and layout design.

Table of Contents

Chapter 1

Designing the interface for a simple web service

What's in this chapter?

In this chapter you'll learn how to design the interface for a simple web service.

Providing cross platform operations across the Internet

Suppose that you'd like to provide a service to the public or to some business partners: They can send you two strings and you will concatenate them and return the string. Of course, in the real world you provide a more useful service.

There are several major requirements: First, the users may be using different languages (Java, C# and etc.) and using different platforms (Windows, Linux and etc.). Your service must be accessible by different languages and platforms. Second, they will call your service across the Internet and there may be firewalls in between. Your service must be able to go through firewalls.

Given these requirements, the best solution is to provide a so-called "web service". For example, you may make a web service accessible on the host www.ttdev.com and accessible as /SimpleService (see the diagram below), so the full URL is http://www.ttdev.com/SimpleService. This is called the "endpoint" of the web service. Your web service may support one or more operations. One operation may be named "concat":

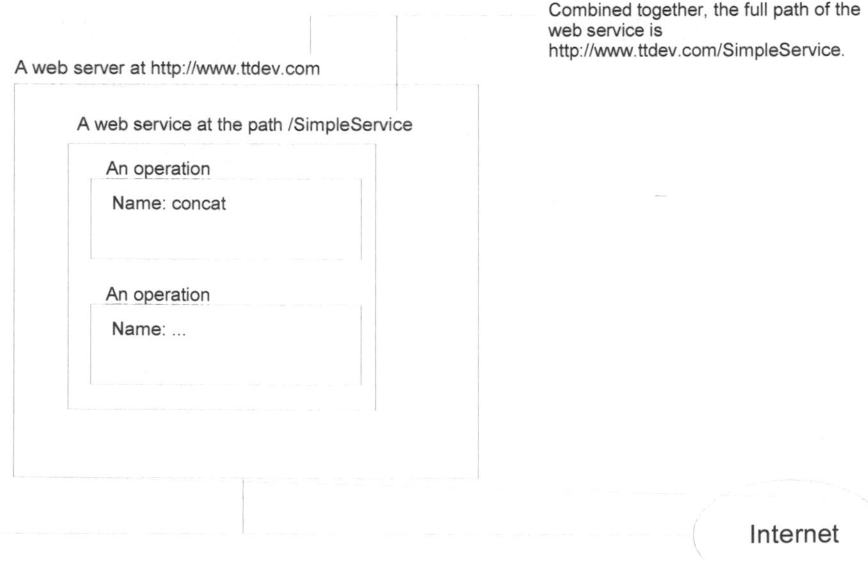

However, you hope to provide a globally unique name to each operation so that you can have your "concat" operation while another person may have his "concat" operation. So, in addition to the name, you may declare that the "concat" name above is in the "namespace" of http://ttdev.com/ss (see the diagram below). A namespace is just like a Java package, but it is not in a dot format like com.ttdev.foo; it is in the format of a URL. So, the full name of the operation will be "concat" in namespace http://ttdev.com/ss. The name "concat" is called the "local name". The full name is called a "QName (qualified name)":

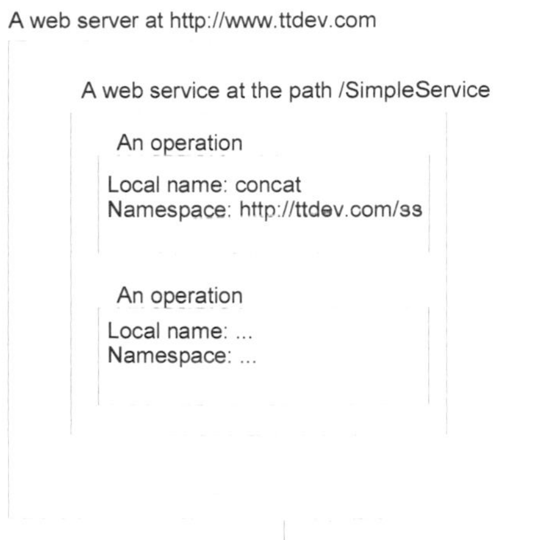

You may wonder what this http://ttdev.com/ss namespace means. The answer is that it has no particular meaning. Even though it is a URL, it does NOT mean that you can use a browser to access this URL to get a web page (if you do, you may get a file not found error). The only important thing is that it must be globally unique. As I have registered the domain name ttdev.com, it must be globally unique.

Note that the namespace is a completely different concept from the endpoint. The endpoint really is the location, while the namespace is just a unique id. I could easily move the web service to another web server and thus it will have a different endpoint, but the namespaces of its operations will remain unchanged.

RPC style web service

Your concat operation may take two parameters. One is named "s1" and is a string. The other is named "s2" and is also a string. The return value is also a string:

An operation

```
Local name: concat
Namespace: http://ttdev.com/ss
Parameters:
   s1: string
   s2: string
Return:
   string
```

However, what does the above "string" type mean? Is it the Java string type? No, you can't say that because it must be language neutral. Fortunately, the XML schema specification defines some basic data types including a string type. Each of these data types has a QName as its id. For example:

Data type	***Local name***	***namespace***
string	string	http://www.w3.org/2001/XMLSchema
integer	int	http://www.w3.org/2001/XMLSchema
...	...	...

So, the interface of your operation should be written as:

An operation

```
Local name: concat
Namespace: http://ttdev.com/ss
Parameters:
   s1: string in http://www.w3.org/2001/XMLSchema
   s2: string in http://www.w3.org/2001/XMLSchema
Return:
   string in http://www.w3.org/2001/XMLSchema
```

Actually, in web services, a method call is called an "input message" and a parameter is called a "part". The return value is called an "output message" and may contain multiple parts. So, it is more correct to say:

An operation

```
Local name: concat
Namespace: http://ttdev.com/ss
Input message:
   Part 1:
      Name: s1
      Type: string in http://www.w3.org/2001/XMLSchema
   Part 2:
      Name: s2
      Type: string in http://www.w3.org/2001/XMLSchema
Output message:
   Part 1:
      Name: return
      Type: string in http://www.w3.org/2001/XMLSchema
```

When someone calls this operation, he can send you an XML element as the input message like:

```
Local name: concat
Namespace: http://ttdev.com/ss
Input message:
   Part 1:
      Name: s1
      Type: string in http://www.w3.org/2001/XMLSchema
   Part 2:
      Name: s2
      Type: string in http://www.w3.org/2001/XMLSchema
Output message:
   Part 1:
      Name: return
      Type: string in http://www.w3.org/2001/XMLSchema
```

There is a child element for each part. Each child element has the same name as that part ("s1" in this case).

The QName of this XML element is exactly that of the operation he is trying to call

foo is a "namespace prefix" representing the http://ttdev.com/ss in the rest of this element including its children.

```
<foo:concat xmlns:foo="http://ttdev.com/ss">
   <s1>abc</s1>
   <s2>123</s2>
</foo:concat>
```

When you return, the output message may be like:

```
Local name: concat
Namespace: http://ttdev.com/ss
Input message:
   Part 1:
      Name: s1
      Type: string in http://www.w3.org/2001/XMLSchema
   Part 2:
      Name: s2
      Type: string in http://www.w3.org/2001/XMLSchema
Output message:
   Part 1:
      Name: return
      Type: string in http://www.w3.org/2001/XMLSchema
```

Each child element has the same name as a part in the output message ("return" in this case).

The QName of this XML element is exactly that of the operation being called

```
<foo:concat xmlns:foo="http://ttdev.com/ss">
   <return>abc123</return>
</foo:concat>
```

This kind of web service is called "RPC style" web service (RPC stands for

"Remote Procedure Call"). That is, the operation QName and the names of the parts are used to create the input and output messages.

Document style web service

The above way is not the only way you design the interface of your web service. For example, you may say that its input message only contains a single part (see the diagram below) which is an element defined in a schema. In that schema, it is defined as an element named "concatRequest" that contains two child elements <s1> and <s2>:

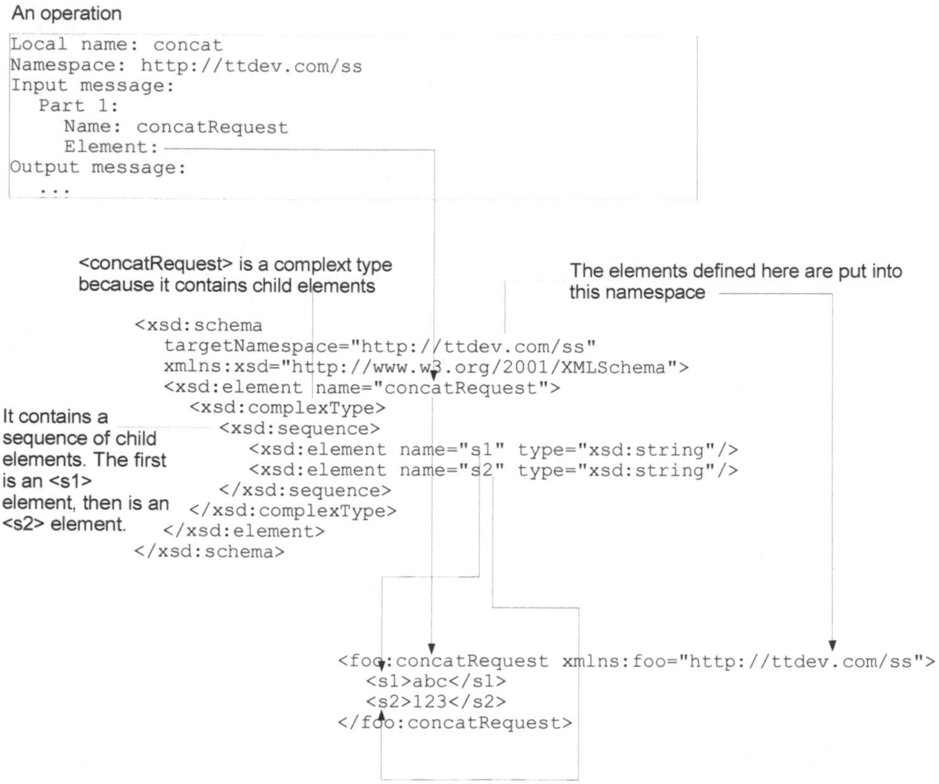

An operation

```
Local name: concat
Namespace: http://ttdev.com/ss
Input message:
   Part 1:
      Name: concatRequest
      Element:
Output message:
   ...
```

<concatRequest> is a complext type because it contains child elements

The elements defined here are put into this namespace

```
<xsd:schema
   targetNamespace="http://ttdev.com/ss"
   xmlns:xsd="http://www.w3.org/2001/XMLSchema">
   <xsd:element name="concatRequest">
      <xsd:complexType>
         <xsd:sequence>
            <xsd:element name="s1" type="xsd:string"/>
            <xsd:element name="s2" type="xsd:string"/>
         </xsd:sequence>
      </xsd:complexType>
   </xsd:element>
</xsd:schema>
```

It contains a sequence of child elements. The first is an <s1> element, then is an <s2> element.

```
<foo:concatRequest xmlns:foo="http://ttdev.com/ss">
   <s1>abc</s1>
   <s2>123</s2>
</foo:concatRequest>
```

Note that the schema is included in the interface of your web service:

A web service

A schema

```
<xsd:schema
  targetNamespace="http://ttdev.com/ss"
  xmlns:xsd="http://www.w3.org/2001/XMLSchema">
  <xsd:element name="concatRequest">
    <xsd:complexType>
      <xsd:sequence>
        <xsd:element name="s1" type="xsd:string"/>
        <xsd:element name="s2" type="xsd:string"/>
      </xsd:sequence>
    </xsd:complexType>
  </xsd:element>
</xsd:schema>
```

An operation

```
Local name: concat
Namespace: http://ttdev.com/ss
Input message:
  Part 1:
    Name: concatRequest
    Element: concatRequest in http://ttdev.com/ss
Output message:
  ...
```

As you can see above, a part may be declared as a particular element (<concatRequest> defined in your schema) or as any element having a particular type (string defined in XML schema specification). In either case it is identified using a QName.

When someone calls this operation, he will send you a <concatRequest> element as the input message like:

```
<foo:concatRequest xmlns:foo="http://ttdev.com/ss">
  <s1>abc</s1>
  <s2>123</s2>
</foo:concatRequest>
```

Similarly, for the output message, you may specify that it contains only one part and that part is a <concatResponse> element:

A web service

A schema

```
<xsd:schema
  targetNamespace="http://ttdev.com/ss"
  xmlns:xsd="http://www.w3.org/2001/XMLSchema">
  <xsd:element name="concatRequest">
    <xsd:complexType>
      <xsd:sequence>
        <xsd:element name="s1" type="xsd:string"/>
        <xsd:element name="s2" type="xsd:string"/>
      </xsd:sequence>
    </xsd:complexType>
  </xsd:element>
  <xsd:element name="concatResponse" type="xsd:string"/>
</xsd:schema>
```

An operation

```
Local name: concat
Namespace: http://ttdev.com/ss
Input message:
  Part 1:
    Name: concatRequest
    Element: concatRequest in http://ttdev.com/ss
Output message:
  Part 1:
    Name: concatResponse
    Element: concatResponse in http://ttdev.com/ss
```

This <concatResponse> element is a "simple type element", meaning that it has no attribute and can't have elements in its body (so only simple string or number in its body).

```
<foo:concatResponse
  xmlns:foo="http://ttdev.com/ss">abc123</foo:concatResponse>
```

This kind of web service is called "document style" web service. That is, the input message will contain a single part only which is well defined in a schema. The same is true of the output message.

If you go back to check the input message for the RPC style service, it should be revised as:

```
<foo:concat>
   xmlns:foo="http://ttdev.com/ss"
   xmlns:xsd="http://www.w3.org/2001/XMLSchema"
   xmlns:xsi="http://www.w3.org/2001/XMLSchema-Instance">
   <s1 xsi:type="xsd:string">abc</s1>
   <s2 xsi:type="xsd:string">123</s2>
</foo:concat>
```

This attribute is used to explicitly state the XML data type of the body of an element ("abc" here). This is useful when the element (<s1>) itself is not defined in a schema. This "type" attribute is defined in the http://www.w3.org/2001/XMLSchema-Instance namespace, so you need to introduce a prefix for it:

This is because <foo:concat>, <s1> and <s2> are not defined in any schema and therefore you must explicitly state the XML element types of the content of <s1> and <s2>.

Now, let's compare the input messages of the RPC style web service and the document style web service:

<table>
<tr><td>RPC style</td><td><pre><foo:concat>
   xmlns:foo="http://ttdev.com/ss"
   xmlns:xsd="http://www.w3.org/2001/XMLSchema"
   xmlns:xsi="http://www.w3.org/2001/XMLSchema-Instance">
   <s1 xsi:type="xsd:string">abc</s1>
   <s2 xsi:type="xsd:string">123</s2>
</foo:concat></pre></td></tr>
<tr><td>Document style</td><td><pre><foo:concatRequest xmlns:foo="http://ttdev.com/ss">
   <s1>abc</s1>
   <s2>123</s2>
</foo:concatRequest></pre></td></tr>
</table>

Not much difference, right? The significant difference is that the former can't be validated with a schema while the latter can. Therefore, document style web service is becoming the dominant style. According to an organization called "WS-I (web services interoperability organization)", you should use document style web services only.

Determining the operation for a document style web service

To call an operation in a document style web service, one will send the single part of the input message only. Note that it does NOT send the operation name in any way. Then if there are more than one operations in the web service (see the diagram below), how can it determine which one is being called? In that case, it will see if the input message is a <concatRequest> or a <someElement> to determine. What if both take a <someElement>? Then it is an error and it won't work:

A web service

A schema

```
...
```

An operation

```
Local name: concat
Namespace: http://ttdev.com/ss
Input message:
   Part 1:
      Name: concatRequest
      Element: concatRequest in http://ttdev.com/ss
Output message:
   ...
```

An operation

```
Local name: bar
Namespace: http://ttdev.com/ss
Input message:
   Part 1:
      Name: barRequest
      Element: someElement in http://ttdev.com/ss
Output message:
   ...
```

Port type

Actually, a web service doesn't directly contain a list of operations. Instead (see the diagram below), operations are grouped into one or more "port types". A port type is like a Java class and each operation in it is like a static method. For example, in the web service above, you could have a port type named "stringUtil" containing operations for strings, while having another port type named "dateUtil" containing operations for dates. The name of a port type must also be a QName:

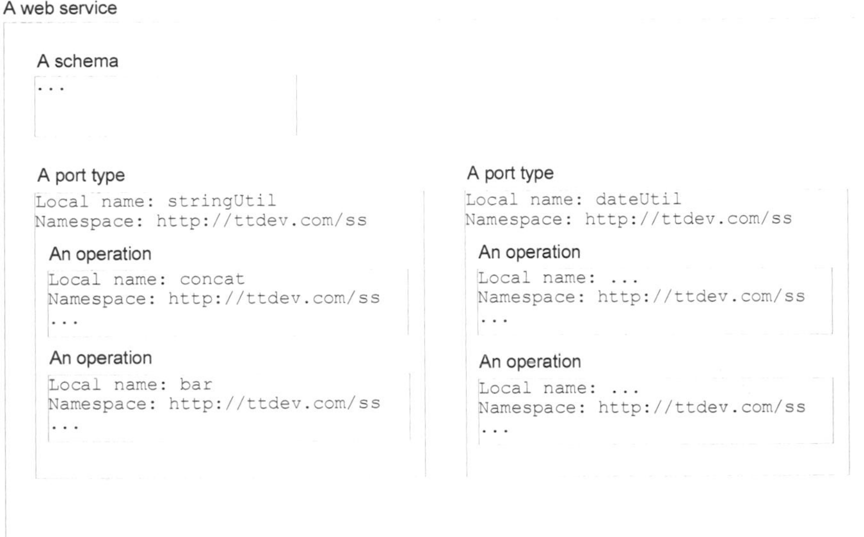

Binding

Actually, a port type may allow you to access it using different message formats. The message format that you have seen is called the "Simple Object Access Protocol (SOAP)" format. It is possible that, say, the stringUtil port type may also support a plain text format:

```
concat(s1='abc', s2='123')
```

In addition to the message format, a port type may allow the message to be carried (transported) in an HTTP POST request or in an email. Each supported combination is called a "binding":

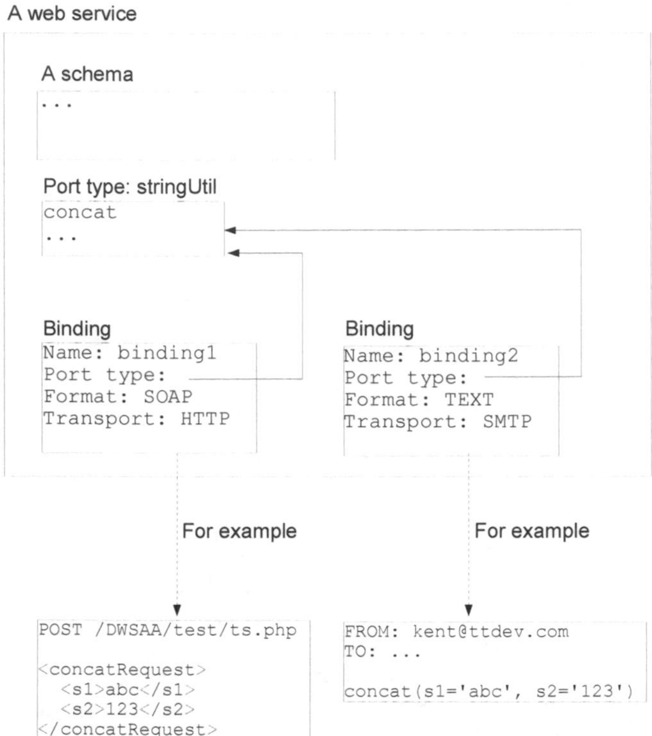

What bindings should your port type support? SOAP+HTTP is the most common combination. So, you should probably use this binding in practice.

Port

Suppose that there are just too many people using your web service, you decide to make it available on more than one computers. For example (see the diagram below), you may deploy the above binding 1 on computers c1, c2 and c3 and deploy binding 2 on c3. In that case it is said that you have four ports. Three ports are using binding 1 and one using binding 2:

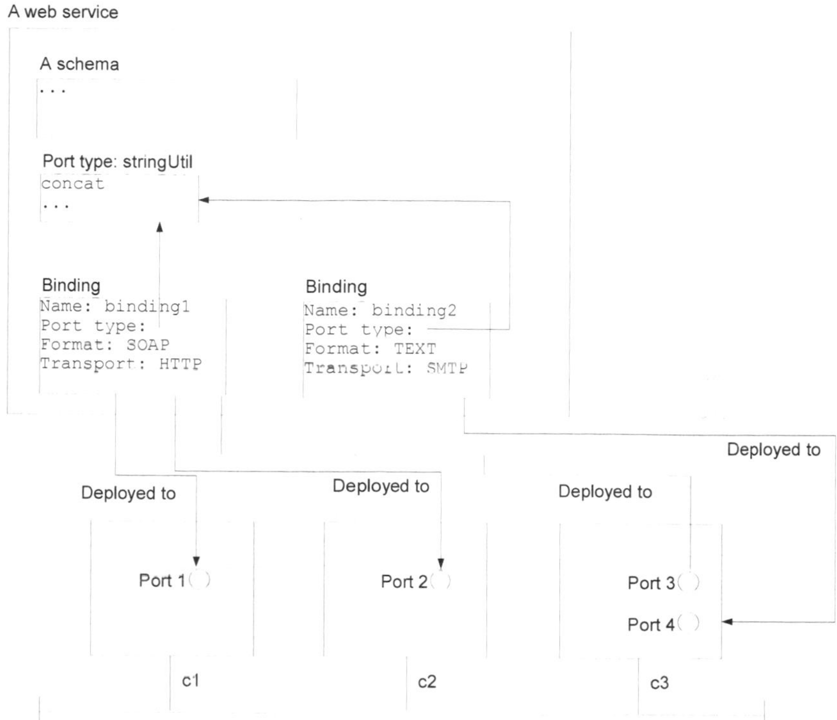

Note that it does NOT mean that the requests received by these three computers will be forwarded to a computer hiding behind for processing. Instead, it means that there is some software implementing the port type installed on these three computers. There is no requirement that the same piece of software is installed onto the different computers. For example, on c1, port 1 may be written in Java, while on c2, port 2 may be written in C#. The important point is that they both support the operations specified in port type stringUtil and the message format and transport specified in the binding 1. Port 4 must also implement the same operations too (same port type) but the message format and transport are different.

To tell others about this arrangement, you include these ports in the interface of the web service:

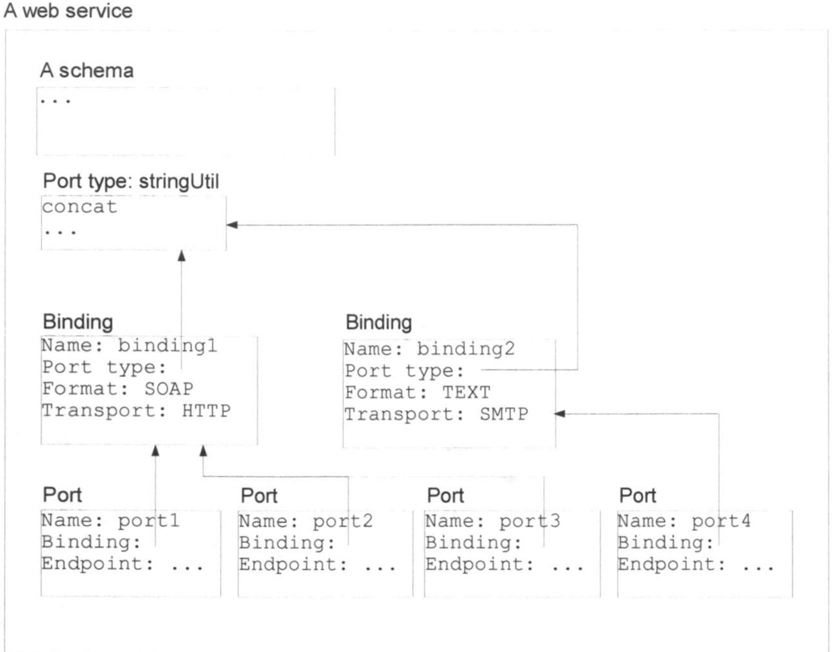

Target namespace

You have been using the same namespace for the operation names, port type names and etc. in this web service. Do they have to be in the same namespace? By default, this is the case: There is a single namespace for a web service to put the names into. This is called the "target namespace" for the web service:

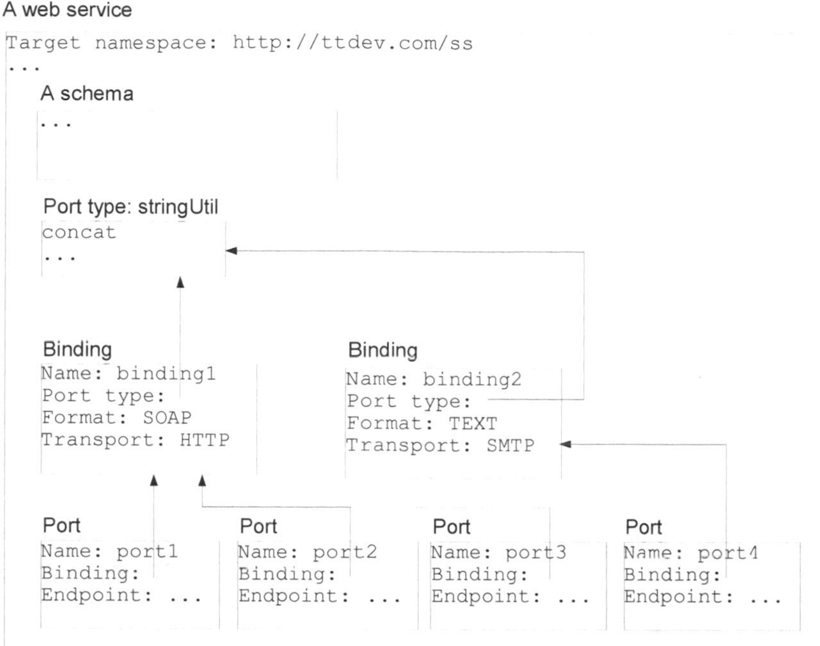

You've been using http://ttdev.com/ss as the target namespace. Is it a good choice? Basically a namespace is good as long as it is globally unique. So this one should be good. However, people may try to download a web page from this URL. When it doesn't work, they may suspect that your web service is out of order. To avoid this confusion, you may use something called URN (Uniform Resource Name) as the namespace.

A namespace must be a URI. URI stands for Uniform Resource Identifier. There are two kinds of URI. One is URL such as http://www.foo.com/bar. The other is URN. A URN takes the format of urn:<some-object-type>:<some-object-id>. For example, International ISBN Agency has made a request to the IANA (International Assigned Numbers Association) that it would like to manage the object type named "isbn". After the request has been approved, the International ISBN Agency can declare that a URN urn:isbn:1-23-456789-0 will identify a book whose ISBN is 1-23-456789-0. It can determine the meaning of the object id without consulting IANA at all.

Similarly, you may submit a request to IANA to register your Internet domain name such as foo.com as the object type. Then on approval you can use URNs like urn:foo.com:xyz to identify an object xyz in your company. What xyz means or its format is completely up to you to decide. For example, you may use urn:foo.com:product:123 (so xyz is product:123) to mean the product #123 produced by your company, or urn:foo.com:patent/123 (so xyz is patent/123) to mean a patent coded 123 in your company.

However, this will create a lot of workload on you and on IANA (one registration per company!). As you have already registered the domain name foo.com, it is unlikely that someone will use it in their URN's. So, you may want to go ahead and use foo.com, or, as many people do, foo-com as the object type without registration with IANA and hope that there won't be any collision.

An XML namespace must be a URI. You can use a URL or a URN. Functionally there is no difference at all. For example, you may use say urn:ttdev.com:ss as the target namespace for your web service instead of http://ttdev.com/ss without changing any functionality.

By the way, if you are going to lookup references on URN, do NOT try to find terms like "object type" or "object id". The official terms are:

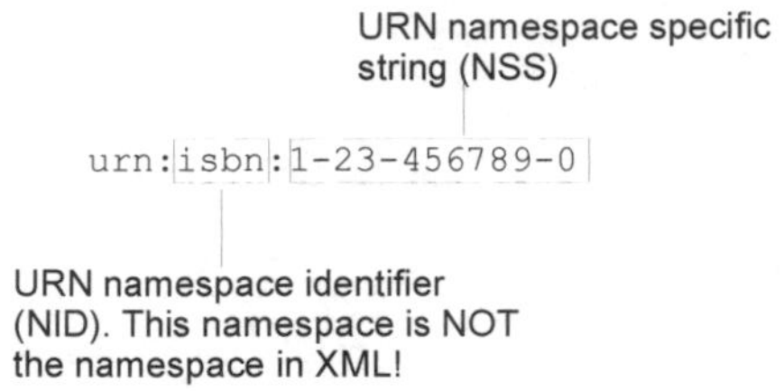

URN namespace specific string (NSS)

```
urn:isbn:1-23-456789-0
```

URN namespace identifier (NID). This namespace is NOT the namespace in XML!

WSDL

By now you have finished designing the interface for your web service:

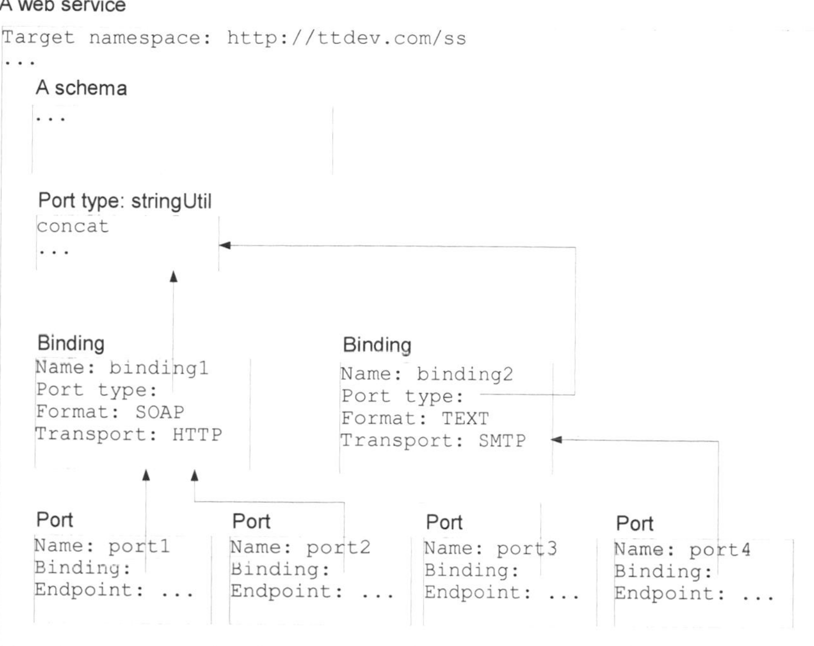

It fully describes your web service. This description language (terms and concepts) is called "WSDL (Web Services Description Language)".

Summary

A web service is platform neutral, language neutral and can be accessed across the Internet.

A web service has one or more ports. Each port is a binding deployed at a certain network address (endpoint). A binding is a port type using a particular message format and a particular transport protocol. A port type contains one or more operations. An operation has an input message and an output message. Each message has one or more parts. Each part is either a certain element defined in the schema of the web service, or any element belonging to a certain element type in that schema. All this information is fully described in WSDL.

To call a RPC style web service, one will create an XML element with the name of the operation and a child element for each of its input message part. To call a document style web service, one will just send the one and only part of its input message. Because the XML element used to call a RPC style web service is not defined in any schema, for better interoperability, one should create document style web services.

The web service, and each of its ports, bindings, port types and operations, has a QName uniquely identifying it. A QName has a local part and an XML namespace. An XML namespace is a URI that is globally unique. By default the names of all these components are put into the target namespace of the web service.

There are two kinds of URI: URL and URN. URN takes the form of urn:<NID>:<NSS>. You can use either as an XML namespace. The only difference is that a URL is suggesting that it is the location of an object, while a URN is purely an id of the object.

Chapter 2

Implementing a web service

What's in this chapter?

In this chapter you'll learn how to implement the web service interface designed in the previous chapter.

Installing Eclipse

You need to make sure you have a recent version Eclipse installed (in this book v3.5 is used) and it is the bundle for Java EE (the bundle for Java SE is NOT enough). If not, go to http://www.eclipse.org to download the Eclipse IDE for Java EE Developers (e.g., eclipse-jee-galileo-SR1-win32.zip). Unzip it into a folder such as c:\eclipse. To see if it's working, run c:\eclipse\eclipse.exe and make sure you can switch to the Java EE perspective:

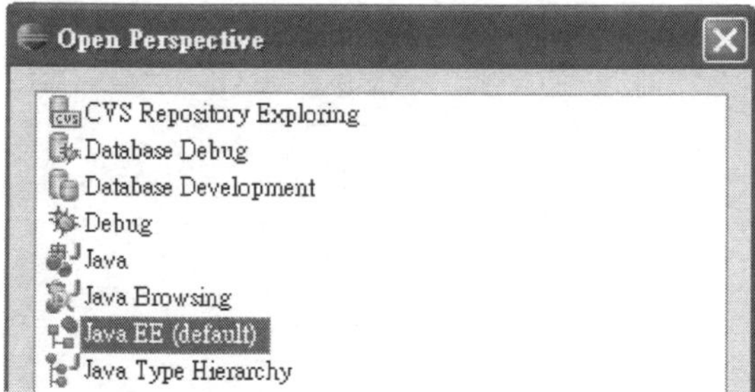

Using a web service library

How to create a web service? You can easily create a Java class that can concatenate two strings together, like:

```
Class Foo {
  String m1(String s1, String s2) {
    ...
  }
}
```

However, when a client calls your web service, it will send a message (probably a SOAP message) as shown below. It will be great if there is a converter that can convert the incoming SOAP message into a Java object and then call a Java object you provide:

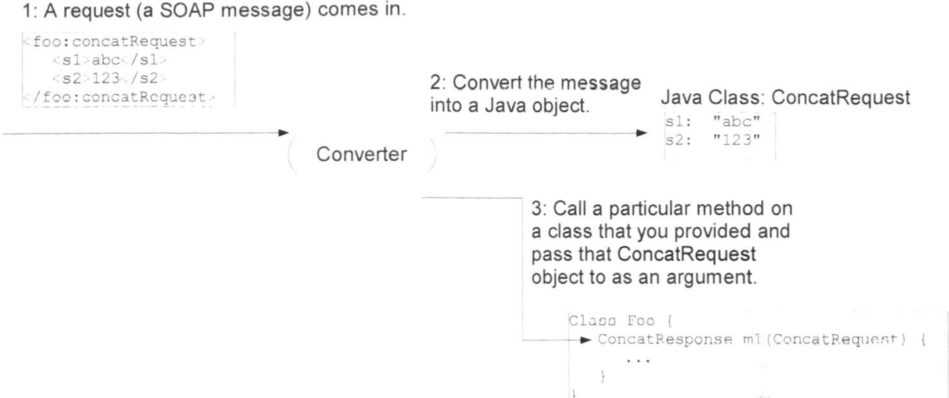
1: A request (a SOAP message) comes in.
<foo:concatRequest>
<s1>abc</s1>
<s2>123</s2>
</foo:concatRequest>
Converter
2: Convert the message into a Java object.
Java Class: ConcatRequest
s1: "abc"
s2: "123"
3: Call a particular method on a class that you provided and pass that ConcatRequest object to as an argument.
Class Foo {
ConcatResponse m1(ConcatRequest) {
...
}
}

The good news is, there are libraries available that can act as such a converter. The most popular ones are Apache CXF, Apache Axis2 and Metro from Sun Microsystems.

Downloading the jar files easily

You're about to download Apache CXF and add its jar files to your Eclipse project. However, CXF itself needs jar files from other 3rd parties so you must download those too.

To do that easily, you can use the Maven2 Eclipse plugin. Once it is installed, you can tell it download CXF. Then it will go to the Internet to download CXF and add its jar files to the classpath of your project. The cool thing is, it will download all jar files needed by CXF automatically. To install this Maven2 Eclipse plugin, choose Help | Install New Software. You'll see:

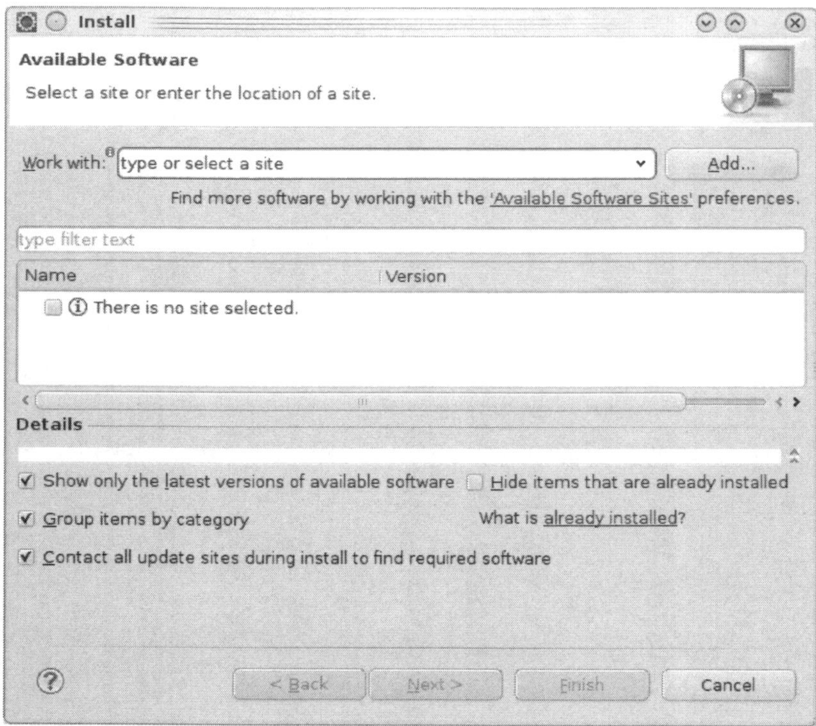

Click Add and define a new update site and input the data as shown below. The name is not really important; the location URL is:

Then choose this m2eclipse site and the available packages on that site will be listed (see below). Choose "Maven integration for Eclipse":

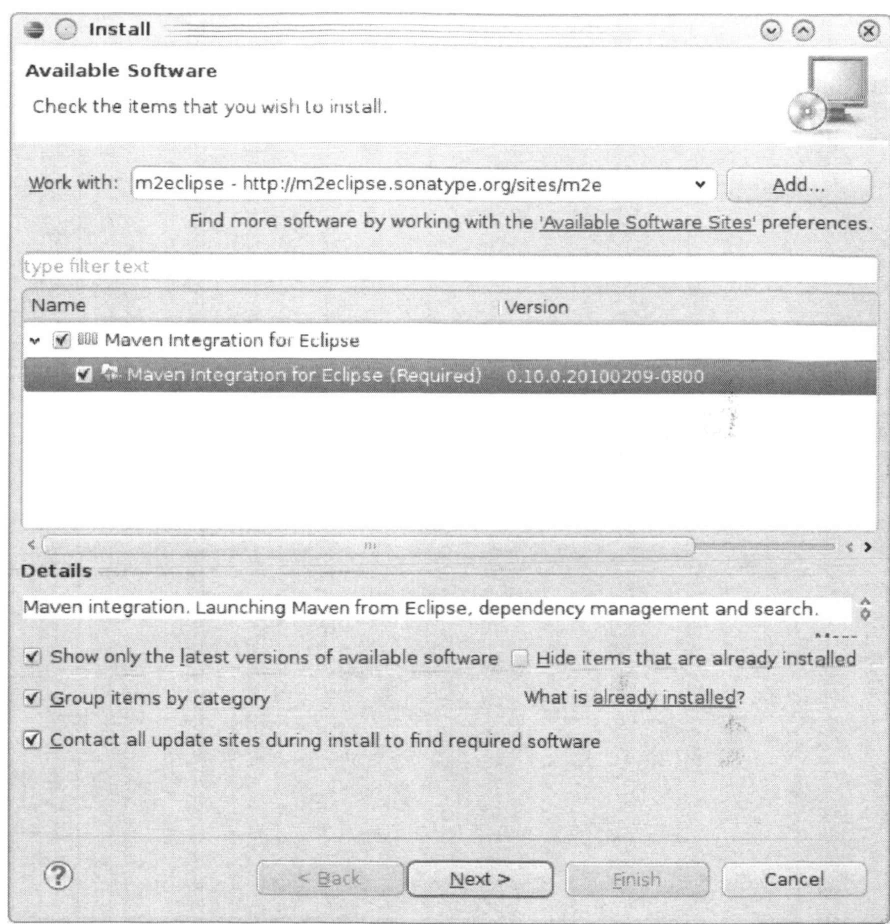

Then continue until you finish the installation. Next, add another site http://m2eclipse.sonatype.org/sites/m2e-extras and choose to install the "Maven integration for WTP":

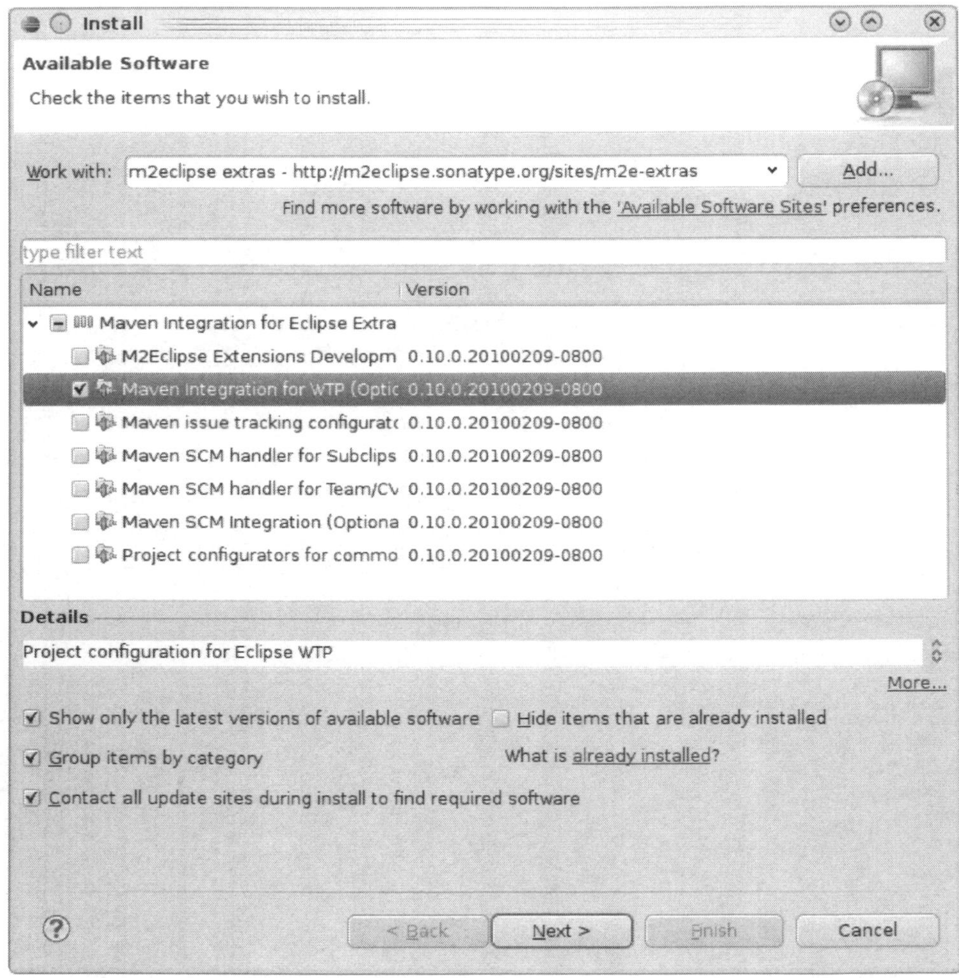

Installing Apache CXF

Note: Even if you are going to use Axis2, you should still follow the steps for working with CXF as many common and important concepts are introduced in the process.

Next, create a Java project as usual in Eclipse. Let's name it SimpleService. Then right click the project and choose Maven | Enable Dependency Management. You'll see:

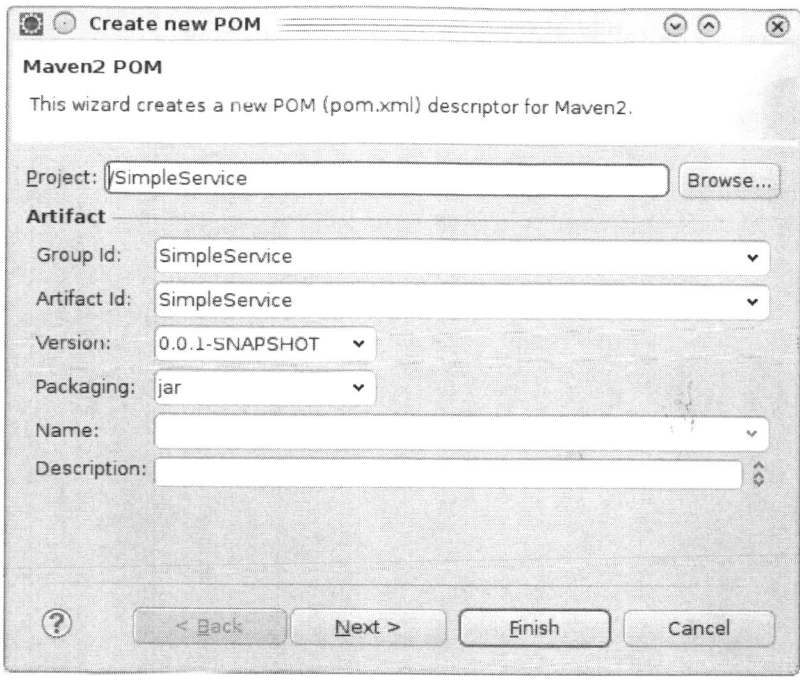

Accept the defaults and click Finish. Then, right click the project and choose Maven | Add Dependency. Enter the "cxf" as the keyword to search for the packages (see below). Then choose the cxf-bundle package:

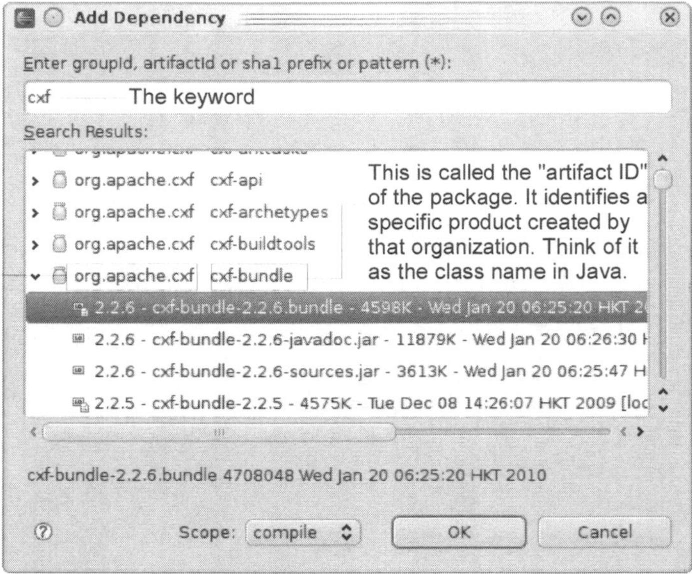

Then open the pom.xml file in the root of your project to make sure that it does NOT contain a line saying <type>bundle</type>. If it does, delete it:

```
<project ...>
  <modelVersion>4.0.0</modelVersion>
  <groupId>SimpleService</groupId>
  <artifactId>SimpleService</artifactId>
  <version>0.0.1-SNAPSHOT</version>
  <dependencies>
    <dependency>
      <groupId>org.apache.cxf</groupId>
      <artifactId>cxf-bundle</artifactId>
      <version>2.2.6</version>
      <type>bundle</type>
    </dependency>
  </dependencies>
</project>
```

Make sure you're connected to the Internet. Then the Maven2 plugin will download all the jar files in Apache CXF and those it needs from a central repository.

In addition, at runtime CXF will perform some logging using the slf4j (simple logging facade for Java) API. The slf4j API works with many different implementations such as log4j or JDK logging. To specify which implementation to use (e.g., log4j), add a new Maven dependency:

Group ID	org.slf4j
Artifact ID	slf4j-log4j12
Version	01/05/10

WSDL file for the web service

Suppose that you'd like to create a web service described in the previous chapter:

```
Target namespace: http://ttdev.com/ss

Schema
<xsd:schema
  targetNamespace="http://ttdev.com/ss
  xmlns:tns="http://ttdev.com/ss"
  xmlns:xsd="http://www.w3.org/2001/XMLSchema">
  <xsd:element name="concatRequest">
    <xsd:complexType>
      <xsd:sequence>
        <xsd:element name="s1" type="xsd:string"/>
        <xsd:element name="s2" type="xsd:string"/>
      </xsd:sequence>
    </xsd:complexType>
  </xsd:element>
  <xsd:element name="concatResponse" type="xsd:string"/>
</xsd:schema>
Port type
Name: ...
Operations:
  Name: concat
  Input msg:
    Part 1:
      Name: concatRequest
      Element: concatRequest element as defined in the schema
  Output msg:
    Part 1:
      Name: concatRequest
      Element: concatResponse element as defined in the schema
Binding
Name: ...
Port type:
Format: SOAP
Transport: HTTP

Port
Name: ...
Binding:
Endpoint: ...
```

To write it using the real WSDL language, it should be:

The names of the port types, operations, bindings and ports will be put into this namespace

All the elements and element types defined in the schema will be put into this namespace

```
<?xml version="1.0" encoding="UTF-8"?>
<wsdl:definitions xmlns:soap="http://schemas.xmlsoap.org/wsdl/soap/"
  xmlns:tns="http://ttdev.com/ss"
  xmlns:wsdl="http://schemas.xmlsoap.org/wsdl/"
  xmlns:xsd="http://www.w3.org/2001/XMLSchema" name="SimpleService"
  targetNamespace="http://ttdev.com/ss">
  <wsdl:types>
    <xsd:schema
      targetNamespace="http://ttdev.com/ss"
      xmlns:tns="http://ttdev.com/ss">
      <xsd:element name="concatRequest">
        <xsd:complexType>
          <xsd:sequence>
          <xsd:element name="s1" type="xsd:string"/>
          <xsd:element name="s2" type="xsd:string"/>
          </xsd:sequence>
        </xsd:complexType>
      </xsd:element>
      <xsd:element name="concatResponse" type="xsd:string"/>
    </xsd:schema>
  </wsdl:types>
  <wsdl:message name="concatRequest">
    <wsdl:part name="concatRequest" element="tns:concatRequest" />
  </wsdl:message>
  <wsdl:message name="concatResponse">
    <wsdl:part name="concatResponse" element="tns:concatResponse" />
  </wsdl:message>
  <wsdl:portType name="SimpleService">
    <wsdl:operation name="concat">
      <wsdl:input message="tns:concatRequest" />
      <wsdl:output message="tns:concatResponse" />
    </wsdl:operation>
  </wsdl:portType>
  ...
</wsdl:definitions>
```

Put the schema into the <types> section

The input message contains a single part. The name of the part is unimportant.

The output message contains a single part. The name of the part is unimportant.

concat operation

This defines the schema and the port type. To define the binding and the port:

```
<?xml version="1.0" encoding="UTF-8"?>
<wsdl:definitions xmlns:soap="http://schemas.xmlsoap.org/wsdl/soap/"
  xmlns:tns="http://ttdev.com/ss"
  xmlns:wsdl="http://schemas.xmlsoap.org/wsdl/"
  xmlns:xsd="http://www.w3.org/2001/XMLSchema" name="SimpleService"
  targetNamespace="http://ttdev.com/ss">
  <wsdl:types>
    ...
  </wsdl:types>
  <wsdl:message name="concatRequest">
    <wsdl:part name="concatRequest" element="tns:concatRequest" />
  </wsdl:message>
  <wsdl:message name="concatResponse">
    <wsdl:part name="concatResponse" element="tns:concatResponse" />
  </wsdl:message>
  <wsdl:portType name="SimpleService">
    <wsdl:operation name="concat">
      <wsdl:input message="tns:concatRequest" />
      <wsdl:output message="tns:concatResponse" />
    </wsdl:operation>
  </wsdl:portType>
  <wsdl:binding name="SimpleServiceSOAP" type="tns:SimpleService">
    <soap:binding style="document"
      transport="http://schemas.xmlsoap.org/soap/http" />
  </wsdl:binding>
  <wsdl:service name="SimpleService">
    <wsdl:port binding="tns:SimpleServiceSOAP"
      name="p1">
      <soap:address
        location="http://localhost:8080/ss/p1" />
    </wsdl:port>
  </wsdl:service>
</wsdl:definitions>
```

The binding uses the SOAP format and HTTP transport. SOAP supports RPC and document styles. Here you use the document style.
This binding implements this port type
The port supports this binding
The port
The endpoint of the port
You'll deploy it on your own computer.
You can use anything as the path, but it is a good convention to include the service name (here a shorthand "ss" is used) and the port name so that, for example, you could deploy another port p2 for the same service on the same host (/ss/p2) or deploy a p1 port for another service (/s2/p1).

In fact, in a SOAP binding, you need to specify some more details:

```
<wsdl:definitions ...>
   ...
   <wsdl:message name="concatRequest">
      <wsdl:part name="concatRequest" element="tns:concatRequest" />
   </wsdl:message>
   <wsdl:message name="concatResponse">
      <wsdl:part name="concatResponse" element="tns:concatResponse " />
   </wsdl:message>
   ...
   <wsdl:binding name="SimpleServiceSOAP" type="tns:SimpleService">
      <soap:binding style="document"
         transport="http://schemas.xmlsoap.org/soap/http" />
      <wsdl:operation name="concat">
         <soap:operation
            soapAction="http://ttdev.com/ss/concat" />
         <wsdl:input>
            <soap:body parts="concatRequest" use="literal" />
         </wsdl:input>
         <wsdl:output>
            <soap:body parts="concatResponse" use="literal" />
         </wsdl:output>
      </wsdl:operation>
   </wsdl:binding>
   ...
</wsdl:definitions>
```

The soap action is used to tell the HTTP server that it is a SOAP message and its purpose. It is up to the HTTP server to interpret the actual meaning. In your case, it is useless because Axis will handle the SOAP message, not Tomcat.

Literal means the message parts are already in XML. No need to convert (encode) it further.

The output message parts listed here will be put into the body of the SOAP response message.

Put the input message parts listed here (just one in this case: the <concatRequest> element) into the body of the SOAP request message:

A SOAP message is like a mail. The outermost is an <Envelope>. The main content is in a <Body>. One or more headers can be put into <Header>.

```
<soap-env:Envelope
   xmlns:soap-env="http://schemas.xmlsoap.org/soap/envelope/">
   <soap-env:Header>
      <...>
      </...>
      <...>
      </...>
   </soap-env:Header>
   <soap-env:Body>
      <foo:concatRequest...>
         <s1>...</s1>
         <s2>...</s2>
      </foo:concatRequest>
      <...>
      </...>
   </soap-env:Body>
</soap-env:Envelope>
```

The <Header> is optional

A "header entry" or "header element". It is used like email headers.

Another header element

It must have a <Body>. The real message content is put there.

This is called a "body entry" or "body element"

Another body element. However, in most cases you should have a single message part and thus a single body element only. Otherwise interoperability will be affected.

RPC version of the web service

If the web service was a RPC style service, then the WSDL file would be like:

```
<wsdl:definitions ...>
  <wsdl:types>
    <xsd:schema ...>
      <xsd:element name="concatRequest">
        <xsd:complexType>
          <xsd:sequence>
            <xsd:element name="s1" type="xsd:string"/>
            <xsd:element name="s2" type="xsd:string"/>
          </xsd:sequence>
        </xsd:complexType>
      </xsd:element>
      <xsd:element name="concatResponse" type="xsd:string"/>
    </xsd:schema>
  <wsdl:types/>
  <wsdl:message name="concatRequest">
    <wsdl:part name="s1" type="xsd:string" />
    <wsdl:part name="s2" type="xsd:string" />
  </wsdl:message>
  <wsdl:message name="concatResponse">
    <wsdl:part name="return" type="xsd:string" />
  </wsdl:message>
  <wsdl:portType name="SimpleService">
    <wsdl:operation name="concat">
      <wsdl:input message="tns:concatRequest" />
      <wsdl:output message="tns:concatResponse" />
    </wsdl:operation>
  </wsdl:portType>
  <wsdl:binding name="SimpleServiceSOAP" type="tns:SimpleService">
    <soap:binding style="rpc"
      transport="http://schemas.xmlsoap.org/soap/http" />
    <wsdl:operation name="concat">
      <soap:operation
        soapAction="http://ttdev.com/ss/concat" />
      <wsdl:input>
        <soap:body parts="s1 s2" use="literal" />
      </wsdl:input>
      <wsdl:output>
        <soap:body parts="return" use="literal" />
      </wsdl:output>
    </wsdl:operation>
  </wsdl:binding>
  ...
</wsdl:definitions>
```

Don't need these any more

The input message has two parts. Each part is of element type xsd:string (not elements).

The output message has one part. It is of element type xsd:string (not elements).

RPC style

Two message parts are listed. So, they will be included into the <Body> (but not directly). As it is a RPC style service, the caller must create an element with the QName of the operation and then add each message part listed here as a child element. So it should still have a single element in the <Body>:

```
<soap-env:Envelope
  xmlns:soap-env="http://schemas.xmlsoap.org/soap/envelope/">
  <soap-env:Header>
    ...
  </soap-env:Header>
  <soap-env:Body>
    <foo:concat ...>
      <s1>...</s1>
      <s2>...</s2>
    </foo:concat>
  </soap-env:Body>
</soap-env:Envelope>
```

No schema to validate it

As RPC style is not good for interoperability, you'll continue to use the document style version.

Creating the WSDL file visually

It may be error prone to manually create such a WSDL file. Instead, you may use the Eclipse to do it. First, create a new folder src/main/resources in the root of your project. Next, right click on that folder and choose New | Other and then Web Services | WSDL:

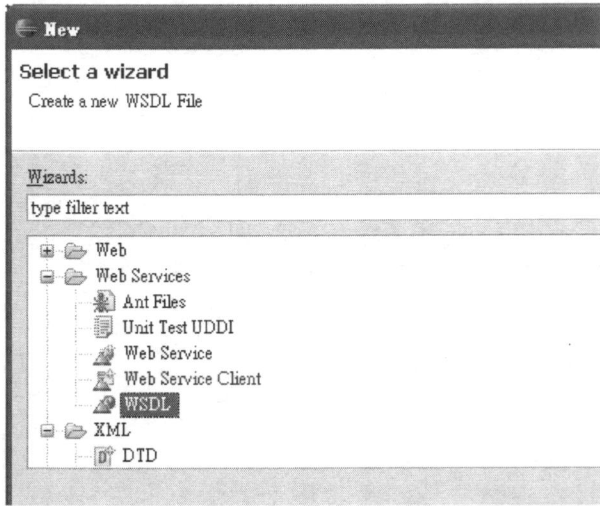

If you don't see this option, it means that you haven't installed the Java EE version of Eclipse. If it is working, click Next and enter SimpleService.wsdl as the filename:

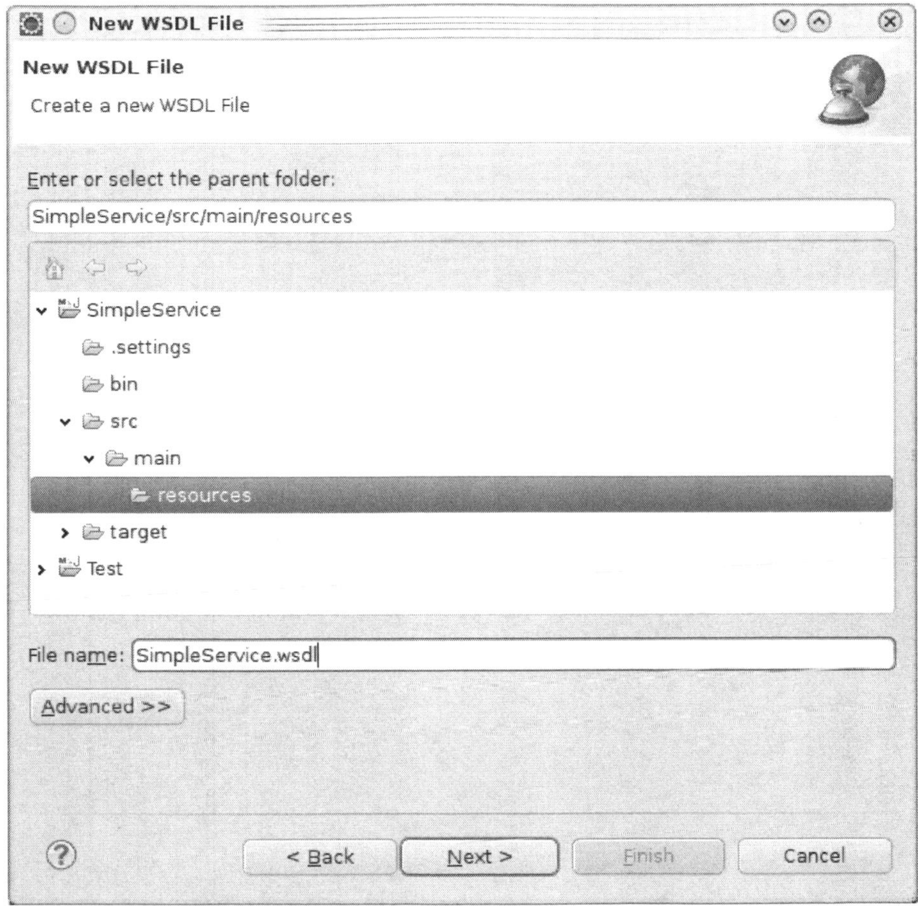

Click Next. Then input as shown below:

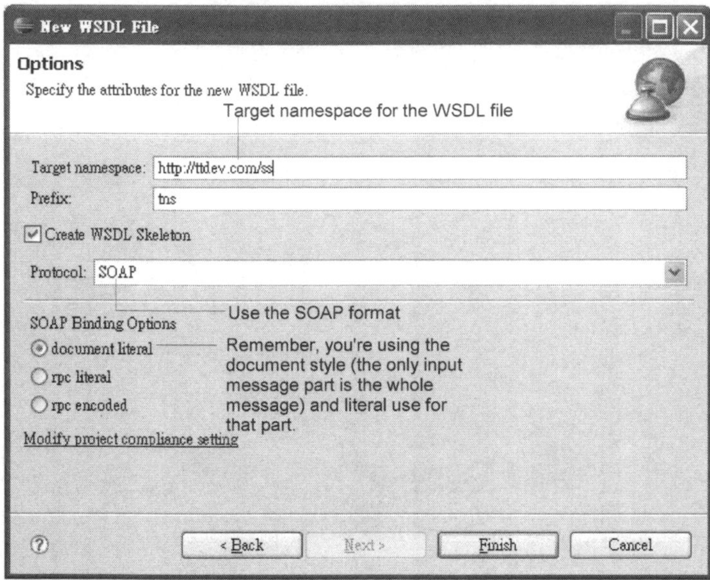

Click Finish. Then you will see something like:

SimpleService.wsdl

```
<?xml version="1.0" encoding="UTF-8"?>
<wsdl:definitions xmlns:wsdl="http://schemas.xmlsoap.org/wsdl/" xmlns:s
  <wsdl:types>
    <xsd:schema targetNamespace="http://ttdev.com/ss" xmlns:xsd="http:/.
      <xsd:element name="NewOperation">
        <xsd:complexType>
          <xsd:sequence>
            <xsd:element name="in" type="xsd:string"/>
          </xsd:sequence>
        </xsd:complexType>
      </xsd:element>
      <xsd:element name="NewOperationResponse">
        <xsd:complexType>
          <xsd:sequence>
            <xsd:element name="out" type="xsd:string"/>
          </xsd:sequence>
        </xsd:complexType>
      </xsd:element>
    </xsd:schema>
  </wsdl:types>
  <wsdl:message name="NewOperationRequest">
    <wsdl:part element="tns:NewOperation" name="parameters"/>
  </wsdl:message>
  <wsdl:message name="NewOperationResponse">
    <wsdl:part element="tns:NewOperationResponse" name="parameters"/>
  </wsdl:message>
  <wsdl:portType name="SimpleService">
    <wsdl:operation name="NewOperation">
      <wsdl:input message="tns:NewOperationRequest"/>
      <wsdl:output message="tns:NewOperationResponse"/>
    </wsdl:operation>
  </wsdl:portType>
```

Design | Source

This is the WSDL code. To edit it visually, click the Design tab at the bottom of the editor window. Then you'll see:

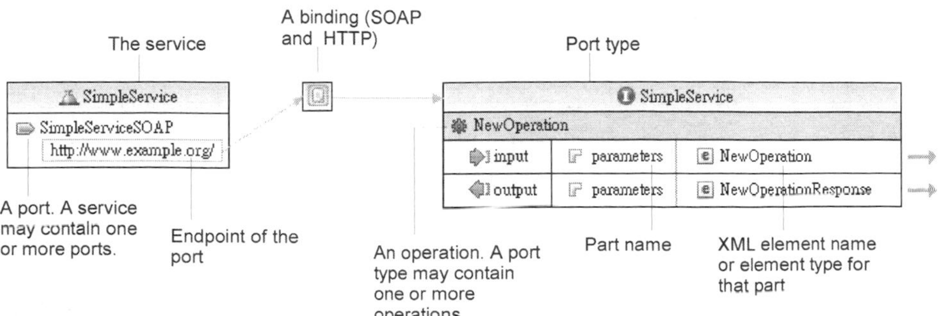

Double click on the endpoint to change it to http://localhost:8080/ss/p1:

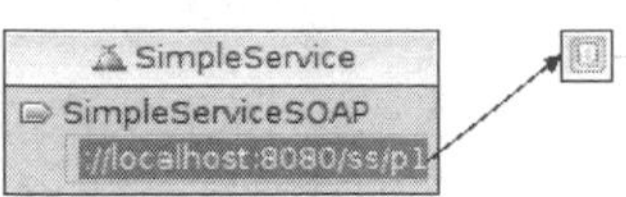

Double click on the name of the port and change it to "p1":

Double click on the name of the operation and change it to "concat":

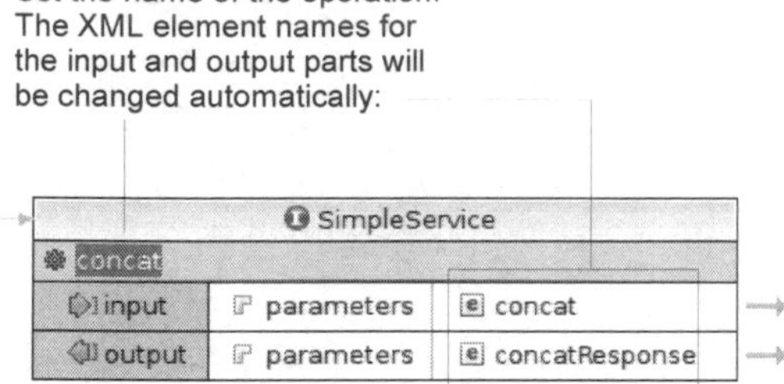

For the moment, the input part is an <concat> element. You'd like to change it to <concatRequest>. But for now, put the cursor on the arrow to its right first. The arrow will turn into blue color. Wait a couple of seconds then a preview window will appear showing the definition of the <concat> element:

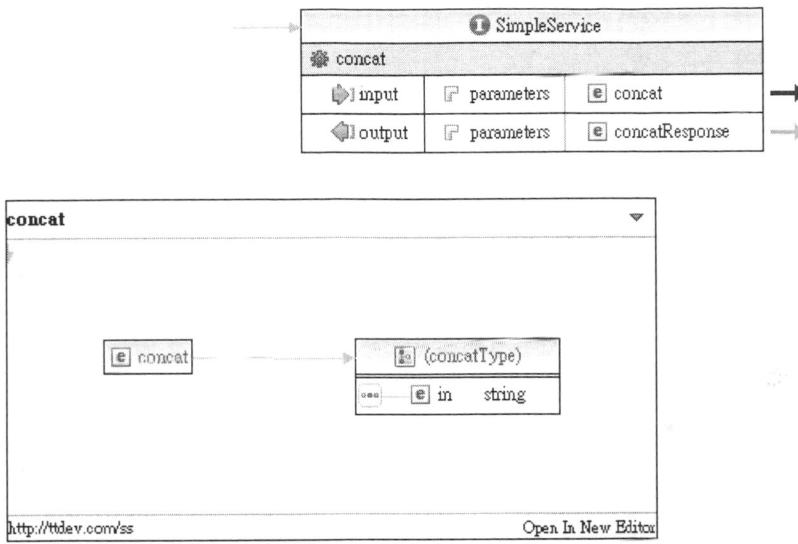

Clicking anywhere else will make that preview window disappear. To edit the schema definition, click on the blue arrow. A new editor window will appear:

```
*SimpleService.wsdl    *Inline Schema of SimpleService.wsdl
<xsd:element name="concat">
  <xsd:complexType>
    <xsd:sequence>
      <xsd:element name="in" type="xsd:string"/>
    </xsd:sequence>
  </xsd:complexType>
</xsd:element>
<xsd:element name="concatResponse">
  <xsd:complexType>
    <xsd:sequence>
      <xsd:element name="out" type="xsd:string"/>
    </xsd:sequence>
```

To edit it visually, click the Design tab at the bottom, you'll see:

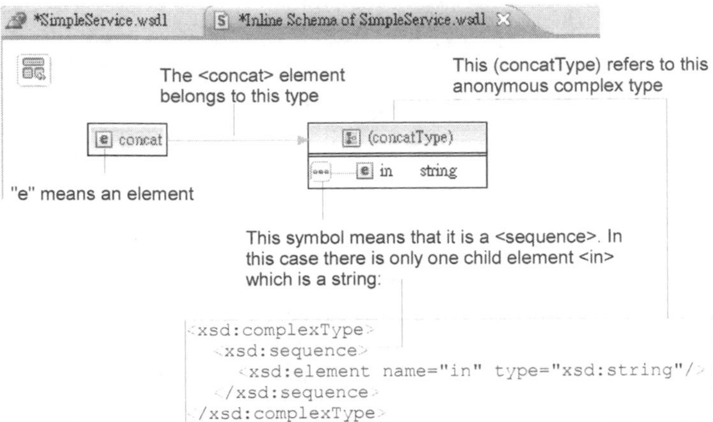

Double click on "in" and change it to "s1":

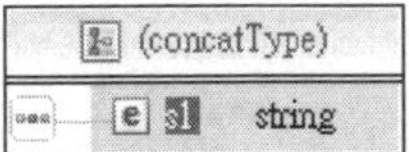

Right click it and choose Insert Element | After and set the name to "s2":

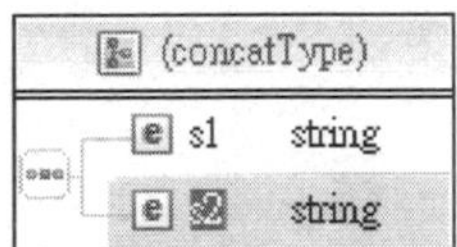

By default the type is already set to string. If you wanted it to be, say, an int instead, you would double click on the type and it would become a combo box and then you could choose "int":

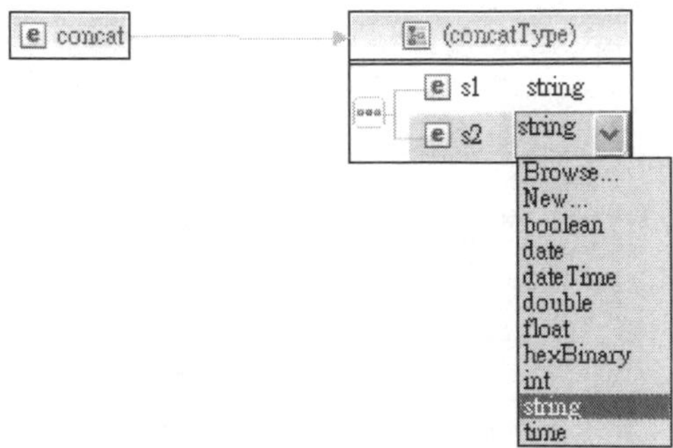

If you wanted s2 to appear before s1 in the sequence, you could drag it and drop it before s1:

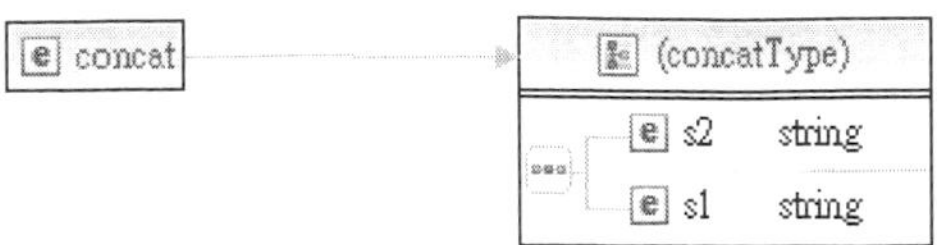

But for now, make sure it is s1 first and then s2. Next, right click on the <concat> element and choose Refactor | Rename, then change its name to concatRequest:

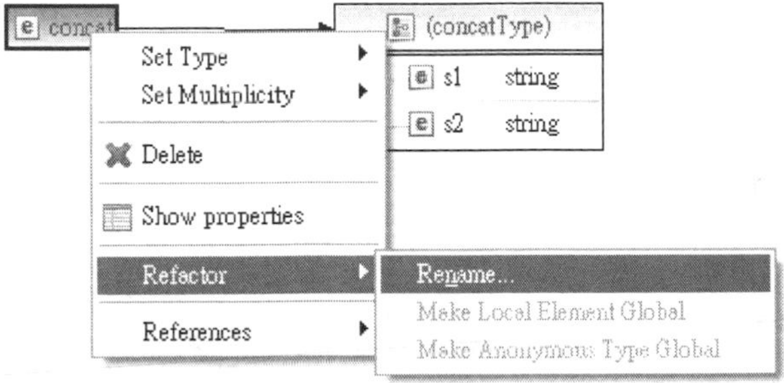

You're done with the <concatRequest> element. Now return to the WSDL editor to work on the response message. For the moment, the <concatResponse> is like:

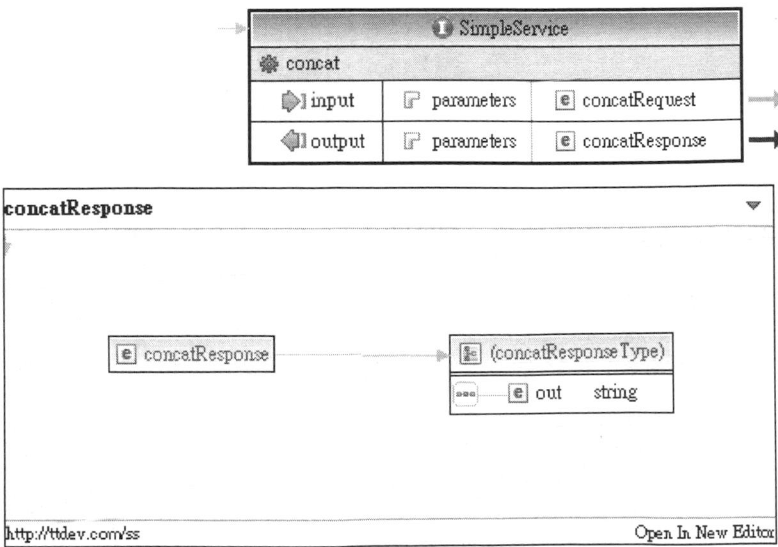

That is, it is an element that contains a sequence of <out> element:

```
<foo:concatResponse>
```

```
    <foo:out>abc</foo:out>
  </foo:concatResponse>
```

However, in your design, the response is simple type element, not a complex type element:

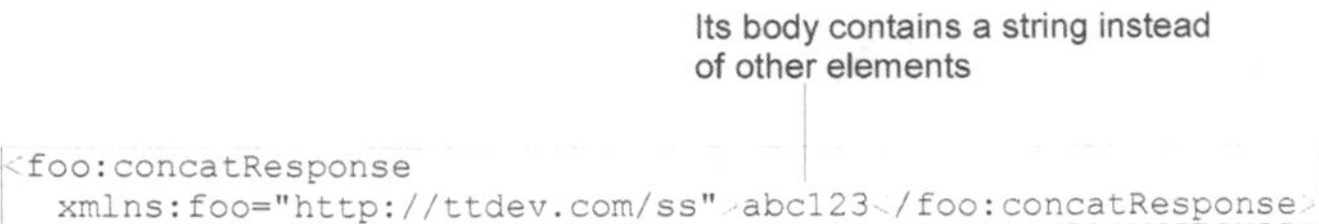

To do that, go into the schema editor to edit the <concatResponse> element:

Right click it and choose Set Type | Browse:

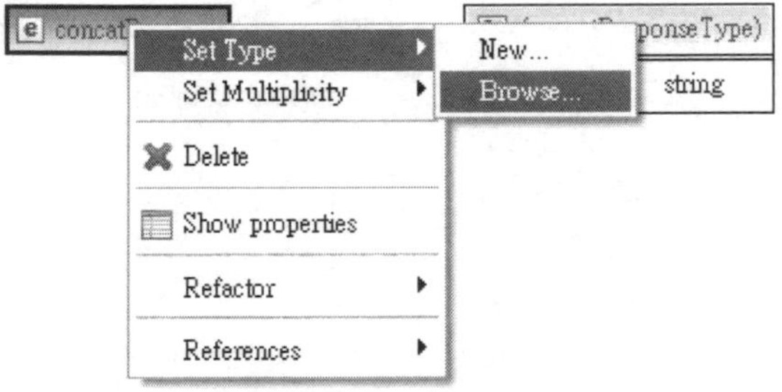

Choose "string":

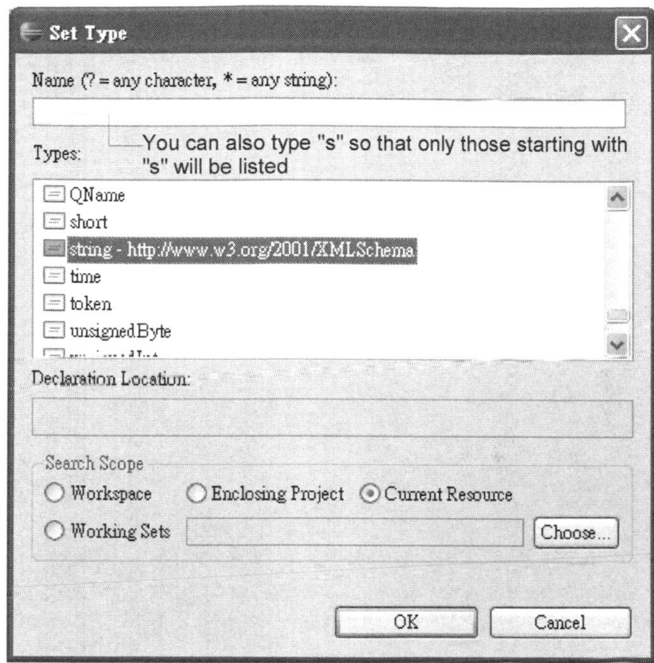

Then it will be like:

That's it. To review the whole schema, click on the icon at the upper left corner:

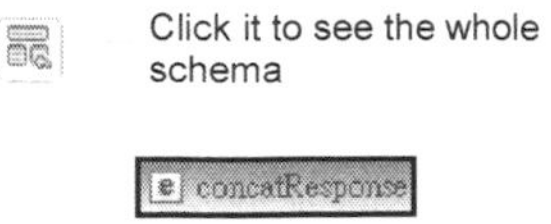

Then you'll see:

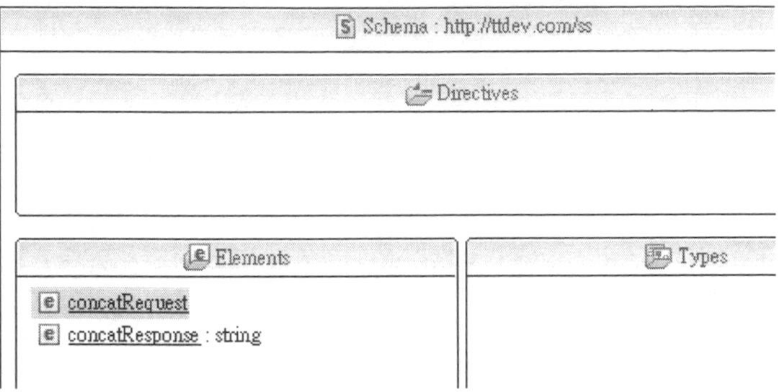
Schema : http://ttdev.com/ss
Directives
Elements
Types
concatRequest
concatResponse : string

This looks fine. Now, save the file.

Validating the WSDL file

The next step is to validate the WSDL file to make sure it conforms to the various web services standards. To do that, right click the SimpleService.wsdl file in Eclipse and choose Validate. If there were anything wrong, they would be reported in the Problems window. For example, here I had introduced an error into the file:

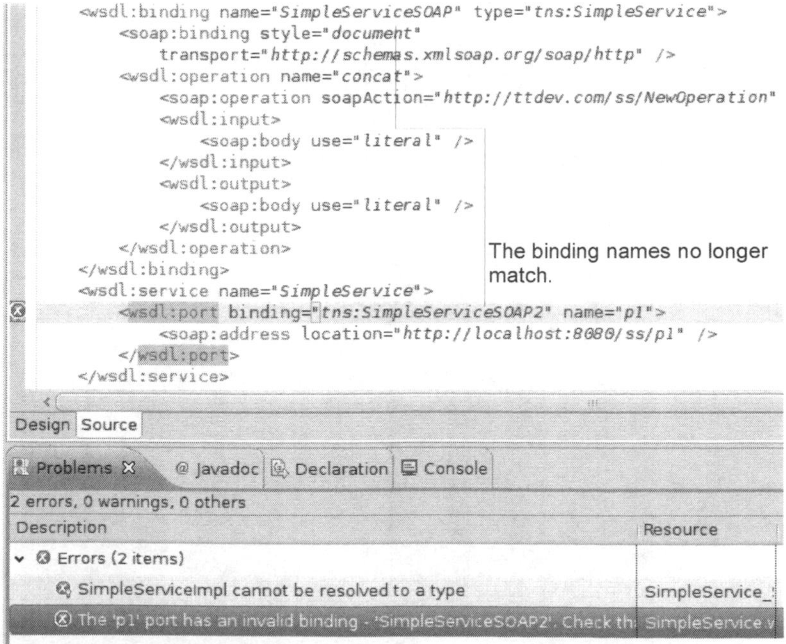
<wsdl:binding name="SimpleServiceSOAP" type="tns:SimpleService">
<soap:binding style="document"
transport="http://schemas.xmlsoap.org/soap/http" />
<wsdl:operation name="concat">
<soap:operation soapAction="http://ttdev.com/ss/NewOperation"
<wsdl:input>
<soap:body use="literal" />
</wsdl:input>
<wsdl:output>
<soap:body use="literal" />
</wsdl:output>
</wsdl:operation>
</wsdl:binding>
<wsdl:service name="SimpleService">
<wsdl:port binding="tns:SimpleServiceSOAP2" name="p1">
<soap:address location="http://localhost:8080/ss/p1" />
</wsdl:port>
</wsdl:service>
The binding names no longer match.
Design
Source
Problems
Javadoc
Declaration
Console
2 errors, 0 warnings, 0 others
Description
Resource
Errors (2 items)
SimpleServiceImpl cannot be resolved to a type
The 'p1' port has an invalid binding - 'SimpleServiceSOAP2'. Check th

Now, correct the error and validate it again. It should pass without any errors.

Generating the service code

As mentioned before, a web service library such as Apache CXF can create a converter to convert an incoming SOAP message into a Java object to be passed as a method argument. To generate this code, create a src/main/java folder and then right click the project root and choose Maven | Update Project Configuration. This will turn that java folder into a source folder in Eclipse (so the Java class files in it will be compiled).

Next, in that src/main/java folder, create a Java class as shown below:

This class comes with Apache CXF. It can be used to convert a WSDL file into Java code.

```
package com.ttdev;

import org.apache.cxf.tools.wsdlto.WSDLToJava;

public class CodeGenerator {
  public static void main(String[] args) {
    WSDLToJava.main(new String[] {
        "-server",
        "-d", "src/main/java",
        "src/main/resources/SimpleService.wsdl" });
    System.out.println("Done!");
  }
}
```

It can be run as a Java application by a user. Here, call its main() method from your own program.

Generate Java code for the server (i.e., the service). If you specify -client, it will generate Java code for the client.

Tell it to put the files into the src/main/java folder. This is a relative path. When this program is run in Eclipse, the current folder will be the project root. So this relative path is correct.

The most important part: Tell the it the path to the WSDL file so that it can read that file. Again, this path is a relative path from the project root.

Run it as a Java application. If you receive an error such as java.lang.AbstractMethodError in a class somewhere inside the org.apache.xerces package, it means that the Xerces library brought in by Apache CXF is too old for your computer (which has its own). To fix this problem, add a new Maven dependency:

Group ID	xerces
Artifact ID	xercesImpl
Version	A recent version such as 2.9.1

After running it successfully, right click the project and choose Refresh. You should see a com.ttdev.ss package has been created and that there are some files in it:

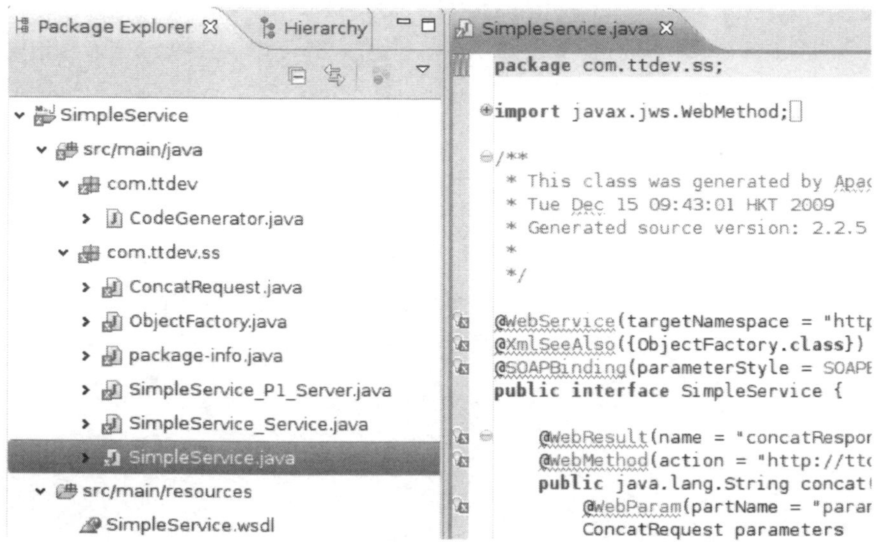

The files are marked as in error because when you updated the project configuration, the Maven Eclipse plugin set the project to use Java 1.4 which doesn't support annotations. To fix the problem, modify the pom.xml file as shown below:

```
<project ...>
  ...
  <dependencies>
    ...
  </dependencies>
  <repositories>
    ...
  </repositories>
  <build>
    <plugins>
      <plugin>
        <groupId>org.apache.maven.plugins</groupId>
        <artifactId>maven-compiler-plugin</artifactId>
        <configuration>
          <source>1.6</source>
          <target>1.6</target>
        </configuration>
      </plugin>
    </plugins>
  </build>
</project>
```

This tells Maven to use Java 1.6 (i.e., Java 6) for this project. Then, update the project configuration again and all the compile errors will be gone except for the SimpleService_P1_Server file, which is a simple class to launch your web service:

```
package com.ttdev.ss;

import javax.xml.ws.Endpoint;

public class SimpleService_P1_Server {

   protected SimpleService_P1_Server() throws Exception {
      System.out.println("Starting Server");
      Object implementor = new SimpleServiceImpl();
      String address = "http://localhost:8080/ss/p1";
      Endpoint.publish(address, implementor);
   }

   public static void main(String args[]) throws Exception {
      new SimpleService_P1_Server();
      System.out.println("Server ready...");
      Thread.sleep(5 * 60 * 1000);
      System.out.println("Server exiting");
      System.exit(0);
   }
}
```

This class is to be implemented by you. It needs to implement the concat() method.

The endpoint address taken from the WSDL file.

This main() method simply launches the server, waits for 5 minutes and then terminates the JVM (and thus ending the HTTP server).

This is the most important part: This method starts an HTTP server on port 8080 (these pieces of information will have been extracted from the endpoint address). If someone sends a request to /ss/p1, it will take it as a SOAP message, try to convert it to a Java object and pass it to the concat() method of the SimpleServiceImpl object.

It is in error because there is no such a SimpleServiceImpl class yet. So, create this class in the com.ttdev.ss package:

The <concatRequest> element will have been converted to an object of this class.

```
package com.ttdev.ss;

public class SimpleServiceImpl implements SimpleService {

  @Override
  public String concat(ConcatRequest parameters) {
    return parameters.getS1() + parameters.getS2();
  }

}
```

Access the <s1> element inside the <concatRequest> element.. As it only contains a string in its body, just access it as a string.

Implement this interface. This interface was generated by WSDLToJava and corresponds to the port type in the WSDL file. It is called the service endpoint interface (SEI).

As these annotations are defined under avax, you can see that they have been standardized. The specification is called JAX-WS (Java API for XML-based Web Services). It means the code here is not limited to CXF.

This annotation marks this interface as corresponding to a port type and attaches information from the WSDL file (e.g., the target namespace).

```
package com.ttdev.ss;

import javax.jws.WebMethod;
import javax.jws.WebParam;
import javax.jws.WebResult;
import javax.jws.WebService;
import javax.jws.soap.SOAPBinding;
import javax.xml.bind.annotation.XmlSeeAlso;

@WebService(targetNamespace = "http://ttdev.com/ss", name = "SimpleService")
@XmlSeeAlso( { ObjectFactory.class })
@SOAPBinding(parameterStyle = SOAPBinding.ParameterStyle.BARE)
public interface SimpleService {

  @WebResult(
    name = "concatResponse",
    targetNamespace = "http://ttdev.com/ss",
    partName = "parameters")
  @WebMethod(action = "http://ttdev.com/ss/NewOperation")
  public java.lang.String concat(
      @WebParam(
        partName = "parameters",
        name = "concatRequest",
        targetNamespace = "http://ttdev.com/ss") ConcatRequest parameters);
}
```

Use SOAP as the message format. You can ignore the parameterStyle for now.

This parameter corresponds to a message part named "parameters" that is an <concatRequest> element.

This method corresponds to an operation in the port type.

In fact, you must also mark your implementation class (SimpleServiceImpl) as a web service and link the SEI (port type) to it:

It is implementing this SEI (port type). Why it doesn't follow the "implements" keyword to find out SEI? If you don't specify the endpoint interface explicitly, CXF will assume that take the public methods defined in this class as the SEI.

This class implements a web service.

```
package com.ttdev.ss;

import javax.jws.WebService;

@WebService(endpointInterface = "com.ttdev.ss.SimpleService")
public class SimpleServiceImpl implements SimpleService {

  @Override
  public String concat(ConcatRequest parameters) {
    return parameters.getS1() + parameters.getS2();
  }
}
```

The ConcatRequest class (also generated by WSDLToJava) is shown below. You can ignore the precise meaning of annotations. Basically they are mapping the Java elements (class, fields) to XML elements (element, child-elements):

```
package com.ttdev.ss;

import javax.xml.bind.annotation.XmlAccessType;
import javax.xml.bind.annotation.XmlAccessorType;
import javax.xml.bind.annotation.XmlElement;
import javax.xml.bind.annotation.XmlRootElement;
import javax.xml.bind.annotation.XmlType;

@XmlAccessorType(XmlAccessType.FIELD)
@XmlType(name = "", propOrder = { "s1", "s2" })
@XmlRootElement(name = "concatRequest")
public class ConcatRequest {

  @XmlElement(required = true)
  protected String s1;
  @XmlElement(required = true)
  protected String s2;

  public String getS1() {
    return s1;
  }
  public void setS1(String value) {
    this.s1 = value;
  }
  public String getS2() {
    return s2;
  }
  public void setS2(String value) {
    this.s2 = value;
  }
}
```

Now, run the SimpleService_P1_Server class as a Java application. You should see some output in the console and finally a "Server ready" message:

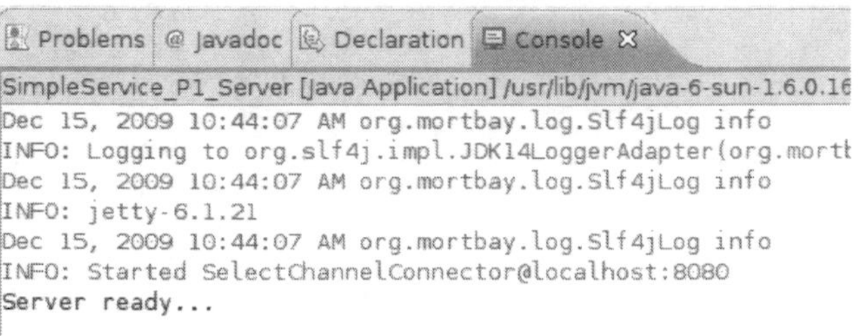

To test if it is working, go to a browser and try to access http://localhost:8080/ss/p1?wsdl (that is, the endpoint address with a query parameter named "wsdl" appended). Then it should return the WSDL file to the browser:

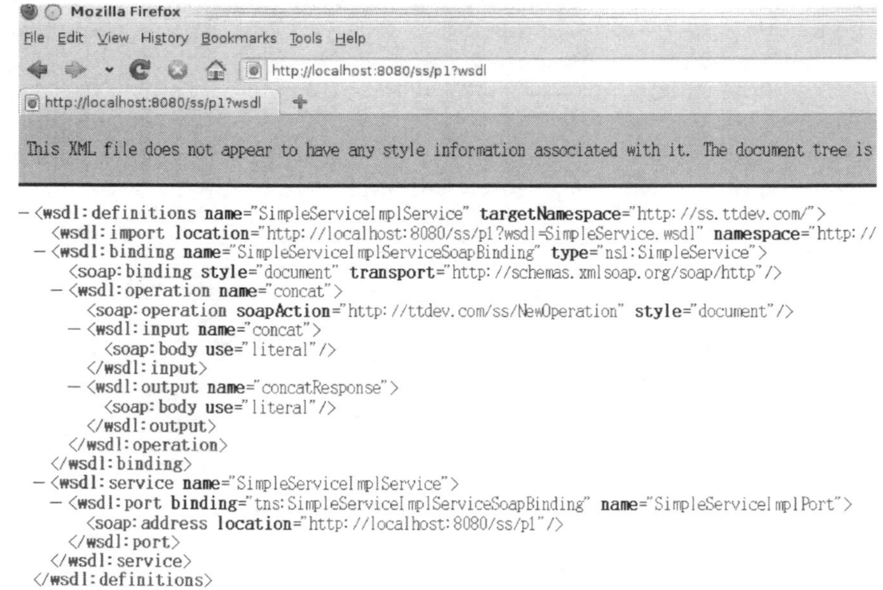

To end the service, just wait 5 minutes or kill the application in Eclipse by clicking the red button in the console window.

Creating a client

To call this web service, again you can ask Apache CXF to generate a converter running on the client side (called a service stub). When you call a method on the stub, it will convert your Java data/objects into the right format (XML) and send it to the real web service. When it gets the response, it will convert it back from XML to Java.

So, copy the SimpleService project and paste it as a new project named

SimpleClient. Then modify the CodeGenerator class so that it converts the WSDL file to Java code for the client, not for the service:

```
package com.ttdev;

import org.apache.cxf.tools.wsdlto.WSDLToJava;

public class CodeGenerator {
  public static void main(String[] args) {
    WSDLToJava.main(new String[] {
        "-client",
        "-d", "src/main/java",
        "src/main/resources/SimpleService.wsdl" });
    System.out.println("Done!");
  }
}
```

Delete the whole com.ttdev.ss as the client shouldn't have access to the code implementing the service (which could have been written in, say, C#); all it has is access to the WSDL file.

Now, run the CodeGenerator class and it should generate some files into the com.ttdev.ss package (refresh the project to see them). Among them, the SimpleService_P1_Client class is the client:

```
package com.ttdev.ss;
...
public final class SimpleService_P1_Client {

   private static final QName SERVICE_NAME = new QName("http://ttdev.com/ss",
        "SimpleService");

   private SimpleService_P1_Client() {
   }
   public static void main(String args[]) throws Exception {
     URL wsdlURL = SimpleService_Service.WSDL_LOCATION;
     if (args.length > 0) {
        File wsdlFile = new File(args[0]);
        try {
           if (wsdlFile.exists()) {
             wsdlURL = wsdlFile.toURI().toURL();
           } else {
             wsdlURL = new URL(args[0]);
           }
        } catch (MalformedURLException e) {
           e.printStackTrace();
        }
     }
     SimpleService_Service ss = new SimpleService_Service(wsdlURL, SERVICE_NAME);
     SimpleService port = ss.getP1();
     {
        System.out.println("Invoking concat...");
        com.ttdev.ss.ConcatRequest _concat_parameters = null;
        java.lang.String _concat__return = port.concat(_concat_parameters);
        System.out.println("concat.result=" + _concat__return);
     }
     System.exit(0);
   }
}
```

This code is to allow you to specify another WSDL file on the command line.

You can specify a path to the WSDL file and the QName of the service (in case the WSDL file contains multiple services). You can simply omit these and use the default.

Create the service stub. It is simulating the service on the client side. This is the most important thing.

Get the p1 port.

Call the operation.

You'll need to create a ConcatRequest object.

The resulting XML element will have been converted into a Java string.

Next, modify the code to create a ConcatRequest object:

```
public final class SimpleService_P1_Client {
```

```
...
public static void main(String args[]) throws Exception {
  ...
  {
    System.out.println("Invoking concat...");
    com.ttdev.ss.ConcatRequest _concat_parameters = new ConcatRequest();
    _concat_parameters.setS1("abc");
    _concat_parameters.setS2("123");
    java.lang.String _concat__return = port.concat(_concat_parameters);
    System.out.println("concat.result=" + _concat__return);
  }
  System.exit(0);
}
}
```

Now, run the service first and then run this client. It should work and print the following output to the console:

```
...
Invoking concat...
concat.result=abc123
```

Controlling the package name

You may wonder why WSDLToJava puts the files into the com.ttdev.ss package. This is because the target namespace of the WSDL file is http://ttdev.com/ss, it simply reverses the domain name and turn the slash(es) into dots:

Of course this is just the default. If you'd like to put them into, say, the com.ttdev.simple package, just invoke the WSDLToJava class like:

```
package com.ttdev;

import org.apache.cxf.tools.wsdlto.WSDLToJava;

public class CodeGenerator {
  public static void main(String[] args) {
    WSDLToJava.main(new String[] {
          "-client",
          "-d", "src/main/java",
          "-p", "http://ttdev.com/ss=com.ttdev.simple",
          "src/main/resources/SimpleService.wsdl" });
    System.out.println("Done!");
  }
}
```

Map this namespace to this package.

Then run it again and it will put the files into the com.ttdev.simple package.

Practical significance of the annotations

You've seen the web service related annotations in the SEI:

```
@WebService(targetNamespace = "http://ttdev.com/ss", name = "SimpleService")
@XmlSeeAlso( { ObjectFactory.class })
@SOAPBinding(parameterStyle = SOAPBinding.ParameterStyle.BARE)
public interface SimpleService {
```

```
    @WebResult(
      name = "concatResponse",
      targetNamespace = "http://ttdev.com/ss",
      partName = "parameters")
    @WebMethod(action = "http://ttdev.com/ss/NewOperation")
    public java.lang.String concat(
        @WebParam(
          partName = "parameters",
          name = "concatRequest",
          targetNamespace = "http://ttdev.com/ss") ConcatRequest parameters);
}
```

Do they serve any practical purpose? For example, when an incoming SOAP message arrives at http://localhost:8080/ss/p1 (see below), CXF will use the relative path in the HTTP request to find the implementor object. But then which which method should it call on that implementor object? It will first try to use the SOAP action HTTP header (only if the HTTP transport is used to send the SOAP message) and use the value to find a method. In this case, it will find the concat() so that it can call that method. What if it didn't match? Then it would use the XML element's QName (concatRequest in the http://ttdev.com/ss namespace) to find a matching method.

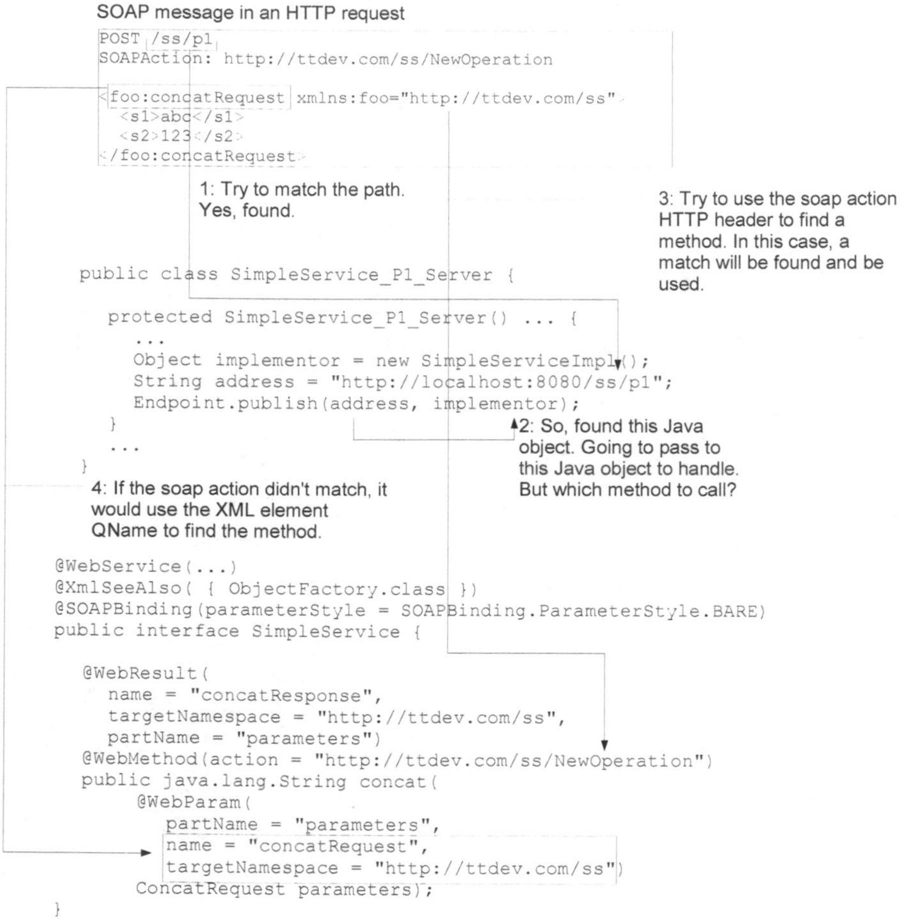

SOAP message in an HTTP request

```
POST /ss/p1
SOAPAction: http://ttdev.com/ss/NewOperation

<foo:concatRequest xmlns:foo="http://ttdev.com/ss">
  <s1>abc</s1>
  <s2>123</s2>
</foo:concatRequest>
```

1: Try to match the path. Yes, found.

3: Try to use the soap action HTTP header to find a method. In this case, a match will be found and be used.

```
public class SimpleService_P1_Server {

   protected SimpleService_P1_Server() ... {
      ...
      Object implementor = new SimpleServiceImpl();
      String address = "http://localhost:8080/ss/p1";
      Endpoint.publish(address, implementor);
   }
   ...
}
```

2: So, found this Java object. Going to pass to this Java object to handle. But which method to call?

4: If the soap action didn't match, it would use the XML element QName to find the method.

```
@WebService(...)
@XmlSeeAlso( { ObjectFactory.class })
@SOAPBinding(parameterStyle = SOAPBinding.ParameterStyle.BARE)
public interface SimpleService {

   @WebResult(
      name = "concatResponse",
      targetNamespace = "http://ttdev.com/ss",
      partName = "parameters")
   @WebMethod(action = "http://ttdev.com/ss/NewOperation")
   public java.lang.String concat(
        @WebParam(
           partName = "parameters",
           name = "concatRequest",
           targetNamespace = "http://ttdev.com/ss")
        ConcatRequest parameters);
}
```

To verify this behavior, try renaming both the SOAP action and the XML local name such as:

```
@WebService(...)
@XmlSeeAlso( { ObjectFactory.class })
@SOAPBinding(parameterStyle = SOAPBinding.ParameterStyle.BARE)
public interface SimpleService {

   @WebResult(
     name = "concatResponse",
     targetNamespace = "http://ttdev.com/ss",
     partName = "parameters")
   @WebMethod(action = "http://ttdev.com/ss/bar")
   public java.lang.String concat(
       @WebParam(
         partName = "parameters",
         name = "baz",
         targetNamespace = "http://ttdev.com/ss")
       ConcatRequest parameters);
}
```

Run the service again. Then run the client and the client will fail as the service will not recognize the message.

Creating the web service with Apache Axis2

If you'd like to use Apache Axis2 instead of Apache CXF, you can follow this section.

First, copy the SimpleService and paste it as a new project named Axis2SimpleService. Then modify the pom.xml file to add the Axis2 dependency (this is an alternative to using the Add Dependency GUI):

```
<project ...>
  ...
  <dependencies>
    <dependency>
      <groupId>org.apache.cxf</groupId>
      <artifactId>cxf-bundle</artifactId>
      <version>2.2.5</version>
    </dependency>
    <dependency>
      <groupId>xerces</groupId>
      <artifactId>xercesImpl</artifactId>
      <version>2.9.1</version>
    </dependency>
    <dependency>
      <groupId>org.apache.axis2</groupId>
      <artifactId>axis2-codegen</artifactId>
      <version>1.5.1</version>
    </dependency>
    <dependency>
      <groupId>org.apache.axis2</groupId>
      <artifactId>axis2-adb-codegen</artifactId>
      <version>1.5.1</version>
    </dependency>
  </dependencies>
  <repositories>
    <repository>
      <id>apache-incubating</id>
      <name>Apache Incubating Repository</name>
      <url>http://people.apache.org/repo/m2-incubating-repository/</url>
    </repository>
  </repositories>
  <build>
    <plugins>
      <plugin>
        <groupId>org.apache.maven.plugins</groupId>
        <artifactId>maven-compiler-plugin</artifactId>
        <configuration>
          <source>1.6</source>
          <target>1.6</target>
        </configuration>
      </plugin>
    </plugins>
  </build>
</project>
```

Save the file. Then the Maven Eclipse plugin will download the files for Axis2. After it's done, modify the CodeGenerator class:

```
package com.ttdev;

import org.apache.axis2.wsdl.WSDL2Code;

public class CodeGenerator {
  public static void main(String[] args) throws Exception {
    WSDL2Code.main(new String[] {
        "-ss",
        "-sd",
        "-S", "src/main/java",
        "-R", "src/main/resources/META-INF",
        "-ns2p", "http://ttdev.com/ss=com.ttdev.ss",
        "-uri", "src/main/resources/SimpleService.wsdl" });
    System.out.println("Done!");
  }
}
```

Put the source files and resource files into these two folders respectively. What is a resource file? By default it will try to copy the WSDL file into there as a resource file.

Generate code for the server side.

Map the namespace to the package. This is not really needed here as it is the default.

Tell it the path to the WSDL file so that it can read that file.

Generate the "service descriptor" file. This file controls how to deploy your service.

Delete the com.ttdev.ss package. Then run the CodeGenerator class. Refresh the project and you should have some files in the com.ttdev.ss package and some files in the src/main/resources/META-INF folder. In particular, the services.xml file is the service descriptor. For now, you don't need to modify it and the default will work just fine.

To implement the web service, modify the SimpleServiceSkeleton class which is the service skeleton:

```
package com.ttdev.ss;

public class SimpleServiceSkeleton {

  public com.ttdev.ss.ConcatResponse concat(
      com.ttdev.ss.ConcatRequest concatRequest) {
    String result = concatRequest.getS1() + concatRequest.getS2();
    ConcatResponse response = new ConcatResponse();
    response.setConcatResponse(result);
    return response;
  }
}
```

To run the web service, you need to run it inside the Axis2 server. To do that, go to http://ws.apache.org/axis2 to download the Standard Binary Distribution (e.g. axis2-1.5.1-bin.zip). Unzip it into, say, a folder named axis in your home folder. To run the Axis server, change into axis/bin and run axis2server.bat. Make sure the JAVA_HOME environment variable has been set to point to the location of your JDK/JRE. When it is started, it should print something like the following to the console:

```
 Using AXIS2_HOME:   /home/kent/axis2-1.5.1
 Using JAVA_HOME:        /usr/lib/jvm/java-6-sun-1.6.0.16
[INFO] [SimpleAxisServer] Starting
[INFO] [SimpleAxisServer] Using the Axis2 Repository/home/kent/axis2-
1.5.1/repository
[SimpleAxisServer] Using the Axis2 Repository/home/kent/axis2-1.5.1/repository
[SimpleAxisServer] Using the Axis2 Configuration File/home/kent/axis2-
1.5.1/conf/axis2.xml
[INFO] Clustering has been disabled
[INFO] Deploying module: mtompolicy-1.5.1 - file:/home/kent/axis2-
1.5.1/repository/modules/mtompolicy-1.5.1.mar
[INFO] Deploying module: script-1.5.1 - file:/home/kent/axis2-
```

```
1.5.1/repository/modules/scripting-1.5.1.mar
[INFO] Deploying module: soapmonitor-1.5.1 - file:/home/kent/axis2-
1.5.1/repository/modules/soapmonitor-1.5.1.mar
[INFO] Deploying module: addressing-1.5.1 - file:/home/kent/axis2-
1.5.1/repository/modules/addressing-1.5.1.mar
[INFO] Deploying module: ping-1.5.1 - file:/home/kent/axis2-
1.5.1/repository/modules/ping-1.5.1.mar
[INFO] Deploying module: metadataExchange-1.5.1 - file:/home/kent/axis2-
1.5.1/repository/modules/mex-1.5.1.mar
[INFO] Deploying module: metadataExchange-1.5.1 - file:/home/kent/axis2-
1.5.1/lib/mex-1.5.1.jar
[INFO] Deploying Web service: version.aar - file:/home/kent/axis2-
1.5.1/repository/services/version.aar
[INFO] [SimpleAxisServer] Started
[SimpleAxisServer] Started
[INFO] Listening on port 8080
```

To deploy your web service, right click the project and choose Run As | Maven package. It will create a file SimpleService-0.0.1-SNAPSHOT.jar in the target folder in your project. This jar file combines the class files compiled from src/main/java and the files in src/main/resources (see below).

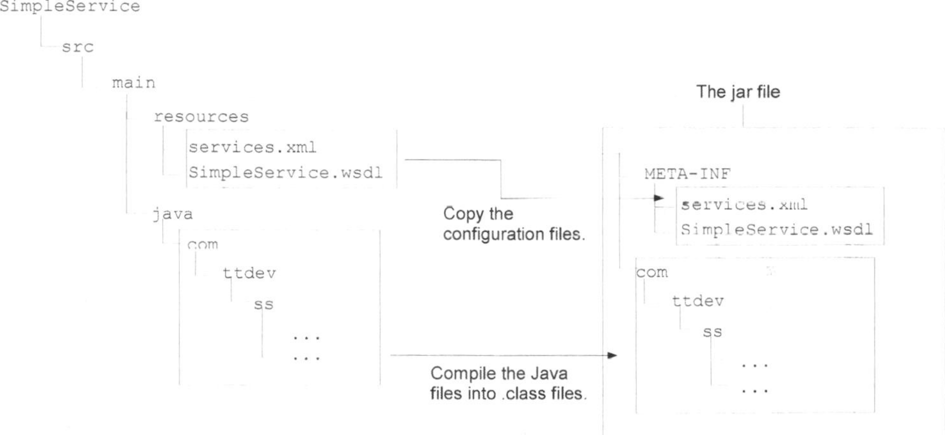

To deploy this jar file, copy it into the axis/repository/services folder and rename rename it to have an .aar extension (aar stands for Axis2 ARchive), such as SimpleService.aar. Note that this can be done while Axis2 server is still running (hot deployment). The Axis2 server will pick up your .aar file and deploy it:

```
...
[INFO] Deploying Web service: SimpleService.aar - file:/home/kent/axis2-
1.5.1/repository/services/SimpleService.aar
...
```

To test it, open a browser and access http://localhost:8080. You should see:

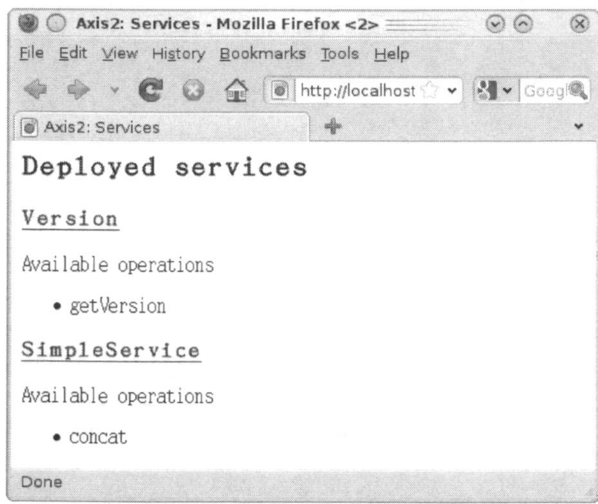

To see its WSDL file, just click the SimpleService link.

Creating a client using Apache Axis2

To create a client using Apache Axis2, copy the Axis2SimpleService project and paste it as a new project named Axis2SimpleClient. Then add two new dependencies in pom.xml:

```
<project ...>
  ...
  <dependencies>
    <dependency>
      <groupId>xerces</groupId>
      <artifactId>xercesImpl</artifactId>
      <version>2.9.1</version>
    </dependency>
    <dependency>
      <groupId>org.apache.axis2</groupId>
      <artifactId>axis2-codegen</artifactId>
      <version>1.5.1</version>
    </dependency>
    <dependency>
      <groupId>org.apache.axis2</groupId>
      <artifactId>axis2-adb-codegen</artifactId>
      <version>1.5.1</version>
    </dependency>
    <dependency>
      <groupId>org.apache.axis2</groupId>
      <artifactId>axis2-transport-http</artifactId>
      <version>1.5.1</version>
    </dependency>
    <dependency>
      <groupId>org.apache.axis2</groupId>
      <artifactId>axis2-transport-local</artifactId>
      <version>1.5.1</version>
    </dependency>
  </dependencies>
  ...
</project>
```

Then modify the CodeGenerator class so that it converts the WSDL file to Java code for the client, not for the service:

```
package com.ttdev;

import org.apache.axis2.wsdl.WSDL2Code;

public class CodeGenerator {
  public static void main(String[] args) throws Exception {
    WSDL2Code.main(new String[] {
        "-ss",
        "-sd",
        "-S", "src/main/java",
        "-R", "src/main/resources/META-INF",
        "-ns2p", "http://ttdev.com/ss=com.ttdev.ss",
        "-uri", "src/main/resources/SimpleService.wsdl" });
    System.out.println("Done!");
  }
}
```

Delete the whole com.ttdev.ss and run the CodeGenerator class. It should generate some files into the com.ttdev.ss package (refresh the project to see them). Among them, the SimpleServiceStub class is the client stub.

Next, create a SimpleClient.java file in the com.ttdev.ss package:

```
<wsdl:definitions ...>
  ...
  <wsdl:service name="SimpleService">
    <wsdl:port binding="tns:SimpleServiceSOAP" name="p1">
      <soap:address
location="http://localhost:8080/ss/p1" />
    </wsdl:port>
  </wsdl:service>
</wsdl:definitions>
```

This is the name of the service as defined in the WSDL file.

```
package com.ttdev.ss;
...
import com.ttdev.ss.SimpleServiceStub.ConcatRequest;
import com.ttdev.ss.SimpleServiceStub.ConcatResponse;

public class SimpleClient {
  public static void main(String[] args) throws RemoteException {
    SimpleServiceStub service = new SimpleServiceStub(
        "http://localhost:8080/axis2/services/SimpleService");
      ConcatRequest request = new ConcatRequest();
    request.setS1("abc");
    request.setS2("123");
    ConcatResponse response = service.concat(request);
    System.out.println(response.getConcatResponse());
  }
}
```

Note that this is the endpoint, not http://localhost:8080/ss/p1. This is because your service must be run inside the Axis2 server and it determines the URL for you.

Run it and it should print "abc123" successfully.

Undeploying a web service from Axis2

If you'd like to undeploy a web service from the Axis2 server, all you need to do is to delete the .aar file. This works even when the Axis2 server is running.

Summary

Most usually your input message or output message is sent in a SOAP message. A SOAP message is always an <Envelope> element. It may contain a <Header> which contains one or more header entries/elements. The <Envelope> must contain a <Body> which may contain one or more body entries/elements. For a document style web service, the one and only input message part is usually the single body entry. For a RPC style web service, the element named after the operation will usually contain all message parts and is then included as the single body entry.

A web service library such as Apache CXF and Axis2 will convert the XML elements in a request message into Java data/objects, pass them to your Java method and convert the Java objects returned back to XML elements and put them into the response message.

To create a web service with Apache CXF, you first create a WSDL file describing its interface. This can be done manually or using a tool like Eclipse. Then run the WSDLToJava class to read the WSDL file to generate the corresponding Java code. This includes a Java interface representing the port type (SEI), a Java class to represent the incoming XML message element, a Java class to represent the outgoing XML message element (if not a simple type like a String), a main program to start the service. Then all you need to do is to create a class to implement that SEI.

The generated Java code, in particular, the SEI contains many standard Java web service annotations to associate information taken from WSDL to the various Java elements (class, fields and etc.). This way, the CXF runtime can find out, say, which method should be called to handle a given SOAP message.

To deploy a web service with CXF, just run the main program. The endpoint is specified by you (in the WSDL file).

To call a web service, run the WSDLToJava class again to generate a service stub simulating the web service on the client side. Then, can create an instance of the service stub and call its methods as if it were the web service. The service stub will convert the Java data/objects into XML elements, create the request message in the right format, send it to the right endpoint using the right transport protocol and convert the XML elements in the response message back into Java data/objects.

Creating a web service with Axis2 is very similar, except that it doesn't use the standard web services annotations. Instead, this mapping information is converted into Java code.

To deploy a web service it with Axis2, package the class files and the services.xml file into a .aar file and copy it into the services folder in Axis2 server. To undeploy a web service, just delete that .aar file. The Axis2 server supports hot deployment. It means you can deploy or undeploy a service while it is running. The endpoint of the deployed web service is http://localhost:8080/axis2/services/<name-of-your-service>.

Chapter 3

Viewing the SOAP messages

What's in this chapter?

In this chapter you'll learn how to capture and view the SOAP messages sent between the client and the web service.

Seeing the SOAP messages

To see the SOAP messages, you'll use a program called "TCP Monitor". It works like this (see the diagram below). You tell the client to treat the TCP Monitor as the destination. Then when the client needs to send the request message, it will send it to the TCP Monitor. Then TCP Monitor will print it to the console and then forward it to the real destination (the web service). When the web service returns a response message, it will return it to the TCP Monitor. It will print it to the console and then forward it to the client:

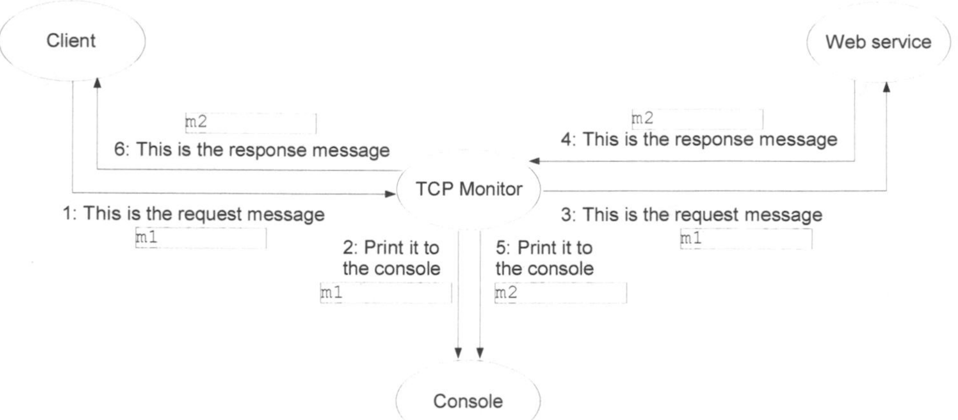

To implement this idea, go to http://ws.apache.org/commons/tcpmon to download the binary distribution of TCP Monitor. Suppose that it is tcpmon-1.0-bin.zip. Unzip it into a folder, say, tcpmon. Then change into the tcpmon/build folder and run tcpmon.bat:

```
C:\>cd tcpmon\build

C:\tcpmon\build>tcpmon.bat
```

Note that directly running tcpmon/build/tcpmon.bat will NOT work; it requires the current folder to be tcpmon/build. Next, you'll see a window. Enter the data as shown below:

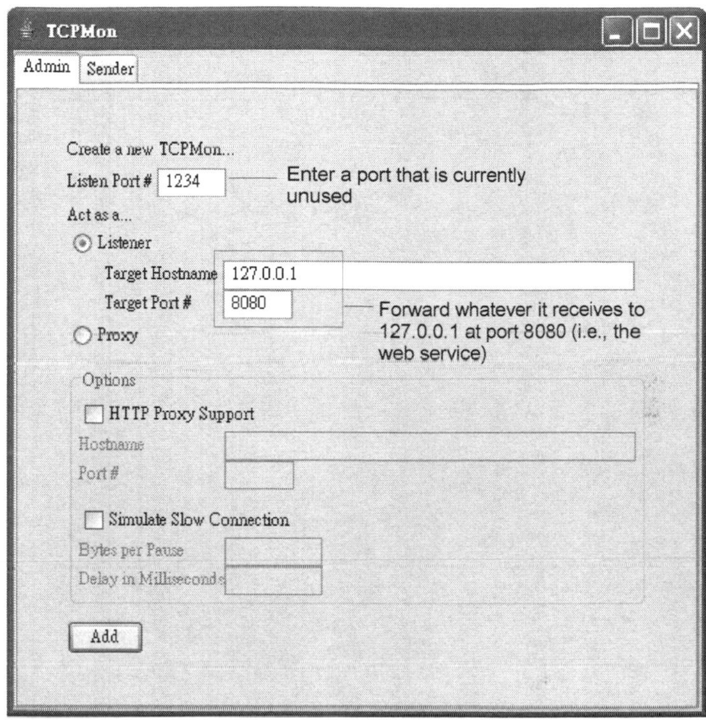

Click Add. This will open a new tab (shown below). Then it will listen on port 1234. Check the XML Format option. This way it will format the content of the TCP connection (an HTTP request containing a SOAP request, but it doesn't know that) nicely as XML:

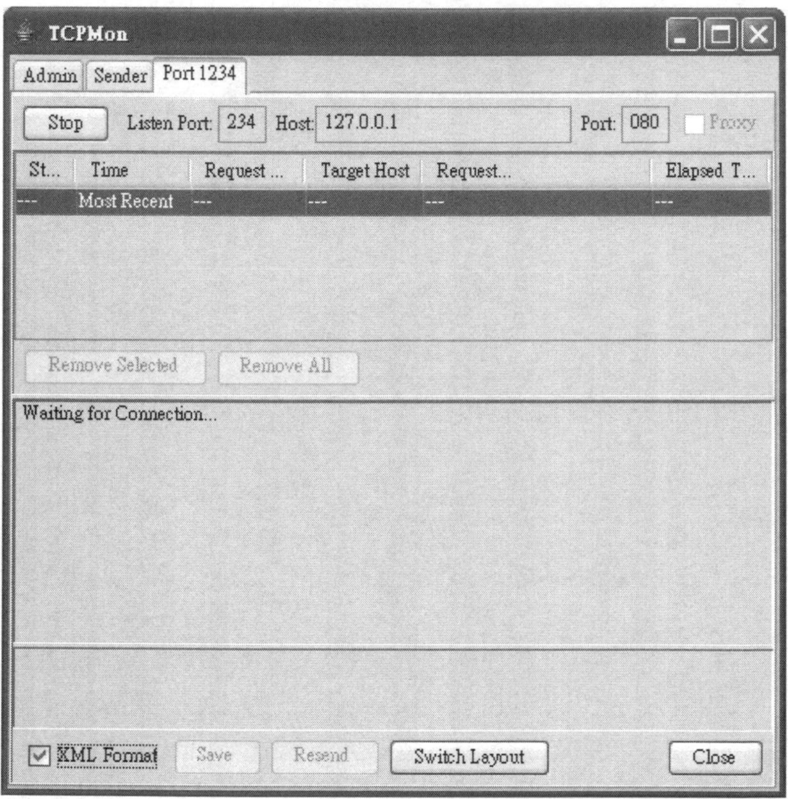

For the client, you need to tell it to use localhost:1234 as the endpoint. For example, modify the SimpleService_P1_Client class as shown below:

```
public final class SimpleService_P1_Client {
   ...
   public static void main(String args[]) throws Exception {
      ...
      SimpleService_Service ss = new SimpleService_Service(...);
      SimpleService port = ss.getP1();
      BindingProvider bp = (BindingProvider) port;
      Map<String, Object> context = bp.getRequestContext();
      context.put(BindingProvider.ENDPOINT_ADDRESS_PROPERTY,
            "http://localhost:1234/ss/p1");
      {
         System.out.println("Invoking concat...");
         ...
      }
      System.exit(0);
   }
}
```

The port object is mainly a proxy for the service at that port (endpoint and binding). Therefore, it contains information about the binding and is called a binding provider in this context..

The binding provider allows you to customize some options regarding the binding (formating and transport) by setting some properties in the "request context".

Here, you set the endpoint address.

Run the client and you will see the messages in TCP Monitor:

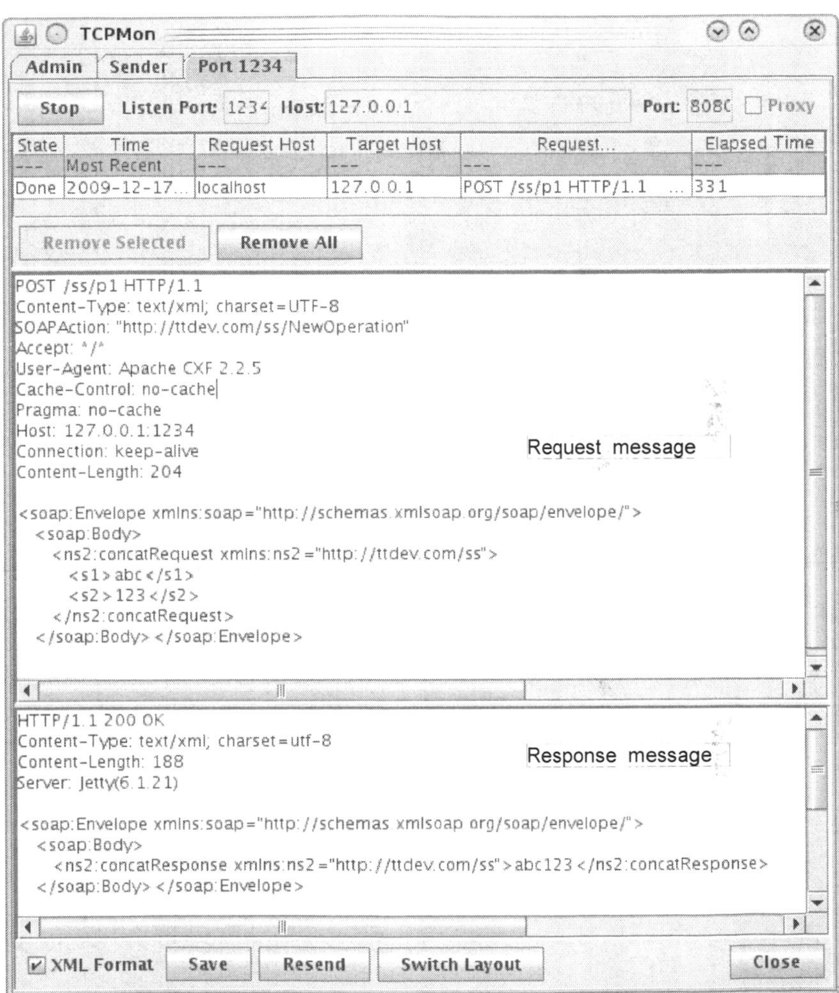

Similarly, for Axis2, you can modify the SimpleClient class to specify the endpoint address:

```
public class SimpleClient {
    public static void main(String[] args) throws RemoteException {
        SimpleServiceStub service = new SimpleServiceStub(
          "http://localhost:1234/axis2/services/SimpleService");
        ConcatRequest request = new ConcatRequest();
        request.setS1("abc");
        request.setS2("123");
        ConcatResponse response = service.concat(request);
        System.out.println(response.getConcatResponse());
    }
}
```

Summary

To check the SOAP messages, you can use the TCP Monitor and modify the client to use a different endpoint address.

To change the endpoint address (part of the binding information), you first obtain the port (a proxy) which is a binding provider. Then configure the request context in it by setting a endpoint address property.

In Axis2, just specify the endpoint address when creating the service stub.

Chapter 4

Accepting multiple parameters

What's in this chapter?

In this chapter you'll learn how to accept multiple parameters in your implementation class.

Splitting the XML element into multiple parameters

For the moment, for the concat operation, the incoming <concatRequest> is converted into a single Java object (ConcatRequest) as pass to the method as the single argument (see below). But wouldn't it be nicer if each child element such as <s1> and <s2> is individually converted into Java objects to be passed as individual arguments? This would make it a little bit easier to write the concat() method as you wouldn't need to call getS1() and getS2() anymore:

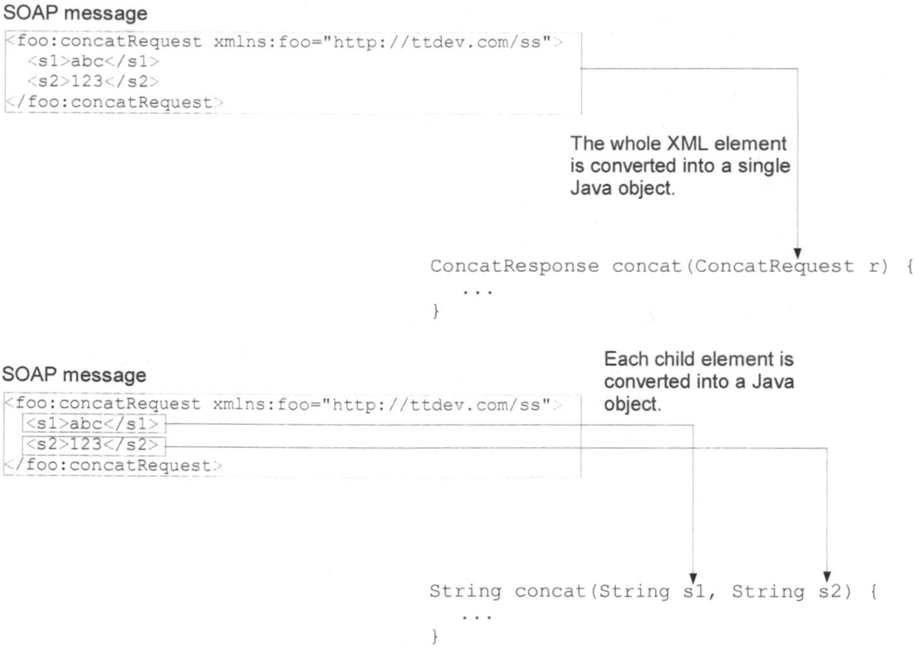

SOAP message

```
<foo:concatRequest xmlns:foo="http://ttdev.com/ss">
  <s1>abc</s1>
  <s2>123</s2>
</foo:concatRequest>
```

The whole XML element is converted into a single Java object.

```
ConcatResponse concat(ConcatRequest r) {
   ...
}
```

SOAP message

```
<foo:concatRequest xmlns:foo="http://ttdev.com/ss">
  <s1>abc</s1>
  <s2>123</s2>
</foo:concatRequest>
```

Each child element is converted into a Java object.

```
String concat(String s1, String s2) {
   ...
}
```

To tell Apache CXF to do that, you need to make two changes to the WSDL file:

```
<?xml version="1.0" encoding="UTF-8"?>
<wsdl:definitions ...>
  <wsdl:types>
    <xsd:schema ...>
      <xsd:element name="concatRequest concat">
        <xsd:complexType>
          <xsd:sequence>
            <xsd:element name="s1" type="xsd:string" />
            <xsd:element name="s2" type="xsd:string" />
          </xsd:sequence>
        </xsd:complexType>
      </xsd:element>
      <xsd:element name="concatResponse" type="xsd:string" />
    </xsd:schema>
  </wsdl:types>
  <wsdl:message name="concatRequest">
    <wsdl:part name="parameters" element="tns:concatRequest concat" />
  </wsdl:message>
  <wsdl:message name="concatResponse">
    <wsdl:part name="parameters" element="tns:concatResponse" />
  </wsdl:message>
  <wsdl:portType name="SimpleService">
    <wsdl:operation name="concat">
      <wsdl:input message="tns:concatRequest" />
      <wsdl:output message="tns:concatResponse" />
    </wsdl:operation>
  </wsdl:portType>
  ...
</wsdl:definitions>
```

The element must be a sequence, which is indeed the case here.

Make sure the element name of that single part in the input message is the same as that of the operation.

Similarly, for the output message, you hope to have Apache CXF wrap the return value as a child element:

SOAP message

```
<foo:concatResponse xmlns:foo="http://ttdev.com/ss">
  <r>abc123</r>
</foo:concatResponse>
```

The return value is converted into a child element.

```
String concat(String s1, String s2) {
  ...
}
```

To do that, in the WSDL file, the element name of the output message must be the name of the operation with the word "Response" appended and it must be a sequence (containing a single child element):

```
<?xml version="1.0" encoding="UTF-8"?>
<wsdl:definitions ...>
  <wsdl:types>
    <xsd:schema ...>
      <xsd:element name="concat">
        <xsd:complexType>
          <xsd:sequence>
            <xsd:element name="s1" type="xsd:string" />
            <xsd:element name="s2" type="xsd:string" />
          </xsd:sequence>
        </xsd:complexType>
      </xsd:element>
      <xsd:element name="concatResponse" type="xsd:string" >
        <xsd:complexType>
          <xsd:sequence>
            <xsd:element name="r" type="xsd:string" />
          </xsd:sequence>
        </xsd:complexType>
      </xsd:element>
    </xsd:schema>
  </wsdl:types>
  <wsdl:message name="concatRequest">
    <wsdl:part name="parameters" element="tns:concat" />
  </wsdl:message>
  <wsdl:message name="concatResponse">
    <wsdl:part name="parameters" element="tns:concatResponse" />
  </wsdl:message>
  <wsdl:portType name="SimpleService">
    <wsdl:operation name="concat">
      <wsdl:input message="tns:concatRequest" />
      <wsdl:output message="tns:concatResponse" />
    </wsdl:operation>
  </wsdl:portType>
  ...
</wsdl:definitions>
```

It must not be a simple type such as string. It must be a sequence.

The sequence must contain a single element. The element name (<r> here) is unimportant.

The element name must be "concat" + "Response", which happens to be the case already.

This style of parameter handling is called wrapped style or wrapper style. In contrast, passing the whole XML element as the single parameter is called the bare style.

Note that this service described by this WSDL file is still a 100% document style service. The clients can still call it the same way (except that <concatRequest> is changed to <concat>). The difference is how the Apache CXF runtime calls your implementation and how it handles your return value. There is no difference seen by the client.

To implement this idea, modify the SimpleService.wsdl file (in the src/main/resources folder):

```
<?xml version="1.0" encoding="UTF-8" standalone="no"?>
<wsdl:definitions xmlns:soap="http://schemas.xmlsoap.org/wsdl/soap/"
  xmlns:tns="http://ttdev.com/ss" xmlns:wsdl="http://schemas.xmlsoap.org/wsdl/"
  xmlns:xsd="http://www.w3.org/2001/XMLSchema" name="WrappedService"
  targetNamespace="http://ttdev.com/ss">
  <wsdl:types>
    <xsd:schema targetNamespace="http://ttdev.com/ss">
      <xsd:element name="concat">
        <xsd:complexType>
          <xsd:sequence>
            <xsd:element name="s1" type="xsd:string" />
            <xsd:element name="s2" type="xsd:string" />
          </xsd:sequence>
        </xsd:complexType>
```

```
      </xsd:element>
      <xsd:element name="concatResponse">
        <xsd:complexType>
          <xsd:sequence>
            <xsd:element name="r" type="xsd:string">
            </xsd:element>
          </xsd:sequence>
        </xsd:complexType>
      </xsd:element>
    </xsd:schema>
  </wsdl:types>
  <wsdl:message name="concatRequest">
    <wsdl:part element="tns:concat" name="parameters" />
  </wsdl:message>
  <wsdl:message name="concatResponse">
    <wsdl:part element="tns:concatResponse" name="parameters" />
  </wsdl:message>
  <wsdl:portType name="WrappedService">
    <wsdl:operation name="concat">
      <wsdl:input message="tns:concatRequest" />
      <wsdl:output message="tns:concatResponse" />
    </wsdl:operation>
  </wsdl:portType>
  <wsdl:binding name="WrappedServiceSOAP" type="tns:WrappedService">
    <soap:binding style="document"
      transport="http://schemas.xmlsoap.org/soap/http" />
    <wsdl:operation name="concat">
      <soap:operation soapAction="http://ttdev.com/ss/NewOperation" />
      <wsdl:input>
        <soap:body use="literal" />
      </wsdl:input>
      <wsdl:output>
        <soap:body use="literal" />
      </wsdl:output>
    </wsdl:operation>
  </wsdl:binding>
  <wsdl:service name="WrappedService">
    <wsdl:port binding="tns:WrappedServiceSOAP" name="p1">
      <soap:address location="http://localhost:8080/ss/p1" />
    </wsdl:port>
  </wsdl:service>
</wsdl:definitions>
```

Delete the whole com.ttdev.ss package and then run the CodeGenerator program again. Note the SEI generated (the WrappedService interface):

```
@WebService(targetNamespace = "http://ttdev.com/ss", name = "WrappedService")
@XmlSeeAlso( { ObjectFactory.class })
public interface WrappedService {

   @WebResult(name = "r", targetNamespace = "")
   @RequestWrapper(
     localName = "concat",
     targetNamespace = "http://ttdev.com/ss",
     className = "com.ttdev.ss.Concat")
   @ResponseWrapper(
     localName = "concatResponse",
     targetNamespace = "http://ttdev.com/ss",
     className = "com.ttdev.ss.ConcatResponse")
   @WebMethod(action = "http://ttdev.com/ss/NewOperation")
   public java.lang.String concat(
        @WebParam(name = "s1", targetNamespace = "") java.lang.String s1,
        @WebParam(name = "s2", targetNamespace = "") java.lang.String s2);
}
```

It tells CXF that when a <concat> element is received, unwrap it to get its child elements and pass them to this method as individual arguments.

Similar to request handling, it tells the CXF runtime to wrap the return value into a <concatResponse> element.

Now the arguments are Strings, not a complex data structure.

To implement the service, create a WrappedServiceImpl class:

```
@WebService(endpointInterface="com.ttdev.ss.WrappedService")
public class WrappedServiceImpl implements WrappedService {

  @Override
  public String concat(String s1, String s2) {
    return s1 + s2;
  }
}
```

To create a client, copy the SimpleClient project and paste it as WrappedClient. Copy the SimpleService.wsdl from the WrappedService project into the WrappedClient project (in the src/main/resources folder). Delete the whole com.ttdev.ss package and then run the CodeGenerator program again. Modify the client code in WrappedService_P1_Client:

```
public final class WrappedService_P1_Client {
  ...
  public static void main(String args[]) throws Exception {
    ...
    WrappedService_Service ss = new WrappedService_Service(wsdlURL,
        SERVICE_NAME);
    WrappedService port = ss.getP1();
    {
      System.out.println("Invoking concat...");
      java.lang.String _concat_s1 = "abc";
      java.lang.String _concat_s2 = "123";
      java.lang.String _concat__return = port.concat(_concat_s1,
          _concat_s2);
      System.out.println("concat.result=" + _concat__return);
    }
    System.exit(0);
  }
}
```

Note that the concat() method in the service stub is now accepting two Strings, not a complex data structure.

Finally, run the service and then run the client. The client should print the "abc123" successfully.

Using the wrapped style in Axis2

To do it in Axis2, copy the Axis2SimpleService and paste it as Axis2WrappedService, copy the Axis2SimpleClient and paste it as Axis2WrappedClient. Copy the SimpleService.wsdl file from the WrappedService project into both of these two new projects.

Next, modify the CodeGenerator class in the Axis2WrappedService project to enable unwrapping:

```
  public static void main(String[] args) throws Exception {
    WSDL2Code.main(new String[] {
        "-ss",
        "-sd",
        "-uw",
        "-S", "src/main/java",
        "-R", "src/main/resources/META-INF",
        "-ns2p", "http://ttdev.com/ss=com.ttdev.ss",
        "-uri", "src/main/resources/SimpleService.wsdl" });
    System.out.println("Done!");
  }
}
```

Do the same thing in the Axis2WrappedClient project:

```
public class CodeGenerator {
  public static void main(String[] args) throws Exception {
    WSDL2Code.main(new String[] {
        "-uw",
        "-S", "src/main/java",
        "-R", "src/main/resources/META-INF",
        "-ns2p", "http://ttdev.com/ss=com.ttdev.ss",
        "-uri", "src/main/resources/SimpleService.wsdl" });
    System.out.println("Done!");
  }
}
```

Delete the com.ttdev.ss package and the src/main/resources/META-INF folder in both projects. Then run CodeGenerator in both projects. Fill in the code in the SimpleServiceSkeleton class:

```
public class SimpleServiceSkeleton {

  public java.lang.String concat(java.lang.String s1, java.lang.String s2) {
    return s1 + s2;
  }
}
```

Note that the concat() method is now taking two Strings and returning a String. Run the project as Maven package. It will still create a SimpleService-0.0.1-SNAPSHOT.jar file in the target folder because the pom.xml file still uses SimpleService as the artifact ID:

```
<project ...>
  <modelVersion>4.0.0</modelVersion>
  <groupId>SimpleService</groupId>
  <artifactId>SimpleService</artifactId>
  <version>0.0.1-SNAPSHOT</version>
  ...
</project>
```

Copy it into the Axis2 server (in the axis2/repository/services folder) as

WrappedService.aar.

Then, in the client project, create a WrappedClient class:

```
public class WrappedClient {
  public static void main(String[] args) throws RemoteException {
    WrappedServiceStub service = new WrappedServiceStub(
        "http://localhost:8080/axis2/services/WrappedService");
    System.out.println(service.concat("abc", "123"));
  }
}
```

Run it and it should print "abc123" successfully.

Interoperability

The wrapped style is a good idea. It is the only kind of web service supported by the .NET framework. Obviously CXF and Axis2 have also implemented this style. The good news is, from the viewpoint of the caller, it is just a document+literal style service. So if the caller doesn't understand the wrapped convention, it can still access it as a regular document style service.

Summary

The wrapped parameter style means that the web service runtime should extract the child XML elements in the input message and pass them as individual arguments to your method. It does the opposite when it receives the return value: wrap it as a child XML element in the output message.

To allow the wrapped style, the XML element in the input message should be a sequence and should have the same name as the operation. For the XML element in the output message, it should be a sequence (containing one element only) and should have the same name as the operation with the word "Response" appended.

The code generation tool in CXF will recognize this pattern automatically and uses the wrapped style. To enable the wrapped style in Axis2, you need to specify an option to the code generation tool.

The clients understanding the wrapped style can also call the service using multiple parameters. For those not understanding it, they can still call it as a regular document style service.

To ensure interoperability with .NET, you should use the wrapped style.

Chapter 5

Sending and receiving complex data structures

What's in this chapter?

In this chapter you'll learn how to send and receive complex data structures to and from a web service.

Product query

Suppose that your company would like to use web service to let your customers query the product availability and place orders with you. For this you need to discuss with them to decide on the interface. It doesn't make sense to say that "When doing query, please send me an object of such a Java class. In this class there are this and that fields..." because perhaps the people involved aren't programmers or don't use Java. Instead, XML is what is designed for this. It is platform neutral and programming language neutral. So, suppose that you all agree on the following schema:

Use the XML schema namespace as the default namespace. It defines elements such as <element>, <complexType> needed for you to define new elements.

Put your elements and types into this namespace

A <productQuery> contains one or more <queryItem> elements. Here is an example:

```
<?xml version="1.0"?>
<schema
   xmlns="http://www.w3.org/2001/XMLSchema"
   targetNamespace="http://foo.com">
   <element name="productQuery">
      <complexType>
         <sequence>
            <element name="queryItem" minOccurs="1" maxOccurs="unbounded">
               <complexType>
                  <attribute name="productId" type="string"/>
                  <attribute name="qty" type="int"/>
               </complexType>
            </element>
         </sequence>
      </complexType>
   </element>
</schema>
```

Define an element <productQuery>

The string type and int type are defined in the XML schema. They are usually shown as xsd:string and xsd:int, but the XML schema namespace here is the default namespace, so no prefix is needed.

A <queryItem> must appear at least once (1). There is no upper limit of its occurrence.

A <productQuery> has two attributes named "productId" and "qty" respectively.

```
<?xml version="1.0"?>
<foo:productQuery xmlns:foo="http://foo.com">
   <queryItem productId="p01" qty="100"/>
   <queryItem productId="p02" qty="200"/>
   <queryItem productId="p03" qty="500"/>
</foo:productQuery>
```

That is, when they need to find out the availability of some products, they will send you a <productQuery> element. For example if they'd like to check if you have 100 pieces of p01, 200 pieces of p02 and 500 pieces of p03, they may send you a request like this:

```
<foo:productQuery
  xmlns:foo="http://foo.com">
  <queryItem productId="p01" qty="100"/>
  <queryItem productId="p02" qty="200"/>
  <queryItem productId="p03" qty="500"/>
</foo:productQuery>
```

Your web service ← Client

How does your web service reply? Use an XML element of course. So, in the schema you may have:

```
<?xml version="1.0"?>
<schema
  xmlns="http://www.w3.org/2001/XMLSchema"
  targetNamespace="http://foo.com">
  <element name="productQuery">
    ...
  </element>
  <element name="productQueryResult">
    <complexType>
      <sequence>
        <element name="resultItem" minOccurs="1" maxOccurs="unbounded">
          <complexType>
            <attribute name="productId" type="string"/>
            <attribute name="price" type="int"/>
          </complexType>
        </element>
      </sequence>
    </complexType>
  </element>
</schema>
```

For each <queryItem>, if the product is available, create a <resultItem> telling the unit price.

So, for the sample query above, if you have over 100 pieces of p01 and 500 pieces of p03 but only 150 pieces of p02, and you're willing to sell p01 at 5 dollars each and p03 at 8 dollars each, you may reply:

```
<foo:productQueryResult
  xmlns:foo="http://foo.com">
  <resultItem productId="p01" price="5"/>
  <resultItem productId="p03" price="8"/>
</foo:productQueryResult>
```

Your web service → Client

To implement this idea, create a new project named BizService as usual (You may copy an old one). Delete the existing WSDL file and create a BizService.wsdl file (use Eclipse or manually):

```
<?xml version="1.0" encoding="UTF-8" standalone="no"?>
<wsdl:definitions xmlns:soap="http://schemas.xmlsoap.org/wsdl/soap/"
  xmlns:tns="http://foo.com" xmlns:wsdl="http://schemas.xmlsoap.org/wsdl/"
  xmlns:xsd="http://www.w3.org/2001/XMLSchema" name="BizService"
  targetNamespace="http://foo.com">
  <wsdl:types>
```

```
      <xsd:schema targetNamespace="http://foo.com">
        <xsd:element name="productQuery" type="tns:productQueryComplexType">
        </xsd:element>
        <xsd:element name="productQueryResult">
          <xsd:complexType>
            <xsd:sequence>
              <xsd:element name="resultItem" maxOccurs="unbounded" minOccurs="1">
                <xsd:complexType>
                  <xsd:attribute name="productId" type="xsd:string" />
                  <xsd:attribute name="price" type="xsd:int" />
                </xsd:complexType>
              </xsd:element>
            </xsd:sequence>
          </xsd:complexType>
        </xsd:element>
        <xsd:complexType name="productQueryComplexType">
          <xsd:sequence>
            <xsd:element name="queryItem" maxOccurs="unbounded" minOccurs="1">
              <xsd:complexType>
                <xsd:attribute name="productId" type="xsd:string"/>
                <xsd:attribute name="qty" type="xsd:int"/>
              </xsd:complexType>
            </xsd:element>
          </xsd:sequence>
        </xsd:complexType>
      </xsd:schema>
    </wsdl:types>
    <wsdl:message name="queryRequest">
      <wsdl:part element="tns:productQuery" name="parameters" />
    </wsdl:message>
    <wsdl:message name="queryResponse">
      <wsdl:part element="tns:productQueryResult" name="parameters" />
    </wsdl:message>
    <wsdl:portType name="BizService">
      <wsdl:operation name="query">
        <wsdl:input message="tns:queryRequest" />
        <wsdl:output message="tns:queryResponse" />
      </wsdl:operation>
    </wsdl:portType>
    <wsdl:binding name="BizServiceSOAP" type="tns:BizService">
      <soap:binding style="document"
        transport="http://schemas.xmlsoap.org/soap/http" />
      <wsdl:operation name="query">
        <soap:operation soapAction="http://foo.com/BizService/NewOperation" />
        <wsdl:input>
          <soap:body use="literal" />
        </wsdl:input>
        <wsdl:output>
          <soap:body use="literal" />
        </wsdl:output>
      </wsdl:operation>
    </wsdl:binding>
    <wsdl:service name="BizService">
      <wsdl:port binding="tns:BizServiceSOAP" name="BizServiceSOAP">
        <soap:address location="http://localhost:8080/bs/p1" />
      </wsdl:port>
    </wsdl:service>
  </wsdl:definitions>
```

If you edit it visually, here are the key steps: First, rename the operation to "query". The input element is automatically renamed to <query>. Double click on the arrow to right of the <query> element in order to edit it. Then right click on it and choose Refactor | Rename:

Rename it to "productQuery":

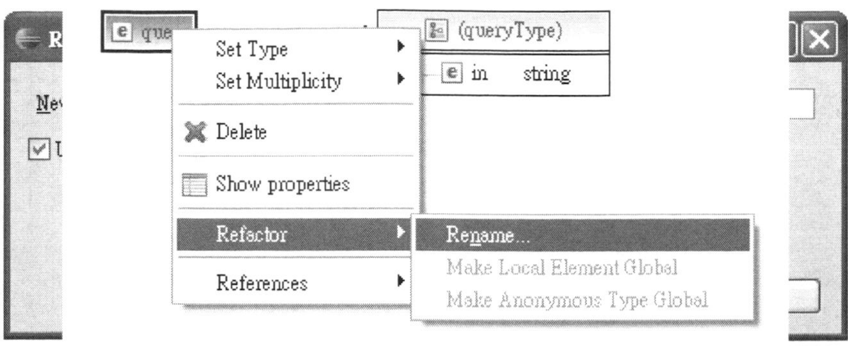

Note that the name of its type will be changed from (queryType) to (productQueryType) automatically.

Also note the meaning of the parentheses: (fooType) means that it is the anonymous type for the <foo> element:

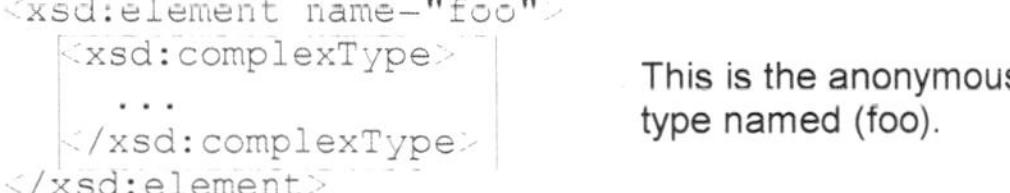

It is possible to name this type explicitly. For example, right click (productQueryType) and choose Refactor | Make Anonymous Type Global:

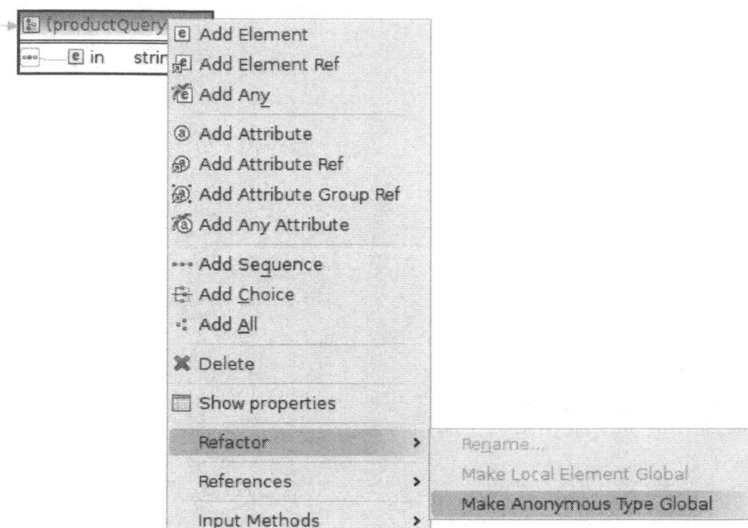

Then it will be given a name (by default, productQueryComplexType) and the XML schema will become:

```
<xsd:schema targetNamespace="http://foo.com">
  <xsd:element name="productQuery"
    type="tns:productQueryComplexType">
  </xsd:element>
  <xsd:complexType name="productQueryComplexType">
    ...
  </xsd:complexType>
</xsd:schema>
```


Anyway, now, Rename the "in" element to "queryItem":

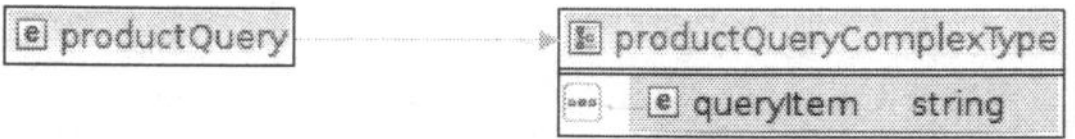

For the moment the <queryItem> element is a string. Right click on it and choose Set Type | New:

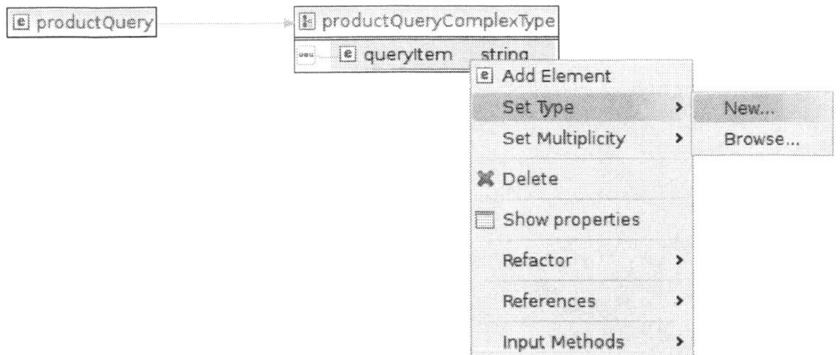

Choose to create an anonymous local complex type:

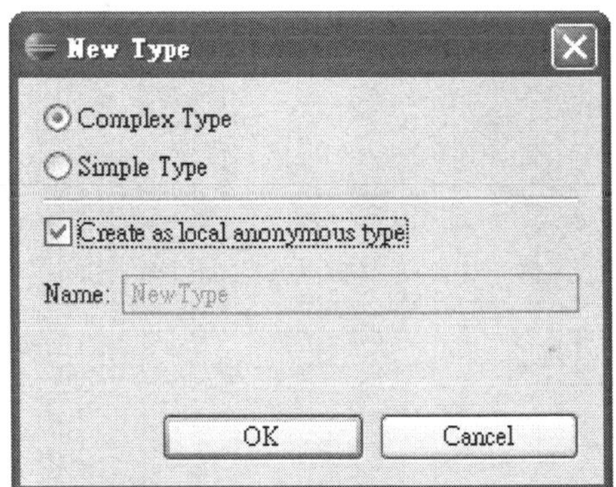

It will be like:

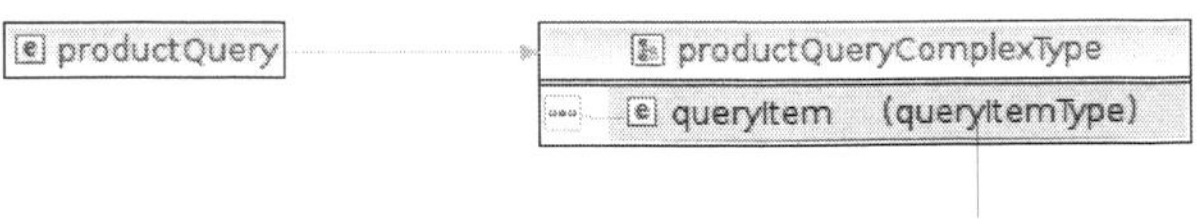

You need to edit it next

Next, you'd like to edit the (queryItemType). But clicking on it will NOT allow you to edit it. Instead, it will only let you choose another type for <queryItem>:

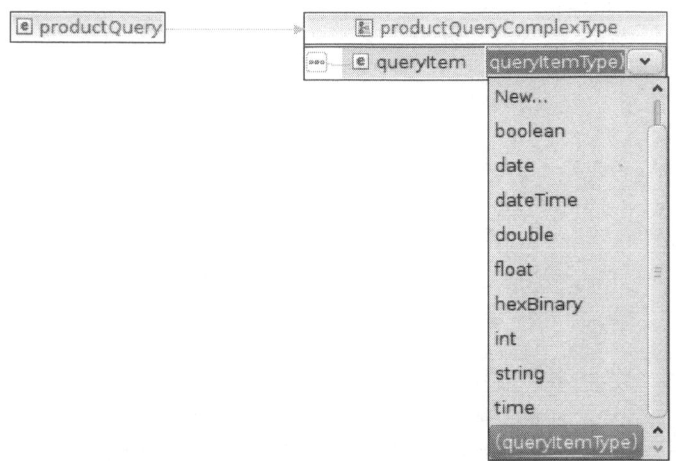

This is because Eclipse will not allow you to directly edit something too deep. Instead, it requires you to drill down by one level. So, double click on productQueryComplexType (Note: NOT (queryItemType)) to drill down. You'll see that the (queryitemType) is available for editing:

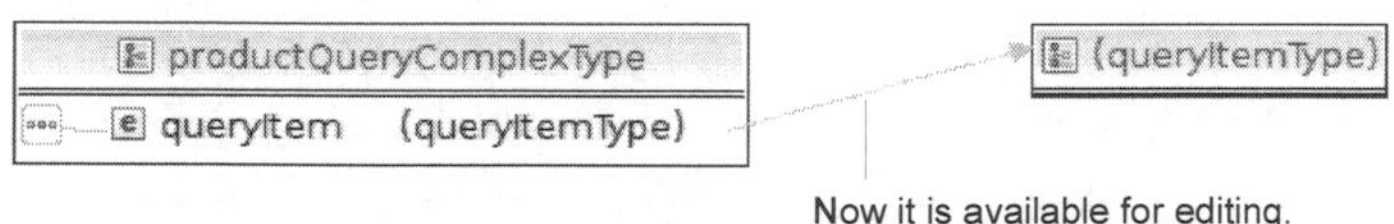

Right click on (queryItemType) and choose Add Attribute:

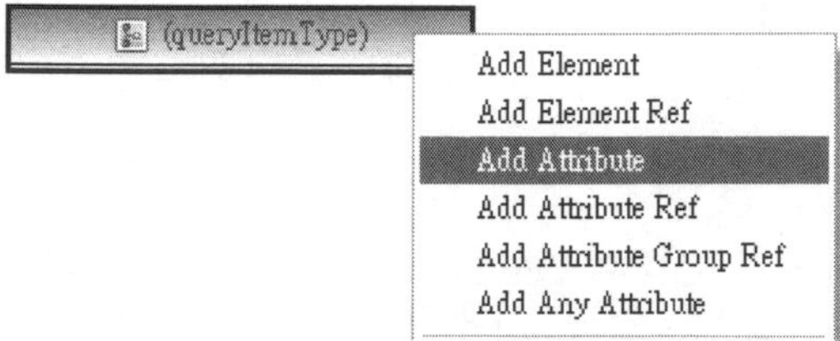

Rename the attribute to "productId". The type is by default string which is what you want:

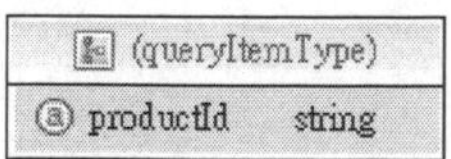

Similarly, add another attribute "qty" and set its type to int:

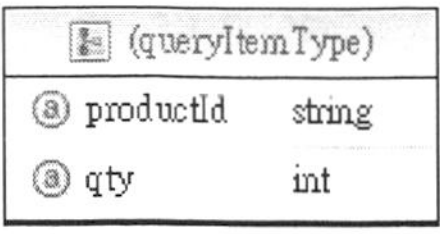

To tell that there can be 1 to many <queryItem> elements, right click the <queryItem> element and choose Set Multiplicity | 1..* (One or More):

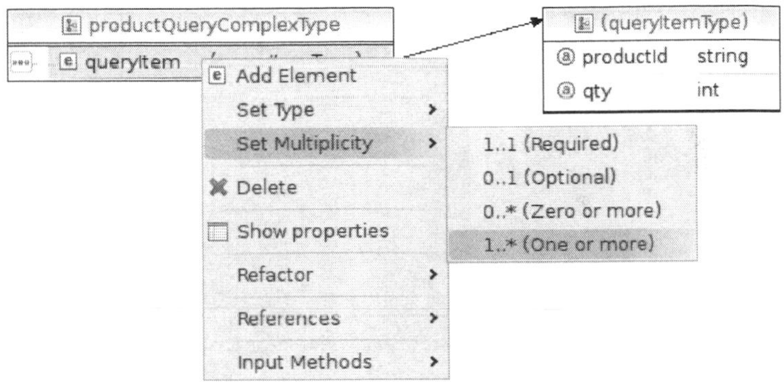

You'll see:

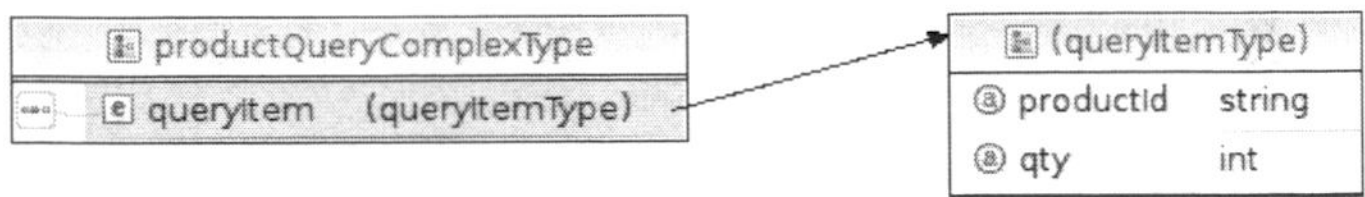

Now, it is done. To return to one level up, click the left arrow icon as if it were a browser:

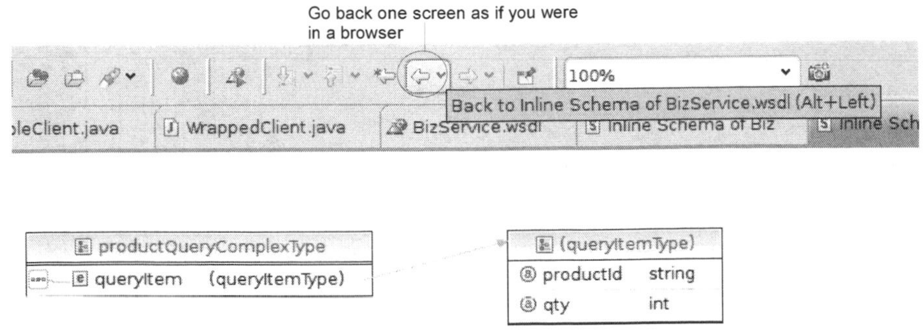

Similarly, create the <productQueryResult> element. As usual, validate it when you're done.

Next, modify the CodeGenerator class:

```
public class CodeGenerator {
  public static void main(String[] args) {
    WSDLToJava.main(new String[] {
        "-server",
        "-p", "http://foo.com=com.ttdev.biz",
        "-d", "src/main/java",
        "src/main/resources/BizService.wsdl" });
    System.out.println("Done!");
  }
}
```

Delete the whole com.ttdev.ss (if any). Run the CodeGenerator class. Note that top level XML types have been converted to Java classes. If the XML type is named such as productQueryComplexType, the name will be used as the Java class name. If an XML type is anonymous such as (productQueryResult), the element name will be used as the Java class name:

```
public interface BizService {
  ...
  public ProductQueryResult query(ProductQueryComplexType parameters);
}
```

XML types have been mapped to Java classes.

```
<xsd:schema ...>
  <xsd:element name="productQuery" type="tns:productQueryComplexType">
    ...
  </xsd:element>
  <xsd:element name="productQueryResult">
    ...
  </xsd:element>
  <xsd:complexType name="productQueryComplexType">
    ...
  </xsd:complexType>
</xsd:schema>
```

If you inspect the ProductQueryComplexType class, you'll note the mapping is like this:

```
@XmlAccessorType(XmlAccessType.FIELD)
@XmlType(name = "productQueryComplexType", propOrder = { "queryItem" })
public class ProductQueryComplexType {

   @XmlElement(required = true)
   protected List<ProductQueryComplexType.QueryItem> queryItem;
   ...
   @XmlAccessorType(XmlAccessType.FIELD)
   @XmlType(name = "")
   public static class QueryItem {

      @XmlAttribute
      protected String productId;
      @XmlAttribute
      protected Integer qty;
      ...
   }
}
```

The field name is the element name.

Each element in a <sequence> is mapped to a field in the class. If that element can occur multiple times (i.e., maxOccurs > 1), the type of the field will be a List.

Attributes are also mapped to fields, just like elements in a sequence.

Use the element name as the Java class name.

A named XML type is mapped to a Java class.

```
<xsd:schema ...>
   ...
   <xsd:complexType name="productQueryComplexType">
      <xsd:sequence>
         <xsd:element name="queryItem"
            maxOccurs="unbounded"
            minOccurs="1">
            <xsd:complexType>
               <xsd:attribute name="productId" type="xsd:string" />
               <xsd:attribute name="qty" type="xsd:int" />
            </xsd:complexType>
         </xsd:element>
      </xsd:sequence>
   </xsd:complexType>
</xsd:schema>
```

An anonymous XML type is mapped to a Java inner class.

Similarly, inspect the ProductQueryResult class to see how a top level anonymous XML type is mapped to a Java class:

```
@XmlAccessorType(XmlAccessType.FIELD)
@XmlType(name = "", propOrder = { "resultItem" })
@XmlRootElement(name = "productQueryResult")
public class ProductQueryResult {
   ...
   @XmlElement(required = true)
   protected List<ProductQueryResult.ResultItem> resultItem;

   @XmlAccessorType(XmlAccessType.FIELD)
   @XmlType(name = "")
   public static class ResultItem {
      ...
      @XmlAttribute
      protected String productId;
      @XmlAttribute
      protected Integer price;
   }
}
```

The anonymous XML type of a top level (root) XML element is mapped to a Java class. The class name is the element name.

The anonymous XML type is mapped to an inner class. The class name is the element name.

Again, each element in a <sequence> is mapped to a field. As maxOccurs is > 1, the type of the field is a List.

```
<xsd:schema ...>
   ...
   <xsd:element name="productQueryResult">
      <xsd:complexType>
         <xsd:sequence>
            <xsd:element name="resultItem" maxOccurs="unbounded"
               minOccurs="1">
               <xsd:complexType>
                  <xsd:attribute name="productId" type="xsd:string" />
                  <xsd:attribute name="price" type="xsd:int" />
               </xsd:complexType>
            </xsd:element>
         </xsd:sequence>
      </xsd:complexType>
   </xsd:element>
</xsd:schema>
```

This way of mapping between XML and Java and the annotations like @XmlType or @XmlElement are standardized in the Java Architecture for XML Binding (JAXB).

To implement the service, create a BizServiceImpl class:

```
package com.ttdev.biz;
...
import com.ttdev.biz.ProductQueryComplexType.QueryItem;
import com.ttdev.biz.ProductQueryResult.ResultItem;

@WebService(endpointInterface = "com.ttdev.biz.BizService")
public class BizServiceImpl implements BizService {

   @Override
   public ProductQueryResult query(ProductQueryComplexType parameters) {
      ProductQueryResult result = new ProductQueryResult();
      List<QueryItem> queryItem = parameters.getQueryItem();
      for (QueryItem item : queryItem) {
         if (item.getQty() <= 200) {
            ResultItem resultItem = new ResultItem();
            resultItem.setProductId(item.getProductId());
            resultItem.setPrice(20);
            result.getResultItem().add(resultItem);
         }
      }
      return result;
   }
}
```

Even though it says getQueryItem(), actually it is a List due to the maxOccurs.

Loop through each query item. Assume it's available if qty is <= 200.

Assume the unit price is always 20.

Add the result item to the query result.

Create a project for the client and name it BizClient. Fill in the code in the BizService_BizServiceSOAP_Client class:

```
public final class BizService_BizServiceSOAP_Client {
   ...
   public static void main(String args[]) throws Exception {
      ...
      BizService_Service ss = new BizService_Service(wsdlURL, SERVICE_NAME);
      BizService port = ss.getBizServiceSOAP();
      {
         System.out.println("Invoking query...");
         com.ttdev.biz.ProductQueryComplexType _query_parameters =
            new ProductQueryComplexType();
         QueryItem item = new QueryItem();
         item.setProductId("p01");
         item.setQty(100);
         _query_parameters.getQueryItem().add(item);
         item = new QueryItem();
         item.setProductId("p02");
         item.setQty(200);
         _query_parameters.getQueryItem().add(item);
         item = new QueryItem();
         item.setProductId("p03");
         item.setQty(500);
         _query_parameters.getQueryItem().add(item);
         com.ttdev.biz.ProductQueryResult _query__return = port
               .query(_query_parameters);
         for (ResultItem resultItem : _query__return.getResultItem()) {
            System.out.println(resultItem.getProductId() + ": "
                  + resultItem.getPrice());
         }
      }
      System.exit(0);
   }

}
```

Run the service and then the client. The client should print the result as shown below:

```
Invoking query...
```

```
p01: 20
p02: 20
```

Sending more data in a message

By the way, this query operation demonstrates a good practice in web services: You generally hope to send more data in a message. For example, you may be sending many query items in a single response message. This is more efficient than sending a single query item object in a message. This is because there is a certain overhead involved in sending a message, even if it contains no data:

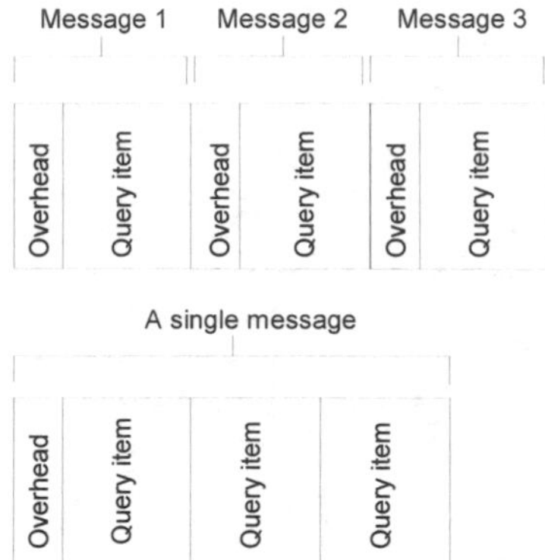

Returning faults

Suppose that a client is calling your query operation but a product id is invalid (not just out of stock, but absolutely unknown) or the quantity is zero or negative. You may want to throw an exception. To return an exception to the client, you send a "fault message", which is very much like an output message. To do that, modify the WSDL file:

```
<?xml version="1.0" encoding="UTF-8" standalone="no"?>
<wsdl:definitions ...>
  <wsdl:types>
    <xsd:schema ...>
      ...
      <xsd:element name="invalidProductId" type="xsd:string" />
      <xsd:element name="invalidQty" type="xsd:int " />
    </xsd:schema>
  </wsdl:types>
  <wsdl:message name="queryRequest">
    <wsdl:part element="tns:productQuery" name="parameters" />
  </wsdl:message>
  <wsdl:message name="queryResponse">
    <wsdl:part element="tns:productQueryResult" name="parameters" />
  </wsdl:message>
  <wsdl:message name="queryInvalidProductId">
    <wsdl:part name="parameters" element="tns:invalidProductId" />
  </wsdl:message>
  <wsdl:message name="queryInvalidQty">
    <wsdl:part name="parameters" element="tns:invalidQty" />
  </wsdl:message>
  <wsdl:portType name="BizService">
    <wsdl:operation name="query">
      <wsdl:input message="tns:queryRequest" />
      <wsdl:output message="tns:queryResponse" />
      <wsdl:fault name="f01" message="tns:queryInvalidProductId" />
      <wsdl:fault name="f02" message="tns:queryInvalidQty" />
    </wsdl:operation>
  </wsdl:portType>
  ...
</wsdl:definitions>
```

The one and only part is a well defined XML element in the schema.

A fault message is like an output message, but it indicates an error.

Unlike an input or output message which doesn't need a name, a fault needs a unique name because there can be multiple fault messages (here you have two). Later you'll refer to a fault using its name.

How to include the fault message in a SOAP message? It is included in the SOAP body, but not directly:

```
<wsdl:definitions ...>
  ...
  <wsdl:portType name="BizService">
    <wsdl:operation name="query">
      <wsdl:input message="tns:queryRequest" />
      <wsdl:output message="tns:queryResponse" />
      <wsdl:fault name="f01" message="tns:queryInvalidProductId" />
      <wsdl:fault name="f02" message="tns:queryInvalidQty" />
    </wsdl:operation>
  </wsdl:portType>
  <wsdl:binding name="BizServiceSOAP" type="tns:BizService">
    <soap:binding style="document"
      transport="http://schemas.xmlsoap.org/soap/http" />
    <wsdl:operation name="query">
      <soap:operation soapAction="http://foo.com/BizService/NewOperation" />
      <wsdl:input>
        <soap:body use="literal" />
      </wsdl:input>
      <wsdl:output>
        <soap:body use="literal" />
      </wsdl:output>
      <wsdl:fault name="f01">
        <soap:fault name="f01" use="literal" />
      </wsdl:fault>
      <wsdl:fault name="f02">
        <soap:fault name="f02" use="literal" />
      </wsdl:fault>
    </wsdl:operation>
  </wsdl:binding> ...
</wsdl:definitions>
```

How to store this fault message in a binding?

In SOAP, include the fault message into SOAP <Body> | <Fault> | <detail>:

The message part is already in XML.

```
<soap-env:Envelope
  xmlns:soap-env="http://http://schemas.xmlsoap.org/soap/envelope/">
  <soap-env:Header>
    ...
  </soap-env:Header>
  <soap-env:Body>
    <soap-env:Fault>
      <soap-env:faultcode>...</soap-env:faultcode>
      <soap-env:faultstring>...</soap-env:faultstring>
      <soap-env:detail>
        <foo:invalidProductId xmlns:foo="http://foo.com">
          p1000
        </foo:invalidProductId>
      </soap-env:detail>
    </soap-env:Fault>
  </soap-env:Body>
<soap-env:Envelope>
```

The SOAP <Fault> element tells the caller that something is wrong. The <faultcode> is a QName acting as an error code. The <faultstring> is an error message for human reading. The <detail> will contain any information that both sides agree on. In this case, it contains your fault message part.

To make the above changes to the WSDL file visually, right click the query operation and choose Add Fault:

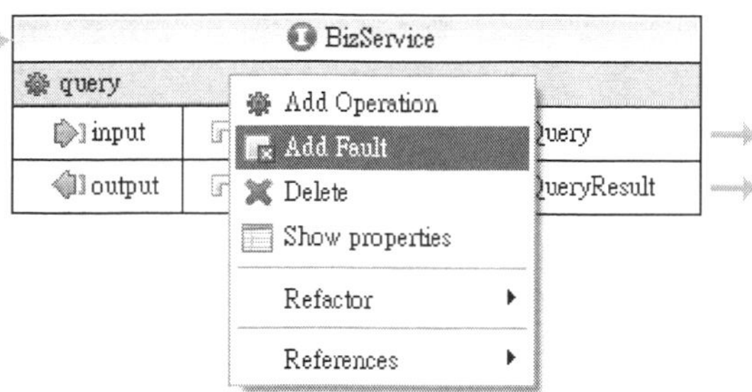

Right click the fault message and choose Show properties. Then in the Properties window, set its name to f01:

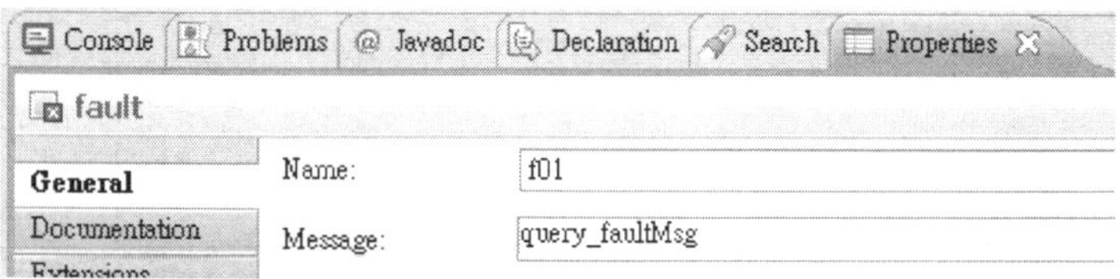

Choose to create a new message:

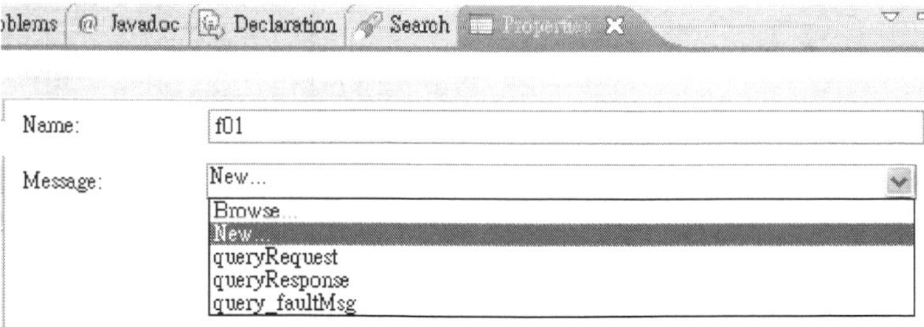

Enter the name for the message:

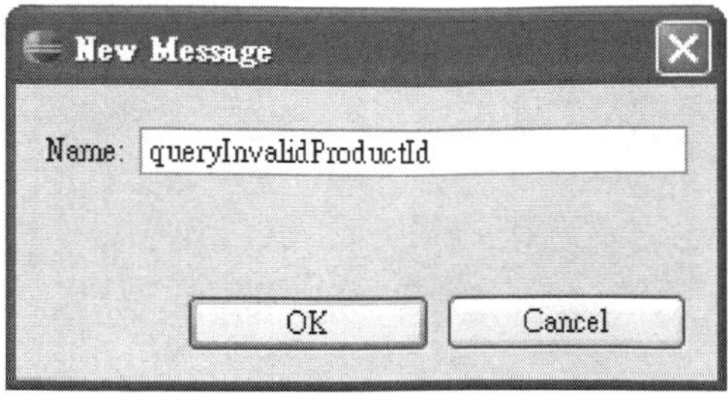

Set the one and only part to a new XML element <invalidProductId>. By default it should be of type xsd:string which is what you want here. Create the second fault similarly. Set the message name to queryInvalidQty, set the XML element to <invalidQty> whose type is xsd:int. Finally it should be like:

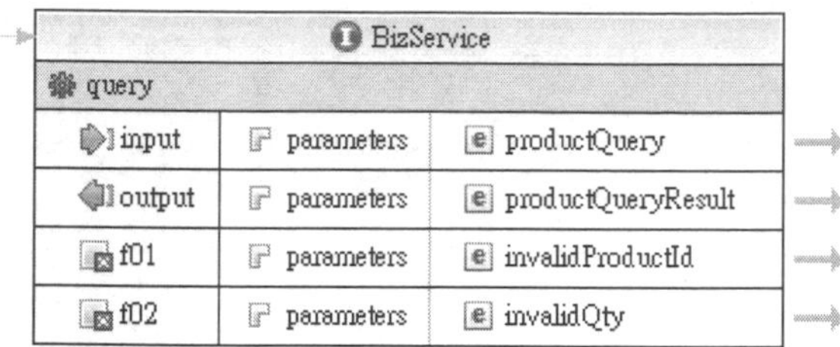

You've done with the port type. Next, create the binding for the two faults. Choose the binding and click Generate Binding Content in the Properties window:

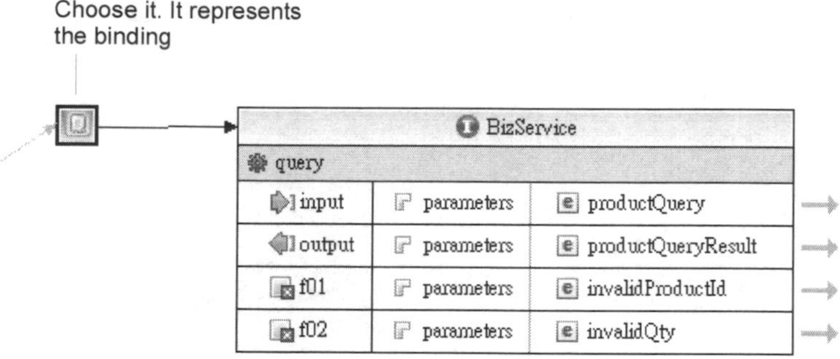

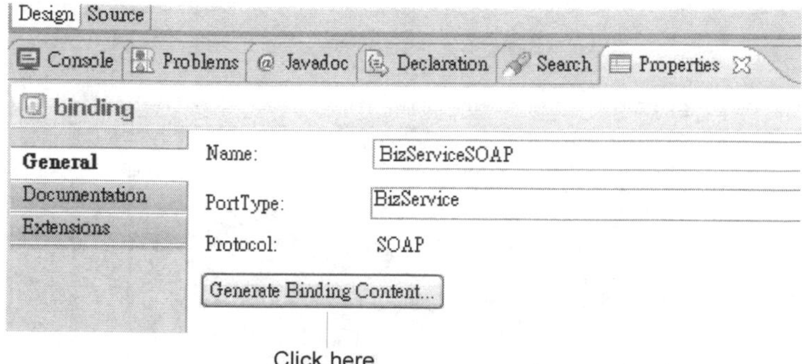

Check Overwrite existing binding information and then click Finish:

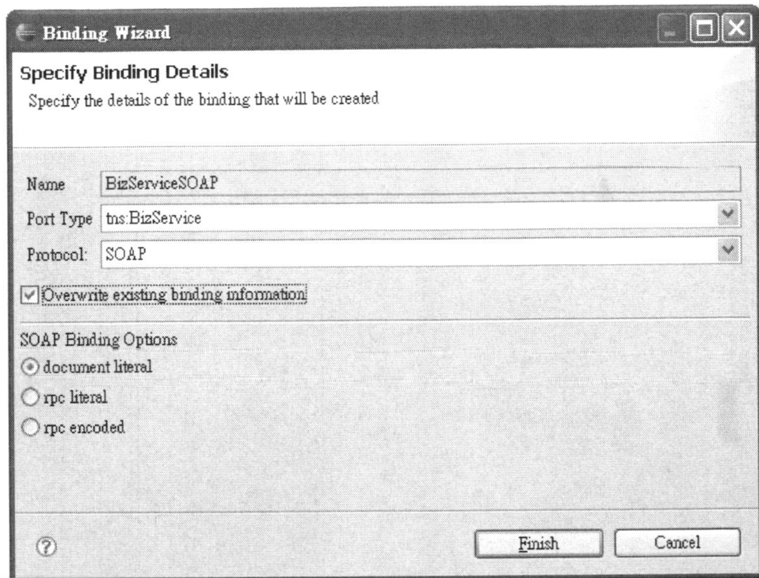

This will generate the binding portion:

```
<wsdl:binding name="BizServiceSOAP" type="tns:BizService">
  <soap:binding style="document"
    transport="http://schemas.xmlsoap.org/soap/http" />
  <wsdl:operation name="query">
    <soap:operation soapAction="http://foo.com/query" />
    <wsdl:input>
      <soap:body use="literal" />
    </wsdl:input>
    <wsdl:output>
      <soap:body use="literal" />
    </wsdl:output>
    <wsdl:fault name="f01">
      <soap:fault use="literal" name="f01" />
    </wsdl:fault>
    <wsdl:fault name="f02">
      <soap:fault use="literal" name="f02" />
    </wsdl:fault>
  </wsdl:operation>
</wsdl:binding>
```

Finally go into the schema index to delete the unused elements created by Eclipse:

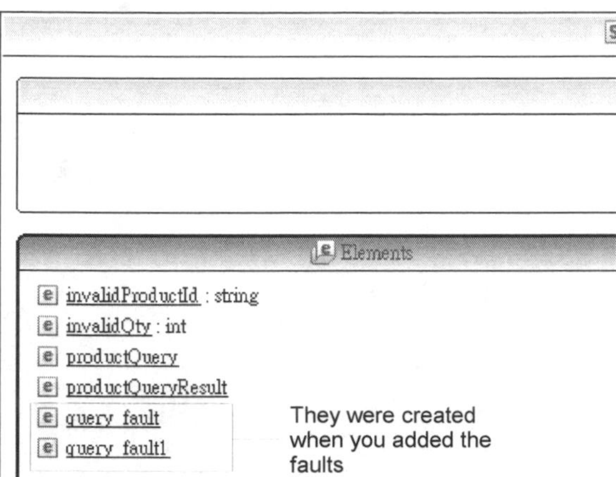

Similarly, choose Window | Show View | Outline to show the outline of the WSDL file as shown below. Right click and delete the unused messages such as query_faultMsg and query_faultMsg1:

Now, copy the WSDL file to the BizClient project. Then generate the service and client code again. The concat() in the SEI will be declared as throwing two types of exceptions:

```
@WebService(targetNamespace = "http://foo.com", name = "BizService")
@XmlSeeAlso( { ObjectFactory.class })
@SOAPBinding(parameterStyle = SOAPBinding.ParameterStyle.BARE)
public interface BizService {

  @WebResult(...)
  @WebMethod(action = "http://foo.com/query")
  public ProductQueryResult query(
       @WebParam(...) ProductQueryComplexType parameters)
       throws QueryInvalidQty, QueryInvalidProductId;
}
```

Take the QueryInvalidProductId exception class as an example, it is defined as:

```
@WebFault(name = "invalidProductId", targetNamespace = "http://foo.com")
public class QueryInvalidProductId extends Exception {
  ...
  private java.lang.String invalidProductId;
  ...
}
```

A fault message is mapped to a Java exception class.

The one and only part of the fault message (an XML element) is mapped to a field. If it was a complex XML type, the field type would be a Java class. But here it is a single string type, so it is mapped to the String class.

```
<wsdl:types>
  <xsd:schema>
    ...
    <xsd:element name="invalidProductId" type="xsd:string" />
    <xsd:element name="invalidQty" type="xsd:int" />
  </xsd:schema>
</wsdl:types>
<wsdl:message name="queryInvalidProductId">
  <wsdl:part name="parameters" element="tns:invalidProductId" />
</wsdl:message>
<wsdl:portType name="BizService">
  <wsdl:operation name="query">
    <wsdl:input message="tns:queryRequest" />
    <wsdl:output message="tns:queryResponse" />
    <wsdl:fault name="f01" message="tns:queryInvalidProductId" />
    <wsdl:fault name="f02" message="tns:queryInvalidQty" />
  </wsdl:operation>
</wsdl:portType>
```

Now modify your implementation code:

```
@WebService(endpointInterface = "com.ttdev.biz.BizService")
public class BizServiceImpl implements BizService {

  @Override
  public ProductQueryResult query(ProductQueryComplexType parameters)
      throws QueryInvalidQty, QueryInvalidProductId {
    ProductQueryResult result = new ProductQueryResult();
    List<QueryItem> queryItem = parameters.getQueryItem();
    for (QueryItem item : queryItem) {
      if (!item.getProductId().startsWith("p")) {
        throw new QueryInvalidProductId("invalid product ID",
          item.getProductId());
      }
      if (item.getQty() <= 0) {
        throw new QueryInvalidQty("invalid qty", item.getQty());
      }
      if (item.getQty() <= 200) {
        ResultItem resultItem = new ResultItem();
        resultItem.setProductId(item.getProductId());
        resultItem.setPrice(20);
        result.getResultItem().add(resultItem);
      }
    }
    return result;
  }
}
```

To see if it's working, modify the BizService_BizServiceSOAP_Client class:

```
public final class BizService_BizServiceSOAP_Client {
   ...
   public static void main(String args[]) throws Exception {
      ...
      BizService_Service ss = new BizService_Service(wsdlURL, SERVICE_NAME);
      BizService port = ss.getBizServiceSOAP();
      {
         System.out.println("Invoking query...");
         try {
            com.ttdev.biz.ProductQueryComplexType _query_parameters =
              new ProductQueryComplexType();
            QueryItem item = new QueryItem();
            item.setProductId("p01");
            item.setQty(100);
            _query_parameters.getQueryItem().add(item);
            item = new QueryItem();
            item.setProductId("p02");
            item.setQty(-200);
            _query_parameters.getQueryItem().add(item);
            item = new QueryItem();
            item.setProductId("p03");
            item.setQty(500);
            _query_parameters.getQueryItem().add(item);
            com.ttdev.biz.ProductQueryResult _query__return = port
                .query(_query_parameters);
            for (ResultItem resultItem : _query__return.getResultItem()) {
              System.out.println(resultItem.getProductId() + ": "
                  + resultItem.getPrice());
            }
         } catch (QueryInvalidQty e) {
            System.out.println("Invalid qty: " + e.getFaultInfo());
         } catch (QueryInvalidProductId e) {
            System.out.println("Invalid product ID: " + e.getFaultInfo());
         }
      }
      System.exit(0);
   }
}
```

This is the Java object representing the XML element. In this case, it is just an int (the quantity).

This is the Java object representing the XML element. In this case, it is just a String (the product ID).

By the way, you should have noted that the BizService_BizServiceSOAP_Client class has been overwritten when you ran the WSDLToJava program again. It means that in practice you shouldn't modify this class. Create your own client class instead.

Now, start the service and then run the client. It should print the following error message in the console:

```
Invoking query...
Invalid qty: -200
```

If you'd like, you can see the messages in TCP Monitor:

```
<?xml version='1.0' encoding='UTF-8'?>
   <soapenv:Envelope xmlns:soapenv="http://schemas.xmlsoap.org/soap/envelope/">
      <soapenv:Body>
         <soapenv:Fault>
            <faultcode>soapenv:Server</faultcode>
            <faultstring>QueryInvalidQty</faultstring>
            <detail>
               <ns1:invalidQty xmlns:ns1="http://foo.com">-200</ns1:invalidQty>
            </detail>
         </soapenv:Fault>
      </soapenv:Body>
   </soapenv:Envelope>
```

Referring to existing XML elements

For the moment you're defining XML elements such as <productQuery> directly in the WSDL file. However, in practice, most likely such elements are defined by a 3rd party such as an industrial consortium or neutral association. Suppose that they are provided in a file purchasing.xsd such as this:

The root element is <schema>.

The default namespace is the XML schema namespace, so you don't need to use the xsd prefix below.

As they are defined by a 3rd party, it should use a different target namespace. Let's assume that it is http://bar.com/purchasing.

Everything else remains unchanged.

```
<?xml version="1.0" encoding="UTF-8"?>
<schema xmlns="http://www.w3.org/2001/XMLSchema"
  targetNamespace="http://bar.org/purchasing"
  xmlns:tns="http://bar.org/purchasing"
  elementFormDefault="qualified">
  <xsd:element name="productQuery" type="tns:productQueryComplexType" />
  <xsd:element name="productQueryResult">
    <xsd:complexType>
      <xsd:sequence>
        <xsd:element name="resultItem" maxOccurs="unbounded"
          minOccurs="1">
          <xsd:complexType>
            <xsd:attribute name="productId" type="xsd:string" />
            <xsd:attribute name="price" type="xsd:int" />
          </xsd:complexType>
        </xsd:element>
      </xsd:sequence>
    </xsd:complexType>
  </xsd:element>
  <xsd:complexType name="productQueryComplexType">
    <xsd:sequence>
      <xsd:element name="queryItem" maxOccurs="unbounded"
        minOccurs="1">
        <xsd:complexType>
          <xsd:attribute name="productId" type="xsd:string" />
          <xsd:attribute name="qty" type="xsd:int" />
        </xsd:complexType>
      </xsd:element>
    </xsd:sequence>
  </xsd:complexType>
  <xsd:element name="invalidProductId" type="xsd:string" />
  <xsd:element name="invalidQty" type="xsd:int" />
</schema>
```

How to refer to those XML elements in your WSDL file? First, put the purchasing.xsd file into the same folder as the WSDL file (i.e., src/main/resources). Then modify the WSDL file:

You're saying: I'd like to refer to the XML elements defined in the http://bar.org/purchasing namespace. Then the XML elements will be visible to this WSDL file. This is like the import statement in Java used to import a package or a class.

How can the WSDL parser find out the XML elements defined there? It will work if the person parsing the WSDL have set up a table like below. Such a table is called an XML catalog.

Namespace	Path to its xsd file
http://bar.org/purchasing	c:\schema\f1.xsd
http://...	c:\...
http://...	c:\...

You don't need to define your own XML elements and XML types anymore.

```
<?xml version="1.0" encoding="UTF-8" standalone="no"?>
<wsdl:definitions xmlns:soap="http://schemas.xmlsoap.org/wsdl/soap/"
  xmlns:tns="http://foo.com"
  xmlns:wsdl="http://schemas.xmlsoap.org/wsdl/"
  xmlns:p="http://bar.org/purchasing"
  xmlns:xsd="http://www.w3.org/2001/XMLSchema"
  name="BizService" targetNamespace="http://foo.com">
  <wsdl:types>
    <xsd:schema targetNamespace="http://foo.com">
      <xsd:import namespace="http://bar.org/purchasing"
        schemaLocation="purchasing.xsd">
      </xsd:import>
      <xsd:element ... />
      <xsd:element ... />
      <xsd:complexType ... />
    </xsd:schema>
  </wsdl:types>
  <wsdl:message name="queryRequest">
    <wsdl:part element="p:productQuery" name="parameters" />
  </wsdl:message>
  <wsdl:message name="queryResponse">
    <wsdl:part element="p:productQueryResult" name="parameters" />
  </wsdl:message>
  <wsdl:message name="queryInvalidProductId">
    <wsdl:part name="parameters" element="p:invalidProductId" />
  </wsdl:message>
  <wsdl:message name="queryInvalidQty">
    <wsdl:part name="parameters" element="p:invalidQty" />
  </wsdl:message>
  ...
</wsdl:definitions>
```

As you'll be giving away this WSDL to many people, it may be too difficult to ask everyone to set up the XML catalog. So you may simply distribute the XSD file and make sure it is in the same folder as the WSDL file and specify the relative path here. In addition to the XML catalog, their WSDL processor will follow this path to find the XSD file.

The elements are now defined in the namespace represented by the prefix "p".

Modify the CodeGenerator class to specify a Java package for the http://bar.org/purchasing namespace (not strictly required. Do it only if you don't want the default):

```
public class CodeGenerator {
  public static void main(String[] args) {
    WSDLToJava.main(new String[] {
        "-server",
        "-p", "http://foo.com=com.ttdev.biz",
        "-p", "http://bar.org/purchasing=com.ttdev.biz.purchasing",
        "-d", "src/main/java",
        "src/main/resources/BizService.wsdl" });
    System.out.println("Done!");
  }
}
```

Delete all the files in the com.ttdev.biz package except BizServiceImpl. Generate the code again. Then BizServiceImpl will be in error. This is because the classes representing the XML types and elements (e.g., ProductQueryComplexType) are now in the com.ttdev.biz.purchasing package.

Just delete the import statements and import the classes again (e.g., by typing Ctrl-Shift-O in Eclipse). Then the errors will be gone.

Copy the WSDL and XSD files to the BizClient project. Modify the CodeGenerator class to specify the package mapping. Delete the generated file and generate the code again. Run the BizClient and it should continue to work.

Doing it in Axis2

To do it in Axis2, copy the Axis2SimpleService and paste it as Axis2BizService, copy the Axis2SimpleClient and paste it as Axis2BizClient. Copy the WSDL file and XSD file from the BizService project into both of these two new projects (and delete the existing WSDL files).

Next, modify the CodeGenerator class in the Axis2BizService project as shown below. Note that the two package mappings are separated by a comma:

```
  public class CodeGenerator {
  public static void main(String[] args) throws Exception {
    WSDL2Code.main(new String[] {
        "-ss",
        "-sd",
        "-S", "src/main/java",
        "-R", "src/main/resources/META-INF",
        "-ns2p",
"http://foo.com=com.ttdev.biz,http://bar.org/purchasing=com.ttdev.biz.purchasing",
        "-uri", "src/main/resources/BizService.wsdl" });
    System.out.println("Done!");
  }
}
```

Do the same thing in the Axis2BizClient project:

```
public class CodeGenerator {
  public static void main(String[] args) throws Exception {
    WSDL2Code.main(new String[] {
        "-S", "src/main/java",
        "-R", "src/main/resources/META-INF",
        "-ns2p",
"http://foo.com=com.ttdev.biz,http://bar.org/purchasing=com.ttdev.biz.purchasing",
        "-uri", "src/main/resources/BizService.wsdl" });
    System.out.println("Done!");
  }
}
```

Delete the com.ttdev.ss package and the src/main/resources/META-INF folder in both projects. Then run CodeGenerator in both projects. Fill in the code in the BizServiceSkeleton class:

```
public class BizServiceSkeleton {
  public com.ttdev.biz.purchasing.ProductQueryResult query(
      com.ttdev.biz.purchasing.ProductQuery productQuery)
      throws QueryInvalidQty, QueryInvalidProductId {
    ProductQueryResult result = new ProductQueryResult();
    QueryItem_type0[] queryItem = productQuery.getProductQuery()
        .getQueryItem();
    for (QueryItem_type0 item : queryItem) {
      if (!item.getProductId().startsWith("p")) {
        InvalidProductId faultMsg = new InvalidProductId();
        faultMsg.setInvalidProductId(item.getProductId());
        QueryInvalidProductId e = new QueryInvalidProductId();
        e.setFaultMessage(faultMsg);
```

```
        throw e;
      }
      if (item.getQty() <= 0) {
        InvalidQty faultMsg = new InvalidQty();
        faultMsg.setInvalidQty(item.getQty());
        QueryInvalidQty e = new QueryInvalidQty();
        e.setFaultMessage(faultMsg);
        throw e;
      }
      if (item.getQty() <= 200) {
        ResultItem_type0 resultItem = new ResultItem_type0();
        resultItem.setProductId(item.getProductId());
        resultItem.setPrice(20);
        result.addResultItem(resultItem);
      }
    }
    return result;
  }
}
```

The mapping from XML to Java as done in Axis2 is very similar to the standard JAXB. The major difference is non-top-level anonymous XML types are mapped to top level Java classes. In order to avoid name clashes, the WSDL2Code program appends a suffix like _type0 to the Java class names.

Modify the pom.xml file to use a new artifact ID:

```
<project ...>
  <modelVersion>4.0.0</modelVersion>
  <groupId>com.ttdev</groupId>
  <artifactId>BizService</artifactId>
  <version>0.0.1-SNAPSHOT</version>
  ...
</project>
```

Run as Maven package and copy the jar file into the Axis2 server (in the axis2/repository/services folder) as BizService.aar.

Then, in the client project, create a BizClient class:

```
public class BizClient {
  public static void main(String[] args) throws RemoteException {
    BizServiceStub service = new BizServiceStub(
        "http://localhost:8080/axis2/services/BizService");
    try {
      ProductQuery _query_parameters = new ProductQuery();
      _query_parameters.setProductQuery(new ProductQueryComplexType());
      QueryItem_type0 item = new QueryItem_type0();
      item.setProductId("p01");
      item.setQty(100);
      _query_parameters.getProductQuery().addQueryItem(item);
      item = new QueryItem_type0();
      item.setProductId("p02");
      item.setQty(-200);
      _query_parameters.getProductQuery().addQueryItem(item);
      item = new QueryItem_type0();
      item.setProductId("p03");
      item.setQty(500);
      _query_parameters.getProductQuery().addQueryItem(item);
      ProductQueryResult _query__return = service
          .query(_query_parameters);
      for (ResultItem_type0 resultItem : _query__return.getResultItem()) {
        System.out.println(resultItem.getProductId() + ": "
            + resultItem.getPrice());
      }
    } catch (QueryInvalidQty e) {
      System.out.println("Invalid qty: "
```

```
            + e.getFaultMessage().getInvalidQty());
      } catch (QueryInvalidProductId e) {
        System.out.println("Invalid product ID: "
            + e.getFaultMessage().getInvalidProductId());
      }
    }
  }
```

Run it and it should print "Invalid qty: -200" successfully.

Summary

You can freely use XML schema elements and XML types to express complex data structures. The code generator will translate them into Java types.

For better performance, you should design the interfaces of your web service operations so that more data is sent in a message.

To report an error from your operation, define a message in the WSDL file and use it as a fault message in the operation. Then add a corresponding child element in the SOAP binding to store it into the SOAP Fault element. The fault message should contain one and only one part which is an XML element describing the fault. The code generator will map a fault message to a Java exception class and the part as a field. The operation will be mapped to a Java method throwing that exception.

If you have existing XML elements in an XSD file that you'd like to use in a WSDL file, you can use <import> to import them. You can specify the relative path to the XSD file so that the WSDL parser can find it.

Chapter 6

Sending binary files

What's in this chapter?

In this chapter you'll learn how to receive and return binary files in your web service.

Providing the image of a product

Suppose that you'd like to have a web service to allow people to upload the image (jpeg) of a product (identified by a product id). The SOAP message may be like below. But how to represent the binary image data? The problem is that SOAP uses XML and XML uses text to represent the data:

```
<Envelope>
  <Body>
    <uploadImage>
      <productId>p01</productId>
      <image>???</image>
    </uploadImage>
  </Body>
</Envelope>
```

How to send the binary image data?

One way to do it is to encode the binary data into a text format. For example, one could encode byte 0 as character 'A', encode byte 1 as character 'B' and etc. One of such an encoding is the base64 encoding. Then the SOAP message will be like:

```
<Envelope>
  <Body>
    <uploadImage>
      <productId>p01</productId>
      <image>kdubn87kamlndy...</image>
    </uploadImage>
  </Body>
</Envelope>
```

The problem is that the base64 encoded data will be much larger than the binary version. This wastes processing time, network bandwidth and transmission time. In fact, if the image is huge, then many XML parsers may not be able to handle it properly. To solve this problem, instead of always representing an XML document as text, people state that it can be represented as a MIME message. For example, the above XML document (SOAP envelope) can be represented as below without changing its meaning:

This is a MIME message. It can contain multiple parts. Here it contains 2 parts. This MIME message represents the XML document (the SOAP envelope).

```
Content-Type: Multipart/Related

--MIME boundary
Content-Type: text/xml

<Envelope>
   <Body>
      <uploadImage>
         <productId>p01</productId>
         <image>
            <xop:Include
               xmlns:xop="http://www.w3.org/2004/08/xop/include"
               href="cid:abc"/>
         </image>
      </uploadImage>
   </Body>
</Envelope>

--MIME boundary
Content-Type: image/jpeg
Content-ID: abc

...binary data here...
...
--MIME boundary
```

A part that contains the "core" of the XML document as text.

This is the xop namespace. xop stands for XML-binary optimized packaging.

Refer to the actual data by content id.

Binary data is allowed in a MIME part.

A part that contains binary data (the image).

The key is that now the XML document (represented as a MIME message) can have textual parts and binary parts. Therefore it can represent binary data efficiently.

To implement this idea, create a new project named ImageService as usual. Rename the WSDL file as ImageService.wsdl and modify it as:

Use a urn as the target namespace.

```
<?xml version="1.0" encoding="UTF-8"?>
<wsdl:definitions xmlns:wsdl="http://schemas.xmlsoap.org/wsdl/"
  xmlns:soap="http://schemas.xmlsoap.org/wsdl/soap/"
  xmlns:tns="urn:ttdev.com:service/img"
  xmlns:xsd="http://www.w3.org/2001/XMLSchema" name="ImageService"
  targetNamespace="urn:ttdev.com:service/img">
  <wsdl:types>
    <xsd:schema targetNamespace="urn:ttdev.com:service/img"
      xmlns:xsd="http://www.w3.org/2001/XMLSchema">
      <xsd:element name="uploadImage">
        <xsd:complexType>
          <xsd:sequence>
            <xsd:element name="productId" type="xsd:string" />
            <xsd:element name="image" type="xsd:base64Binary" />
          </xsd:sequence>
        </xsd:complexType>
      </xsd:element>
    </xsd:schema>
  </wsdl:types>
  <wsdl:message name="uploadImageRequest">
    <wsdl:part name="parameters" element="tns:uploadImage" />
  </wsdl:message>
  <wsdl:portType name="ImageService">
    <wsdl:operation name="uploadImage">
      <wsdl:input message="tns:uploadImageRequest" />
    </wsdl:operation>
  </wsdl:portType>
  <wsdl:binding name="ImageServiceSOAP" type="tns:ImageService">
    <soap:binding style="document"
      transport="http://schemas.xmlsoap.org/soap/http" />
    <wsdl:operation name="uploadImage">
      <soap:operation soapAction="urn:ttdev.com:service/img/uploadImage" />
      <wsdl:input>
        <soap:body use="literal" />
      </wsdl:input>
    </wsdl:operation>
  </wsdl:binding>
  <wsdl:service name="ImageService">
    <wsdl:port binding="tns:ImageServiceSOAP" name="p1">
      <soap:address location="http://localhost:8080/is/p1" />
    </wsdl:port>
  </wsdl:service>
</wsdl:definitions>
```

It will contain binary data. It is basically to be encoded using base64. Later you will tell the code generator to use XOP for it.

The operation doesn't return anything, so there is no output message.

Although this is not required, it uses the wrapped convention. Next, update the CodeGenerator class:

```
public class CodeGenerator {
  public static void main(String[] args) {
    WSDLToJava.main(new String[] {
        "-server",
        "-d", "src/main/java",
        "src/main/resources/ImageService.wsdl" });
    System.out.println("Done!");
  }
}
```

Generate the code again. Check the SEI:

```
@WebService(targetNamespace = "urn:ttdev.com:service/img", name = "ImageService")
@XmlSeeAlso( { ObjectFactory.class })
public interface ImageService {
```

```
    @Oneway
    @RequestWrapper(
      localName = "uploadImage",
      targetNamespace = "urn:ttdev.com:service/img",
      className = "com.ttdev.service.img.UploadImage")
    @WebMethod(action = "urn:ttdev.com:service/img/uploadImage")
    public void uploadImage(
        @WebParam(
          name = "productId",
          targetNamespace = "") java.lang.String productId,
        @WebParam(
          name = "image",
          targetNamespace = "") byte[] image);
  }
```

Note that the binary image data is presented as a byte array. You are NOT using XOP yet. You're just getting the service up and running. Create a ImageServiceImpl class:

```
  package com.ttdev.service.img;
  ...
  @WebService(endpointInterface = "com.ttdev.service.img.ImageService")
  public class ImageServiceImpl implements ImageService {

    @Override
    public void uploadImage(String productId, byte[] image) {
      try {
        FileOutputStream out = new FileOutputStream(productId+".jpg");
        out.write(image);
        out.close();
      } catch (IOException e) {
        throw new RuntimeException(e);
      }
    }
  }
```

It simply saves the image data into a p01.jpg file if the product is p01. Next, create an ImageClient product as usual. Copy any .jpg file in your computer into the src/main/resources folder as sample.jpg. Then modify the ImageService_P1_Client class:

```
  public final class ImageService_P1_Client {
    ...
    public static void main(String args[]) throws Exception {
      ...
      ImageService_Service ss = new ImageService_Service(wsdlURL, SERVICE_NAME);
      ImageService port = ss.getP1();
      {
        System.out.println("Invoking uploadImage...");
        java.lang.String _uploadImage_productId = "p01";
        FileInputStream in = new FileInputStream(
            "src/main/resources/sample.jpg");
        ByteArrayOutputStream out = new ByteArrayOutputStream();
        byte[] buf = new byte[1024];
        for (;;) {
          int noBytesRead = in.read(buf);
          if (noBytesRead == -1) {
            break;
          }
          out.write(buf, 0, noBytesRead);
        }
        port.uploadImage(_uploadImage_productId, out.toByteArray());
        out.close();
        in.close();
      }
      System.exit(0);
    }
```

```
}
```

Run the service and then run the client. Refresh the ImageService project and you should see a p01.jpg file there. Open it with a browser to verify that it is a copy of your sample.jpg.

To verify that it is NOT using XOP, use the TCP Monitor and adjust the client:

```
public final class ImageService_P1_Client {
  ...
  public static void main(String args[]) throws Exception {
    ...
    ImageService_Service ss = new ImageService_Service(wsdlURL, SERVICE_NAME);
    ImageService port = ss.getP1();
    {
      BindingProvider bp = (BindingProvider) port;
      bp.getRequestContext().put(
          BindingProvider.ENDPOINT_ADDRESS_PROPERTY,
          "http://localhost:1234/is/p1");
      System.out.println("Invoking uploadImage...");
      java.lang.String _uploadImage_productId = "p01";
      FileInputStream in = new FileInputStream(
          "src/main/resources/sample.jpg");
      ByteArrayOutputStream out = new ByteArrayOutputStream();
      ...
      port.uploadImage(_uploadImage_productId, out.toByteArray());
      out.close();
      in.close();
    }
    System.exit(0);
  }
}
```

The message captured should be like below. That is, a lot of binary data encoded as base64:

```
POST /is/p1 HTTP/1.1
Content-Type: text/xml; charset=UTF-8
SOAPAction: "urn:ttdev.com:service/img/uploadImage"
Accept: */*
User-Agent: Apache CXF 2.2.5
Cache-Control: no-cache
Pragma: no-cache
Host: 127.0.0.1:1234
Connection: keep-alive
Transfer-Encoding: chunked

ff9
<soap:Envelope xmlns:soap="http://schemas.xmlsoap.org/soap/envelope/">
  <soap:Body>
    <ns2:uploadImage xmlns:ns2="urn:ttdev.com:service/img">
      <productId>p01</productId>
      <image>/9j/4AAQSkZJRgABAgEASABIAAD/7QlCUGhvdG9zaG9wIDMuMAA4QklNA+0AAAAAAB
AASAAAAAEAAgBIAAAAAQACOEJJTQQNAAAAA...zr/2Q==</image>
    </ns2:uploadImage>
  </soap:Body></soap:Envelope>0
```

To enable the use of XOP, modify the WSDL file in the client project:

```
<?xml version="1.0" encoding="UTF-8"?>
<wsdl:definitions xmlns:wsdl="http://schemas.xmlsoap.org/wsdl/"
  xmlns:soap="http://schemas.xmlsoap.org/wsdl/soap/"
  xmlns:tns="urn:ttdev.com:service/img"
  xmlns:xmime="http://www.w3.org/2005/05/xmlmime"
  xmlns:xsd="http://www.w3.org/2001/XMLSchema" name="ImageService"
  targetNamespace="urn:ttdev.com:service/img">
  <wsdl:types>
    <xsd:schema targetNamespace="urn:ttdev.com:service/img"
      xmlns:xsd="http://www.w3.org/2001/XMLSchema">
      <xsd:element name="uploadImage">
        <xsd:complexType>
          <xsd:sequence>
            <xsd:element name="productId" type="xsd:string" />
            <xsd:element name="image" type="xsd:base64Binary"
              xmime:expectedContentTypes="application/octet-stream"/>
          </xsd:sequence>
        </xsd:complexType>
      </xsd:element>
    </xsd:schema>
  </wsdl:types>
  ...
</wsdl:definitions>
```

This XML MIME namespace defines XML attributes used for representing XML in a MIME message.

It states that this element should be sent as a MIME part those content type is application/octet-stream which means a generic (no particular meaning) byte stream.

Generate the code again. Then data type of the binary data will be changed from byte[] to DataHandler:

```
@WebService(targetNamespace = "urn:ttdev.com:service/img", name = "ImageService")
@XmlSeeAlso( { ObjectFactory.class })
public interface ImageService {

  @Oneway
  @RequestWrapper(...)
  @WebMethod(action = "urn:ttdev.com:service/img/uploadImage")
  public void uploadImage(
      @WebParam(...) java.lang.String productId,
      @WebParam(...) javax.activation.DataHandler image);
}
```

How's a DataHandler differ from a byte array? A DataHandler can provide an InputStream on demand, which means that the program doesn't need to load all the data into memory. In addition, a DataHandler can tell you the content type of the data.

As the SEI has changed, you need to modify the ImageService_P1_Client class to pass a DataHandler:

```
public static void main(String args[]) throws Exception {
   ...
   ImageService_Service ss = new ImageService_Service(wsdlURL, SERVICE_NAME);
   ImageService port = ss.getP1();
   {
      BindingProvider bp = (BindingProvider) port;
      bp.getRequestContext().put(
            BindingProvider.ENDPOINT_ADDRESS_PROPERTY,
            "http://localhost:1234/is/p1");
      System.out.println("Invoking uploadImage...");
      java.lang.String _uploadImage_productId = "p01";
      FileDataSource ds = new FileDataSource("src/main/resources/sample.jpg");
      port.uploadImage(_uploadImage_productId, new DataHandler(ds));
   }
   System.exit(0);
}
```

Create a DataSource from this file. A DataSource can also provide an InputStream and a content type (here it will guess from the file extension .jpg to conclude that the content type is image/jpeg).

Let the DataHandler get the data from this DataSource. In addition to providing the data and the content type, a DataHandler can also suggest a list of actions that can be performed on that data (something like when you right click on a file and you'll see a list of menu commands).

However, this is not enough. You need to enable this special packaging in the client:

```
import javax.xml.ws.Binding;
import javax.xml.ws.soap.SOAPBinding;
...
public static void main(String args[]) throws Exception {
   ...
   ImageService_Service ss = new ImageService_Service(wsdlURL, SERVICE_NAME);
   ImageService port = ss.getP1();
   {
      BindingProvider bp = (BindingProvider) port;
      bp.getRequestContext().put(
            BindingProvider.ENDPOINT_ADDRESS_PROPERTY,
            "http://localhost:1234/is/p1");
      Binding binding = bp.getBinding();
      SOAPBinding soapBinding = (SOAPBinding) binding;
      soapBinding.setMTOMEnabled(true);
      System.out.println("Invoking uploadImage...");
      java.lang.String _uploadImage_productId = "p01";
      FileDataSource ds = new FileDataSource("src/main/resources/sample.jpg");
      port.uploadImage(_uploadImage_productId, new DataHandler(ds));
   }
   System.exit(0);
}
```

Get the binding from the binding provider (the port). Cast it to a SOAP binding as you're using SOAP.

Enable MTOM which stands for Message Transmission Optimization Mechanism. It simply means sending a SOAP message using XOP.

Run the client again. In the TCP Monitor, you should see:

```
POST /is/p1 HTTP/1.1
Content-Type: multipart/related; type="application/xop+xml";
boundary="uuid:9223456b-e0fb-4d04-bf15-52793bea1426";
start="<root.message@cxf.apache.org>"; start-info="text/xml"
SOAPAction: "urn:ttdev.com:service/img/uploadImage"
Accept: */*
User-Agent: Apache CXF 2.2.5
Cache-Control: no-cache
Pragma: no-cache
Host: 127.0.0.1:1234
Connection: keep-alive
Transfer-Encoding: chunked

ff9

--uuid:9223456b-e0fb-4d04-bf15-52793bea1426
Content-Type: application/xop+xml; charset=UTF-8; type="text/xml";
Content-Transfer-Encoding: binary
Content-ID: <root.message@cxf.apache.org>

<soap:Envelope xmlns:soap="http://schemas.xmlsoap.org/soap/envelope/">
   <soap:Body>
      <ns2:uploadImage xmlns:ns2="urn:ttdev.com:service/img">
         <productId>p01</productId>
         <image>
            <xop:Include
               xmlns:xop="http://www.w3.org/2004/08/xop/include"
               href="cid:c9796a3a-ea9d-495d-ae5b-b7f854ea26bb-1@http%3A%2F
%2Fcxf.apache.org%2F"/>
         </image>
      </ns2:uploadImage>
   </soap:Body>
</soap:Envelope>
--uuid:9223456b-e0fb-4d04-bf15-52793bea1426
Content-Type: image/jpeg
Content-Transfer-Encoding: binary
Content-ID: <c9796a3a-ea9d-495d-ae5b-b7f854ea26bb-1@http://cxf.apache.org/>

����□JFIF□□H□H□□��      BPhotoshop 3.0□8BIM�□□□□□□H□□□□□H□□□□8BIM
□□□□□□□□x8BIM�□□□□□□□□□□□□□□8BIM
▪ ▪ ▪ ▪ ▪ ▪ ▪ 8BIM' ▪ ▪ ▪ ▪ ▪
...
--uuid:9223456b-e0fb-4d04-bf15-52793bea1426--
0
```

MIME message (multipart/related)

Refer to the binary data using cid (content id).

The binary data

Note that even though you haven't done anything in the service, it can already successfully decode the SOAP message sent using MTOM. This is designed for good compatibility: The receiver can receive all kinds of formats, while explicit configuration determines which format to be initiated by the sender.

Enabling MTOM in the service

For the moment, it is your client that needs to send a file. If it was your web service that needed to do that, you would need to enable MTOM in the service. To do that, copy the WSDL file from the client into the service and generate the code again. Then modify your implementation class to use a DataHandler:

```
public class ImageServiceImpl implements ImageService {

  @Override
  public void uploadImage(String productId, DataHandler image) {
    try {
      FileOutputStream out = new FileOutputStream(productId+".jpg");
      image.writeTo(out);
      out.close();
    } catch (IOException e) {
      throw new RuntimeException(e);
    }
  }
}
```

To initiate MTOM, modify the ImageService_P1_Server class:

```
public class ImageService_P1_Server {

  protected ImageService_P1_Server() throws Exception {
    System.out.println("Starting Server");
    Object implementor = new ImageServiceImpl();
    String address = "http://localhost:8080/is/p1";
    Endpoint endpoint = Endpoint.publish(address, implementor);
    SOAPBinding soapBinding = (SOAPBinding) endpoint.getBinding();
    soapBinding.setMTOMEnabled(true);
  }
  ...
}
```

The way to enable MTOM is very similar to the client: you get the SOAP binding and enable MTOM. For the client you get it from the port, for the service you get it from the endpoint.

Doing it in Axis2

To do it in Axis2, copy the Axis2SimpleService and paste it as Axis2ImageService, copy the Axis2SimpleClient and paste it as Axis2ImageClient. Copy the WSDL file and XSD file from the ImageService project into both of these two new projects (and delete the existing WSDL files).

Next, modify the CodeGenerator class in the Axis2BizService project as shown below. Note that the two package mappings are separated by a comma:

```
public class CodeGenerator {
public static void main(String[] args) throws Exception {
  WSDL2Code.main(new String[] {
      "-ss",
      "-sd",
      "-uw",
      "-S", "src/main/java",
      "-R", "src/main/resources/META-INF",
      "-ns2p", "urn:ttdev.com:service/img=com.ttdev.is",
      "-uri", "src/main/resources/ImageService.wsdl" });
  System.out.println("Done!");
}
}
```

Do the same thing in the Axis2ImageClient project:

```
public class CodeGenerator {
  public static void main(String[] args) throws Exception {
    WSDL2Code.main(new String[] {
        "-uw",
        "-S", "src/main/java",
        "-R", "src/main/resources/META-INF",
```

```
        "-ns2p", "urn:ttdev.com:service/img=com.ttdev.is",
        "-uri", "src/main/resources/ImageService.wsdl" });
    System.out.println("Done!");
  }
}
```

Delete the com.ttdev.ss package and the src/main/resources/META-INF folder in both projects. Then run CodeGenerator in both projects. Fill in the code in the ImageServiceSkeleton class:

```
public class ImageServiceSkeleton {

  public void uploadImage(java.lang.String productId,
      javax.activation.DataHandler image) {
    try {
      FileOutputStream out = new FileOutputStream(productId + ".jpg");
      image.writeTo(out);
      out.close();
    } catch (IOException e) {
      throw new RuntimeException(e);
    }
  }
}
```

To initiate MTOM from the service, modify src/main/resources/META-INF/services.xml:

```
<serviceGroup>
  <service name="ImageService">
    <messageReceivers>
      <messageReceiver mep="http://www.w3.org/ns/wsdl/in-only"
        class="service.com.ttdev.ImageServiceMessageReceiverInOnly" />
    </messageReceivers>
    <parameter name="ServiceClass">service.com.ttdev.ImageServiceSkeleton
    </parameter>
    <parameter name="useOriginalwsdl">true</parameter>
    <parameter name="modifyUserWSDLPortAddress">true</parameter>
    <parameter name="enableMTOM">true</parameter>
    <operation name="uploadImage" mep="http://www.w3.org/ns/wsdl/in-only"
      namespace="urn:ttdev.com:service/img">
      <actionMapping>urn:ttdev.com:service/img/uploadImage
      </actionMapping>
    </operation>
  </service>
</serviceGroup>
```

Modify the pom.xml file to use a new artifact ID:

```
<project ...>
  <modelVersion>4.0.0</modelVersion>
  <groupId>com.ttdev</groupId>
  <artifactId>ImageService</artifactId>
  <version>0.0.1-SNAPSHOT</version>
  ...
</project>
```

Run as Maven package and copy the jar file into the Axis2 server (in the axis2/repository/services folder) as ImageService.aar.

Then, in the client project, create an ImageClient class:

```
package com.ttdev.is;
...
import javax.activation.DataHandler;
import javax.activation.FileDataSource;
import org.apache.axis2.Constants;

public class ImageClient {
  public static void main(String[] args) throws RemoteException {
```

```
        ImageServiceStub service = new ImageServiceStub(
            "http://localhost:1234/axis2/services/ImageService");
        service._getServiceClient().getOptions().setProperty(
            Constants.Configuration.ENABLE_MTOM, "true");
        FileDataSource ds = new FileDataSource("src/main/resources/sample.jpg");
        service.uploadImage("p01", new DataHandler(ds));
    }
}
```

The way to enable MTOM in Axis2 is very similar to that in CXF (which actually is the standard JAX-WS API).

Copy the sample.jpg file into the client package in the src/main/resources folder. Run the client and observe the message in TCP Monitor. It should be packaged in a MIME message.

Interoperability

If you need to send binary files to others, make sure the other side supports MTOM. For example, for .NET, MTOM is supported with WSE (Web Services Enhancements) 3.0 or later.

Summary

XOP stores XML elements that is of the type xsd:base64Binary as MIME parts and represents the whole XML document as a MIME message. When the XML document is a SOAP envelope, it is called MTOM.

To receive a binary file using MTOM, if the receiver is written with CXF or Axis2, for maximum interoperability, it can always handle incoming messages using MTOM without any configuration.

To send a binary file using MTOM, indicate the content type in the schema and set an option to enable MTOM in the sender.

Chapter 7

Invoking lengthy operations

What's in this chapter?

What if your web service involves manual processing that could take days to finish? In this chapter you'll learn what the problems are and how to deal with them.

Invoking a time consuming operation

Suppose that you have a client program that can invoke a web service to perform some kind of statistics (see below). Let's assume that it will take quite some time, say, 20 seconds to calculate the statistics. If the client insists on waiting for the result before proceeding, then the program may appear to have stopped responding.

Menu
1: Get statistics
2: Quit
Command: 1
The result is: ...
Menu
1: Get statistics
2: Quit
Command:
A long silence (e.g., 20s) here

To solve this problem, the client program may create a new thread to invoke the operation (see below), while the main thread will continue to take commands from the user. When that new thread receives the result, it will display the result into the screen "by brute force":

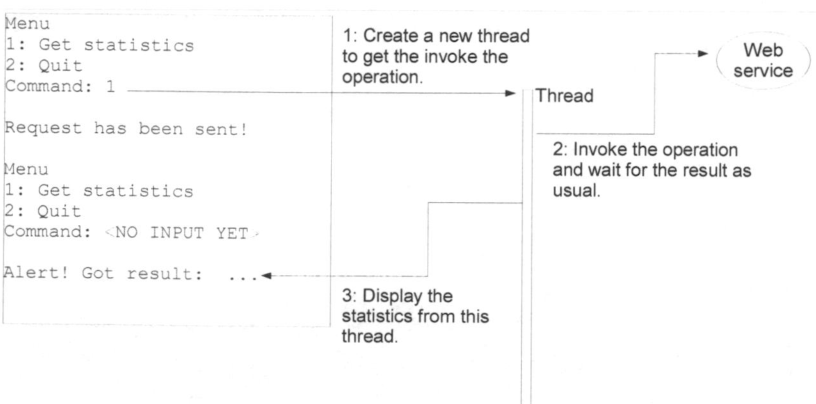

To implement this idea, create a StatService project as usual. Create a StatService.wsdl:

```
<?xml version="1.0" encoding="UTF-8" standalone="no"?>
<wsdl:definitions xmlns:soap="http://schemas.xmlsoap.org/wsdl/soap/"
  xmlns:tns="http://ttdev.com/ss" xmlns:wsdl="http://schemas.xmlsoap.org/wsdl/"
```

```
    xmlns:xsd="http://www.w3.org/2001/XMLSchema" name="StatService"
    targetNamespace="http://ttdev.com/ss">
    <wsdl:types>
      <xsd:schema targetNamespace="http://ttdev.com/ss">
        <xsd:element name="getStatistics" type="xsd:string">
        </xsd:element>
        <xsd:element name="getStatisticsResponse" type="xsd:string">
        </xsd:element>
      </xsd:schema>
    </wsdl:types>
    <wsdl:message name="getStatisticsRequest">
      <wsdl:part element="tns:getStatistics" name="parameters" />
    </wsdl:message>
    <wsdl:message name="getStatisticsResponse">
      <wsdl:part element="tns:getStatisticsResponse" name="parameters" />
    </wsdl:message>
    <wsdl:portType name="StatService">
      <wsdl:operation name="getStatistics">
        <wsdl:input message="tns:getStatisticsRequest" />
        <wsdl:output message="tns:getStatisticsResponse" />
      </wsdl:operation>
    </wsdl:portType>
    <wsdl:binding name="StatServiceSOAP" type="tns:StatService">
      <soap:binding style="document"
        transport="http://schemas.xmlsoap.org/soap/http" />
      <wsdl:operation name="getStatistics">
        <soap:operation soapAction="http://ttdev.com/ss/NewOperation" />
        <wsdl:input>
          <soap:body use="literal" />
        </wsdl:input>
        <wsdl:output>
          <soap:body use="literal" />
        </wsdl:output>
      </wsdl:operation>
    </wsdl:binding>
    <wsdl:service name="StatService">
      <wsdl:port binding="tns:StatServiceSOAP" name="p1">
        <soap:address location="http://localhost:8080/ss/p1" />
      </wsdl:port>
    </wsdl:service>
  </wsdl:definitions>
```

There is nothing special about it. In order to create a new thread for the call, modify the WSDL file as below:

```
<wsdl:definitions
  xmlns:soap="http://schemas.xmlsoap.org/wsdl/soap/"
  xmlns:tns="http://ttdev.com/ss"
  xmlns:wsdl="http://schemas.xmlsoap.org/wsdl/"
  xmlns:jaxws="http://java.sun.com/xml/ns/jaxws"
  xmlns:xsd="http://www.w3.org/2001/XMLSchema"
  name="StatService" targetNamespace="http://ttdev.com/ss">
  ...
  <wsdl:portType name="StatService">
    <wsdl:operation name="getStatistics">
      <wsdl:input message="tns:getStatisticsRequest" />
      <wsdl:output message="tns:getStatisticsResponse" />
      <jaxws:bindings>
        <jaxws:enableAsyncMapping>true</jaxws:enableAsyncMapping>
      </jaxws:bindings>
    </wsdl:operation>
  </wsdl:portType>
  ...
</wsdl:definitions>
```

A JAXWS binding allows you to attach Java meaning to the WSDL elements. For example, here you're saying that the Java method to be generated should be asynchronous (new thread).

You could put the binding here to affect the whole port type instead of just one operation.

By the way, to enable auto-completion for the elements in this JAXWS namespace, you can choose Windows | Preferences, then choose XML | XML Catalog and add a user entry:

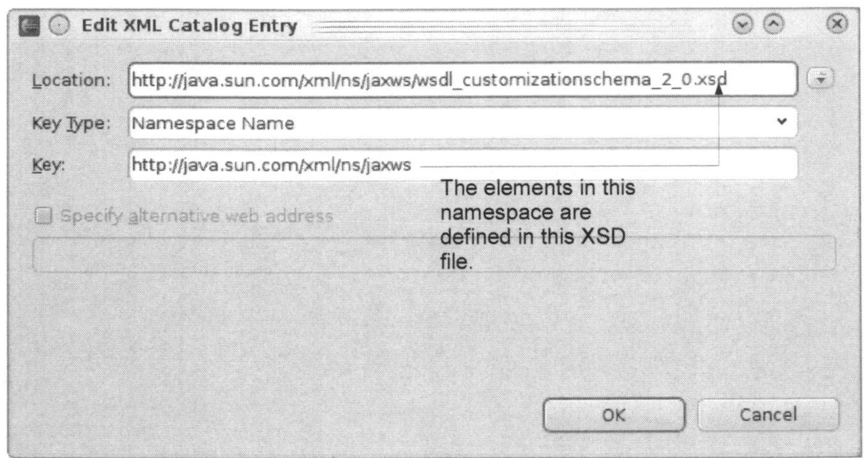

Modify the CodeGenerator class:

```
public class CodeGenerator {
  public static void main(String[] args) {
    WSDLToJava.main(new String[] {
        "-server",
        "-d", "src/main/java",
        "src/main/resources/StatService.wsdl" });
    System.out.println("Done!");
  }
}
```

Delete the com.ttdev.ss package and generate the code again. Observe that the SEI has now two asynchronous method signatures:

```
@WebService(targetNamespace = "http://ttdev.com/ss", name = "StatService")
@XmlSeeAlso( { ObjectFactory.class })
@SOAPBinding(parameterStyle = SOAPBinding.ParameterStyle.BARE)
public interface StatService {

  @WebMethod(operationName = "getStatistics")
  public Response<java.lang.String> getStatisticsAsync(
       @WebParam(...) java.lang.String parameters);

  @WebMethod(operationName = "getStatistics")
  public Future<?> getStatisticsAsync(
       @WebParam(...) java.lang.String parameters,
       @WebParam(
          name = "asyncHandler",
          targetNamespace = "") AsyncHandler<java.lang.String> asyncHandler);

  @WebResult(...)
  @WebMethod(action = "http://ttdev.com/ss/NewOperation")
  public java.lang.String getStatistics(
       @WebParam(...) java.lang.String parameters);
}
```

If you call it, it will create a new thread to call the web service and return a Response object to you immediately. You can poll the Response object from time to time.

Just like the previous method except that you should pass a handler to it. When the result is available, it will notify your handler.

This is the normal synchronous (blocking) method.

This interface is mainly used by the client. For the service, you only need to implement the synchronous method. So, create the StatServiceImpl class:

```
@WebService(endpointInterface = "com.ttdev.ss.StatService")
public class StatServiceImpl implements StatService {

  @Override
  public String getStatistics(String parameters) {
    try {
      Thread.sleep(3000);
      return parameters.toUpperCase();
    } catch (InterruptedException e) {
      throw new RuntimeException(e);
    }
  }
  @Override
  public Response<String> getStatisticsAsync(String parameters) {
    return null;
  }
  @Override
  public Future<?> getStatisticsAsync(String parameters,
      AsyncHandler<String> asyncHandler) {
    return null;
  }
}
```

Here you're simulating a slow processing by sleeping for 3 seconds, then just return the upper case version of the argument. To test it, create a StatClient project as usual. Modify its CodeGenerator class:

```
public class CodeGenerator {
  public static void main(String[] args) {
    WSDLToJava.main(new String[] {
        "-client",
        "-d", "src/main/java",
        "src/main/resources/StatService.wsdl" });
    System.out.println("Done!");
  }
}
```

Delete the com.ttdev.ss package and generate the code. Modify the StatService_P1_Client class:

```
public static void main(String args[]) throws Exception {
   ...
   StatService_Service ss = new StatService_Service(wsdlURL, SERVICE_NAME);
   StatService port = ss.getP1();
   port.getStatisticsAsync("abc", new AsyncHandler<String>() {

     @Override
     public void handleResponse(Response<String> res) {
       try {
         System.out.println("Got result: " + res.get());
       } catch (Exception e) {
         throw new RuntimeException(e);
       }
     }
   });
   System.out.println("Press Enter to quit");
   new BufferedReader(new InputStreamReader(System.in)).readLine();
   System.exit(0);
}
```

When the new thread gets the result, it will call this method.

The result is available here.

Must not quit now as the result may not be available yet. So, ask the user to press Enter to quit.

Run the service and then run the client. The output should be like below:

```
Press Enter to quit
```

```
<A FEW SECOND OF SILENCE>
Got result: ABC
```

Press Enter to terminate the program.

What if you can't modify the WSDL file?

What if the WSDL file is controlled by a 3rd party and you aren't supposed to modify it, then how to do map the operation to an asynchronous Java method? To simulate this situation, delete the binding from the WSDL files in both projects. Then, in the client project, create a file named binding.xml (the name is unimportant) in the src/main/resources folder:

Apply this "binding file" to this WSDL file. It is a URL to the WSDL file. Here it is a relative path.

```
<?xml version="1.0" encoding="UTF-8"?>
<jaxws:bindings
  xmlns:jaxws="http://java.sun.com/xml/ns/jaxws"
  wsdlLocation="StatService.wsdl"
  node="wsdl:definitions/wsdl:portType/wsdl:operation[@name='getStatistics']">
  <jaxws:enableAsyncMapping>true</jaxws:enableAsyncMapping>
</jaxws:bindings>
```

Apply the bindings to this node in the XML element tree. This expression is like a path in a file system. It is called a XPath.

```
<wsdl:definitions>
    <wsdl:portType>
        <wsdl:operation name="getStatistics">
```

You can match the element using its attribute values.

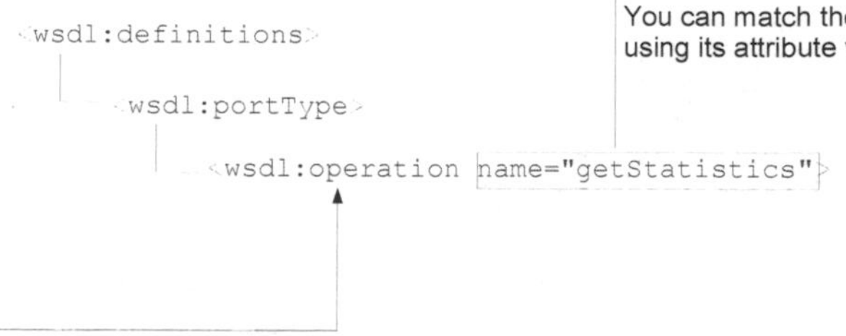

Modify the CodeGenerator class in the client project to apply this binding file:

```
public class CodeGenerator {
  public static void main(String[] args) {
    WSDLToJava.main(new String[] {
         "-client",
         "-d", "src/main/java",
         "-b", "src/main/resources/binding.xml",
         "src/main/resources/StatService.wsdl" });
    System.out.println("Done!");
  }
}
```

Generate the code again. Note that the SEI will still have the asynchronous methods. Fill the code into StatService_P1_Client again to call the asynchronous method.

In the service project, just generate the code again. You don't need the binding file as the asynchronous handling is entirely done on the client side by the service stub. It has got nothing to do with the service implementation at all. The StatServiceImpl class should be adjusted as:

```
public class StatServiceImpl implements StatService {
```

```
    @Override
    public String getStatistics(String parameters) {
      try {
        Thread.sleep(3000);
        return parameters.toUpperCase();
      } catch (InterruptedException e) {
        throw new RuntimeException(e);
      }
    }
}
```

Run the service and then run the client. The client should continue to run in an asynchronous manner.

Extremely lengthy processing

Currently the processing in the service only takes 3 seconds to finish. What if it takes 3 hours or even 3 days? This is possible if it relies on human processing. Then it will be a problem because after sending the HTTP request, the client will expect the HTTP response to arrive "shortly" in the same TCP connection:

If a response isn't received in a short time (e.g., by default 30 seconds in CXF), the HTTP client code in the client will think something is wrong in the server. In order to avoid holding up the resources used by the connection, it will time out and terminate the connection.

To solve this problem, you could use a transport such as SMTP (it is fine for the reply email to arrive days later). However, the use of any transport for web services other HTTP is quite uncommon and thus is not good for interoperability.

An easier solution is to let the web service return a dummy response immediately to acknowledge the request (see below). A few days later, when the result is available, let the web service initiate a call back to the client.

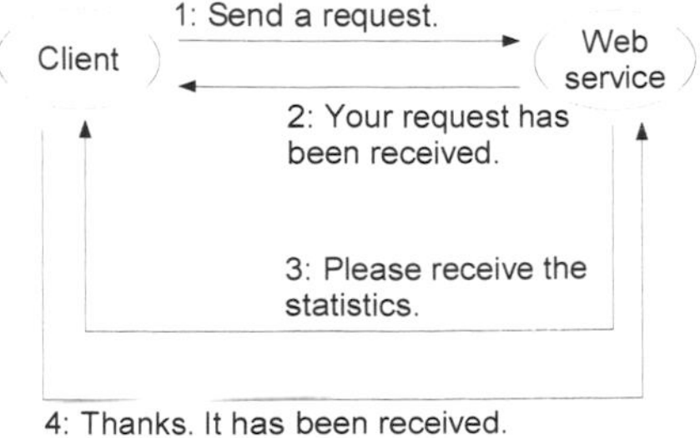

It means that each side will act as both a web service and a client:

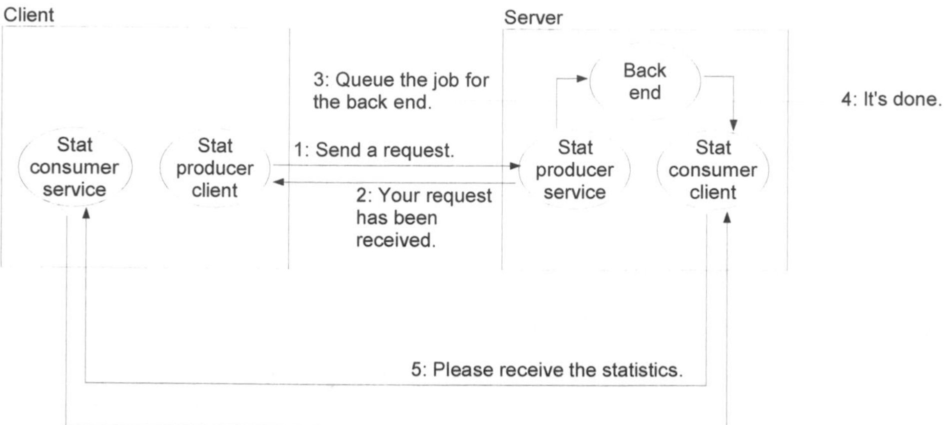

To implement this idea, copy the StatService project as StatProducer. Create two a WSDL file named StatProducer.wsdl:

```
<?xml version="1.0" encoding="UTF-8" standalone="no"?>
<wsdl:definitions xmlns:soap="http://schemas.xmlsoap.org/wsdl/soap/"
  xmlns:tns="http://ttdev.com/sp" xmlns:wsdl="http://schemas.xmlsoap.org/wsdl/"
  xmlns:xsd="http://www.w3.org/2001/XMLSchema" name="StatProducer"
  targetNamespace="http://ttdev.com/sp">
  <wsdl:types>
    <xsd:schema targetNamespace="http://ttdev.com/sp">
      <xsd:element name="getStatistics" type="xsd:string">
      </xsd:element>
    </xsd:schema>
  </wsdl:types>
  <wsdl:message name="getStatisticsRequest">
    <wsdl:part element="tns:getStatistics" name="parameters" />
  </wsdl:message>
  <wsdl:portType name="StatProducer">
    <wsdl:operation name="getStatistics">
      <wsdl:input message="tns:getStatisticsRequest" />
    </wsdl:operation>
  </wsdl:portType>
  <wsdl:binding name="StatProducerSOAP" type="tns:StatProducer">
    <soap:binding style="document"
      transport="http://schemas.xmlsoap.org/soap/http" />
    <wsdl:operation name="getStatistics">
      <soap:operation soapAction="http://ttdev.com/sp/NewOperation" />
      <wsdl:input>
        <soap:body use="literal" />
      </wsdl:input>
    </wsdl:operation>
  </wsdl:binding>
  <wsdl:service name="StatProducer">
    <wsdl:port binding="tns:StatProducerSOAP" name="p1">
      <soap:address location="http://localhost:8080/sp/p1" />
    </wsdl:port>
  </wsdl:service>
</wsdl:definitions>
```

Note that the operation has only an input message but no output message. It means after sending the SOAP message as an HTTP request, it will expect an (successful) HTTP response containing no SOAP message. That will serve as the dummy acknowledgement.

Create another WSDL file named StatConsumer.wsdl in the same folder:

```
<?xml version="1.0" encoding="UTF-8" standalone="no"?>
<wsdl:definitions xmlns:soap="http://schemas.xmlsoap.org/wsdl/soap/"
  xmlns:tns="http://ttdev.com/sc" xmlns:wsdl="http://schemas.xmlsoap.org/wsdl/"
  xmlns:xsd="http://www.w3.org/2001/XMLSchema" name="StatConsumer"
  targetNamespace="http://ttdev.com/sc">
  <wsdl:types>
    <xsd:schema targetNamespace="http://ttdev.com/sc">
      <xsd:element name="putStatistics" type="xsd:string">
      </xsd:element>
    </xsd:schema>
  </wsdl:types>
  <wsdl:message name="putStatisticsRequest">
    <wsdl:part element="tns:putStatistics" name="parameters" />
  </wsdl:message>
  <wsdl:portType name="StatConsumer">
    <wsdl:operation name="putStatistics">
      <wsdl:input message="tns:putStatisticsRequest" />
    </wsdl:operation>
  </wsdl:portType>
  <wsdl:binding name="StatConsumerSOAP" type="tns:StatConsumer">
    <soap:binding style="document"
      transport="http://schemas.xmlsoap.org/soap/http" />
    <wsdl:operation name="putStatistics">
      <soap:operation soapAction="http://ttdev.com/sc/NewOperation" />
      <wsdl:input>
        <soap:body use="literal" />
      </wsdl:input>
    </wsdl:operation>
  </wsdl:binding>
  <wsdl:service name="StatConsumer">
    <wsdl:port binding="tns:StatConsumerSOAP" name="p1">
      <soap:address location="http://localhost:8081/sc/p1" />
    </wsdl:port>
  </wsdl:service>
</wsdl:definitions>
```

Again, the operation has no output message. Also note that the endpoint address is using port 8081 for the consumer side as port 8080 has been used by the producer side.

The CodeGenerator class should be like:

```
public class CodeGenerator {
  public static void main(String[] args) {
    WSDLToJava.main(new String[] {
        "-server",
        "-d", "src/main/java",
        "src/main/resources/StatProducer.wsdl" });
    WSDLToJava.main(new String[] {
        "-client",
        "-d", "src/main/java",
        "src/main/resources/StatConsumer.wsdl" });
    System.out.println("Done!");
  }
}
```

Run the CodeGenerator class. Then create a StatProducerImpl class in the com.ttdev.sp package:

```
@WebService(endpointInterface = "com.ttdev.sp.StatProducer")
public class StatProducerImpl implements StatProducer {
  private Queue<String> statRequestQueue;

  public StatProducerImpl(Queue<String> statRequestQueue) {
    this.statRequestQueue = statRequestQueue;
```

```
    }
    @Override
    public void getStatistics(String parameters) {
      statRequestQueue.add(parameters);
    }
  }
```

It simply adds the request to a queue for later processing and return from the method (so that it won't tie up the thread). As the method ends immediately without error, a dummy successful HTTP response will be returned.

Then create a main program to launch the service and process the request queue. So, create a Main class in the com.ttdev package:

A blocking queue is a queue that will wait (i.e., block) if you're trying to retrieve an item but the queue is empty.

```
package com.ttdev;
...
import java.util.concurrent.BlockingQueue;
import java.util.concurrent.LinkedBlockingDeque;

public class Main {
  private BlockingQueue<String> requestQueue;

  public static void main(String[] args) {
    new StatServer().run();
  }
  public StatServer() {
    requestQueue = new LinkedBlockingDeque<String>();
  }
  private void run() {
    Object implementor = new StatProducerImpl(requestQueue);
    String address = "http://localhost:8080/sp/p1";
    Endpoint.publish(address, implementor);
    processRequeusts();
  }
  private void processRequeusts() {
    System.out.println("Waiting for requests");
    BufferedReader br = new BufferedReader(new InputStreamReader(System.in));
    while (true) {
      try {
        String req = requestQueue.take();
        System.out.println("Got a request: " + req);
        System.out.println("Enter response: ");
        String result = br.readLine();
        StatConsumer_Service ss = new StatConsumer_Service(
            StatConsumer_Service.WSDL_LOCATION, new QName(
                "http://ttdev.com/sc", "StatConsumer"));
        StatConsumer port = ss.getP1();
        port.putStatistics(result);
      } catch (InterruptedException e) {
        continue;
      } catch (IOException e) {
        continue;
      }
    }
  }
}
```

Let the service implementation object put the requests into this global queue.

Wait for and process requests after launching the producer service.

Try to get (and remove) the first item from the queue. If there is none, wait.

Let the user process the request and input the result. This simulates a manual processing that may take days.

Send the result to the client (which hosts the consumer service).

The StatProducer_P1_Server class is trying to create a StatProducerImpl without providing a queue. Either delete this class as it is not used or create a no-argument in the StatProducerImpl class to fix the compile error.

Copy the StatProducer project and paste it as the StatConsumer project. Then modify the CodeGenerator class to reverse the client and server roles:

```
public class CodeGenerator {
  public static void main(String[] args) {
    WSDLToJava.main(new String[] {
        "-client",
        "-d", "src/main/java",
        "src/main/resources/StatProducer.wsdl" });
    WSDLToJava.main(new String[] {
        "-server",
        "-d", "src/main/java",
        "src/main/resources/StatConsumer.wsdl" });
    System.out.println("Done!");
  }
```

Delete the com.ttdev.sp and com.ttdev.sc packages. Run the CodeGenerator class. Create the StatConsumerImpl class:

```
package com.ttdev.sc;
...
@WebService(endpointInterface = "com.ttdev.sc.StatConsumer")
public class StatConsumerImpl implements StatConsumer {

  @Override
  public void putStatistics(String parameters) {
    System.out.println("Got response: " + parameters);
  }

}
```

Here you simply print out the result. Next, modify the Main class as below. It starts the consumer service and then sends a single request to the producer service:

```
public class Main {
  public static void main(String[] args) {
    new Main().run();
  }
  private void run() {
    Object implementor = new StatConsumerImpl();
    String address = "http://localhost:8081/sc/p1";
    Endpoint.publish(address, implementor);
    sendRequeust();
  }
  private void sendRequeust() {
    System.out.println("Sending a request");
    StatProducer_Service ss = new StatProducer_Service(
        StatProducer_Service.WSDL_LOCATION, new QName(
            "http://ttdev.com/sp", "StatProducer"));
    StatProducer port = ss.getP1();
    port.getStatistics("abc");
  }
}
```

Now run the Main program in the StatProducer project. Then run the Main program in the StatConsumer product. Then the producer will prompt you for the response:

```
Waiting for requests
Got a request: abc
Enter response:
```

Enter any string such as "hello" as the response and press Enter. If you'd like, you can wait a very long time beforehand; it won't hurt. Then the client will receive the result and print it:

```
Sending a request
...
Got response: hello
```

Kill both processes in Eclipse (see below if you don't know how). This is necessary because you aren't calling System.exit() in the Main program so they will run indefinitely.

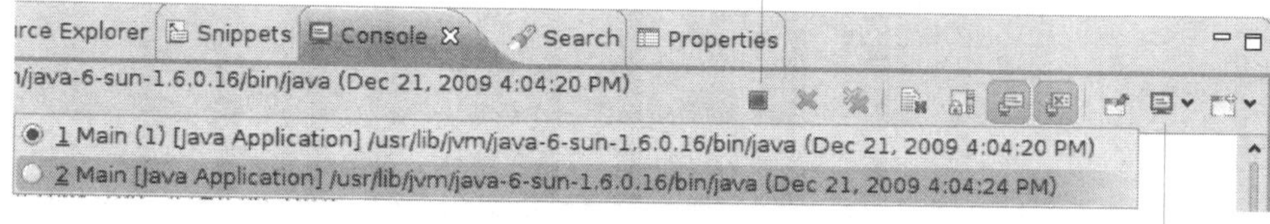

Specifying the reply address

For the moment, the producer will send the result to http://localhost:8081/sc/p1 as specified in the StatConsumer.wsdl file:

```
<wsdl:definitions ...>
  ...
  <wsdl:service name="StatConsumer">
    <wsdl:port binding="tns:StatConsumerSOAP" name="p1">
      <soap:address location="http://localhost:8081/sc/p1" />
    </wsdl:port>
  </wsdl:service>
</wsdl:definitions>
```

This doesn't make sense as there could be many different consumers running on different hosts on the Internet. To solve this problem, the consumer should specify the reply address when sending the request:

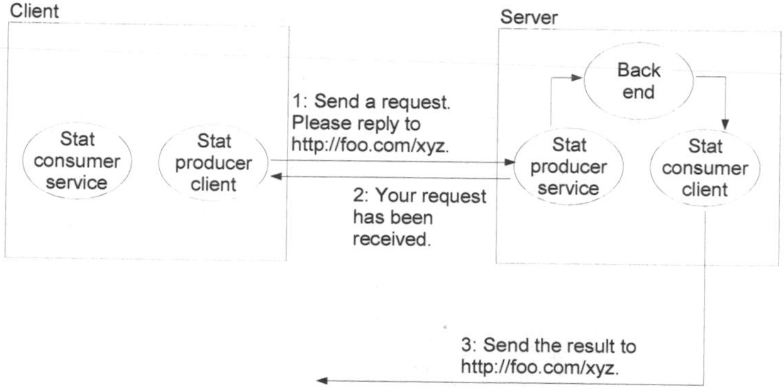

To implement this idea, modify the StatProducer.wsdl in both projects:

```
<?xml version="1.0" encoding="UTF-8" standalone="no"?>
<wsdl:definitions xmlns:soap="http://schemas.xmlsoap.org/wsdl/soap/"
  xmlns:tns="http://ttdev.com/sp" xmlns:wsdl="http://schemas.xmlsoap.org/wsdl/"
  xmlns:xsd="http://www.w3.org/2001/XMLSchema" name="StatProducer"
  targetNamespace="http://ttdev.com/sp">
  <wsdl:types>
    <xsd:schema targetNamespace="http://ttdev.com/sp">
      <xsd:element name="getStatistics">
```

```
        <xsd:complexType>
          <xsd:sequence>
            <xsd:element name="param" type="xsd:string">
            </xsd:element>
            <xsd:element name="replyTo" type="xsd:string">
            </xsd:element>
          </xsd:sequence>
        </xsd:complexType>
      </xsd:element>
    </xsd:schema>
  </wsdl:types>
  <wsdl:message name="getStatisticsRequest">
    <wsdl:part element="tns:getStatistics" name="parameters" />
  </wsdl:message>
  <wsdl:portType name="StatProducer">
    <wsdl:operation name="getStatistics">
      <wsdl:input message="tns:getStatisticsRequest" />
    </wsdl:operation>
  </wsdl:portType>
  <wsdl:binding name="StatProducerSOAP" type="tns:StatProducer">
    <soap:binding style="document"
      transport="http://schemas.xmlsoap.org/soap/http" />
    <wsdl:operation name="getStatistics">
      <soap:operation soapAction="http://ttdev.com/sp/NewOperation" />
      <wsdl:input>
        <soap:body use="literal" />
      </wsdl:input>
    </wsdl:operation>
  </wsdl:binding>
  <wsdl:service name="StatProducer">
    <wsdl:port binding="tns:StatProducerSOAP" name="p1">
      <soap:address location="http://localhost:8080/sp/p1" />
    </wsdl:port>
  </wsdl:service>
</wsdl:definitions>
```

Generate the code in both projects again. Modify the StatProducerImpl class in the producer project:

```
public class StatProducerImpl implements StatProducer {
  private Queue<GetStatistics> statRequestQueue;

  public StatProducerImpl(Queue<GetStatistics> statRequestQueue) {
    this.statRequestQueue = statRequestQueue;
  }
  public StatProducerImpl() {
  }
  @Override
  public void getStatistics(String param, String replyTo) {
    GetStatistics req = new GetStatistics();
    req.setParam(param);
    req.setReplyTo(replyTo);
    statRequestQueue.add(req);
  }
}
```

The GetStatistics class was a generated class to represent the <getStatistics> element. Next, modify the Main program in the producer project to send the result to the reply address:

```
public class Main {
  private BlockingQueue<GetStatistics> requestQueue;

  public static void main(String[] args) {
    new Main().run();
  }
  public Main() {
    requestQueue = new LinkedBlockingDeque<GetStatistics>();
```

```
    }
    private void run() {
      Object implementor = new StatProducerImpl(requestQueue);
      String address = "http://localhost:8080/sp/p1";
      Endpoint.publish(address, implementor);
      processRequeusts();
    }
    private void processRequeusts() {
      System.out.println("Waiting for requests");
      BufferedReader br = new BufferedReader(new InputStreamReader(System.in));
      while (true) {
        try {
          GetStatistics req = requestQueue.take();
          System.out.println("Got a request: " + req.getParam());
          System.out.println("Enter response: ");
          String result = br.readLine();
          StatConsumer_Service ss = new StatConsumer_Service(
              StatConsumer_Service.WSDL_LOCATION, new QName(
                  "http://ttdev.com/sc", "StatConsumer"));
          StatConsumer port = ss.getP1();
          BindingProvider bp = (BindingProvider) port;
          bp.getRequestContext().put(
              BindingProvider.ENDPOINT_ADDRESS_PROPERTY,
              req.getReplyTo());
          port.putStatistics(result);
        } catch (InterruptedException e) {
          continue;
        } catch (IOException e) {
          continue;
        }
      }
    }
  }
```

In the consumer project, modify the Main program as shown below. Note that you are deliberately using a different port (8888) from that specified in the WSDL (8081). Of course, you're also providing the reply address in the call:

```
public class Main {
  public static void main(String[] args) {
    new Main().run();
  }
  private void run() {
    Object implementor = new StatConsumerImpl();
    String address = "http://localhost:8888/sc/p1";
    Endpoint.publish(address, implementor);
    sendRequeust();
  }

  private void sendRequeust() {
    System.out.println("Sending a request");
    StatProducer_Service ss = new StatProducer_Service(
        StatProducer_Service.WSDL_LOCATION, new QName(
            "http://ttdev.com/sp", "StatProducer"));
    StatProducer port = ss.getP1();
    port.getStatistics("abc", "http://localhost:8888/sc/p1");
  }
}
```

Now run the producer and then the consumer. The reply should still be able to reach the consumer.

Using an asynchronous client in Axis2

To use an asynchronous client in Axis2, copy the Axis2SimpleClient and paste it as Axis2StatClient. Copy the WSDL file from the StatClient project (NOT StatConsumer) into the new project (and delete the existing WSDL files).

Next, modify the CodeGenerator class:

```
public class CodeGenerator {
  public static void main(String[] args) throws Exception {
    WSDL2Code.main(new String[] {
        "-S", "src/main/java",
        "-R", "src/main/resources/META-INF",
        "-ns2p", "http://ttdev.com/ss=com.ttdev.ss",
        "-uri", "src/main/resources/StatService.wsdl" });
    System.out.println("Done!");
  }
}
```

Delete the com.ttdev.ss package and the src/main/resources/META-INF folder. Then run CodeGenerator. Then create a StatClient class:

Create a callback object.

Let it call the CXF service.

```
public class StatClient {
  public static void main(String[] args) throws IOException {
    StatServiceStub service = new StatServiceStub("http://localhost:8080/ss/p1");
    GetStatistics req = new GetStatistics();
    req.setGetStatistics("abc");
    StatServiceCallbackHandler callback = new StatServiceCallbackHandler() {
      @Override
      public void receiveResultgetStatistics(GetStatisticsResponse result) {
        String r = result.getGetStatisticsResponse();
        System.out.println("Got result: " + r);
      }
    };
    service.startgetStatistics(req, callback);
    System.out.println("Press Enter to quit");
    new BufferedReader(new InputStreamReader(System.in)).readLine();
  }
}
```

The receiveXXX() method will be called once the result is available.

Adding the word "start" to it will give you the asynchronous method.

getStatistics() is the synchronous method.

Pass the callback object to it.

Note that the WSDL2Code program in Axis2 will create both the synchronous and the asynchronous methods by default and therefore you don't need to explicitly tell it to.

Now, run the StatService_P1_Server class in the StatService (using CXF). As the asynchronous operation entirely happens on the client side, you don't need to do anything on the server side. Then run the StatClient you just written above. It should print the result in a few seconds:

```
Press Enter to quit
Got result: ABC
```

Summary

To let the client program to continue without waiting for the result, use the asynchronous API. With a JAXWS implementation (such as CXF), you can use a binding to tell the code generator to generate the asynchronous API. With Axis2, it is done by default.

However, using a asynchronous API on the client is not enough if the service processing takes a very long time because the underlying HTTP transport connection will time out. In that case, you can split the service into a provider side and a consumer side, then let the server initiate a callback to the consumer once the processing is finished. Most probably the client will need to provide a reply address so that the server knows where to send the reply to.

Chapter 8

Signing and encrypting SOAP messages

What's in this chapter?

In this chapter you'll learn how to sign and encrypt SOAP messages.

Private key and public key

Usually when you encrypt some text using a key, you need the same key to decrypt it:

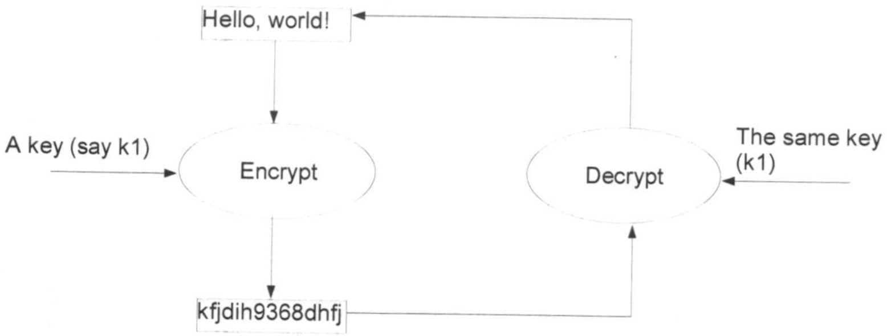

This is called "symmetric encryption". If you would like to send something to me in private, then we need to agree on a key. If you need to send something private to 100 individuals, then you'll need to negotiate with each such individual to agree on a key (so 100 keys in total). This is troublesome.

To solve the problem, an individual may use something called a "private key" and a "public key". First, he uses some software to generate a pair of keys: One is the private key and the other is the public key. There is an interesting relationship between these two keys: If you use the private key to encrypt something, then it can only be decrypted using the public key (using the private key won't work). The reverse is also true: If you use the public key to encrypt something, then it can only be decrypted using the private key:

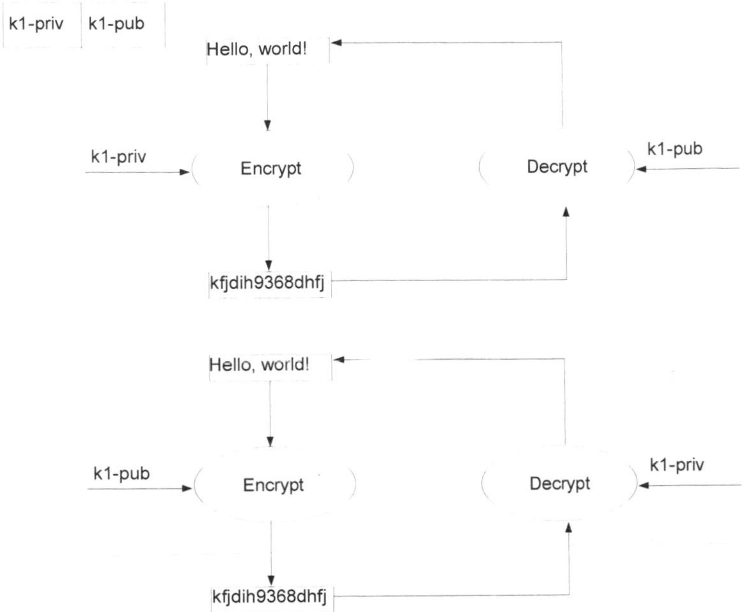

After generating the key pair, he will keep the private key really private (won't tell anyone), but he will tell everyone his public key. Can other people find out the private key from the public key? It is extremely difficult, so there is no worry about it. Now, suppose that you'd like to send something confidential to an individual Paul (see the diagram below), you can use his public key to encrypt it. Even though other people know his public key, they can't decrypt it (as it is encrypted using the public key, only the private key can decrypt it). Only Paul knows the private key and so only he can decrypt it:

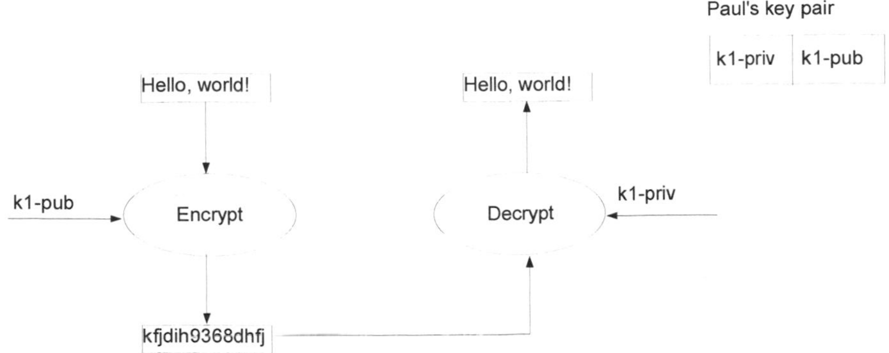

This kind of encryption is called "asymmetric encryption".

Digital signature

Suppose that the message you send to Paul is not confidential. However, Paul really needs to be sure that it is really from you. How to do that? You need to prove to Paul that the creator of the message knows your private key. If he does, then he must be you (remember, nobody else is supposed to know your private key). To prove that, you can use your private key to encrypt the message, then send it to Paul. Paul can try to decrypt it using your public key. If it works, then the creator of the message must know your private key and must be you.

However, this is not a good solution, because if the message is long, the encrypted message may double in size and the encryption takes a lot of time. To solve this problem, you can feed the message to a "one way hash function" (see the diagram below). No matter how long the input is, the output from the one way hash function is always the same small size (e.g., 128 bits). In addition, if two input messages are different (maybe just a single bit is different), then the output will be completely different. Therefore, the output message can be considered a small-sized snapshot of the input message. It is therefore called the "message digest" of the original message:

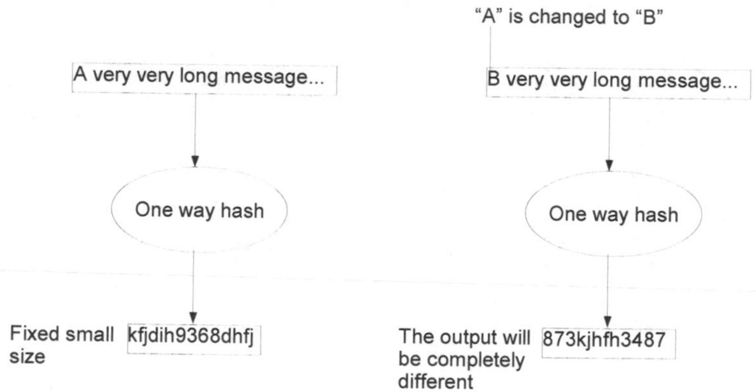

Another feature of the one way hash function is that it is very fast to calculate the digest of a given message, but it is extremely difficult to calculate a message given a digest. Otherwise people would find different messages for a given digest and it is no longer a good snapshot for the message:

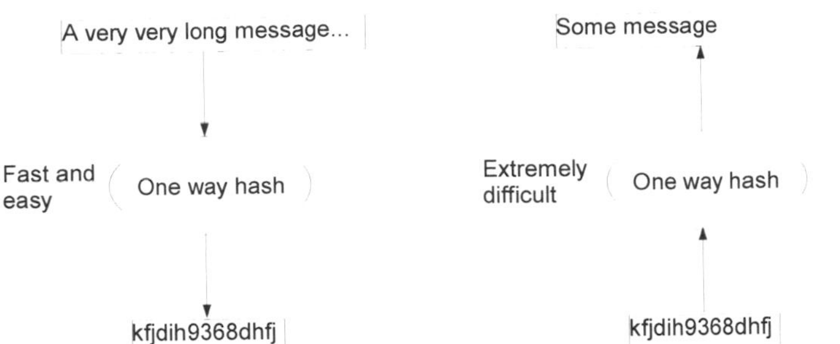

Now, to prove to Paul that you know your private key, you can use your private key to encrypt the message digest (because the digest is small, the result is also small and the encryption process will be fast), then send both the message and the message digest to Paul. He can try to decrypt the digest using your public key. Then he can calculate the digest from the message and compare the two. If the two match, then the person producing the encrypted digest must be you:

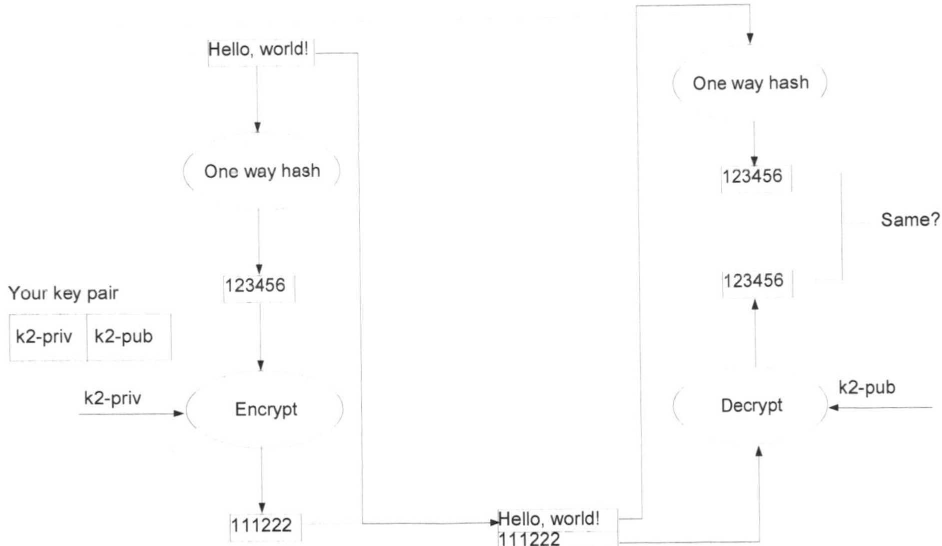

The encrypted digest is called the "digital signature". The whole process of calculating the digest and then encrypting it is called "signing the message".

Signing and encrypting

What if you'd like to sign the message, while keeping the message available to Paul only? Just sign it as usual (see the diagram below) and then encrypt the message and the digest using Paul's public key. When Paul receives it, he uses his private key to decrypt it and then go on to verify the signature as usual:

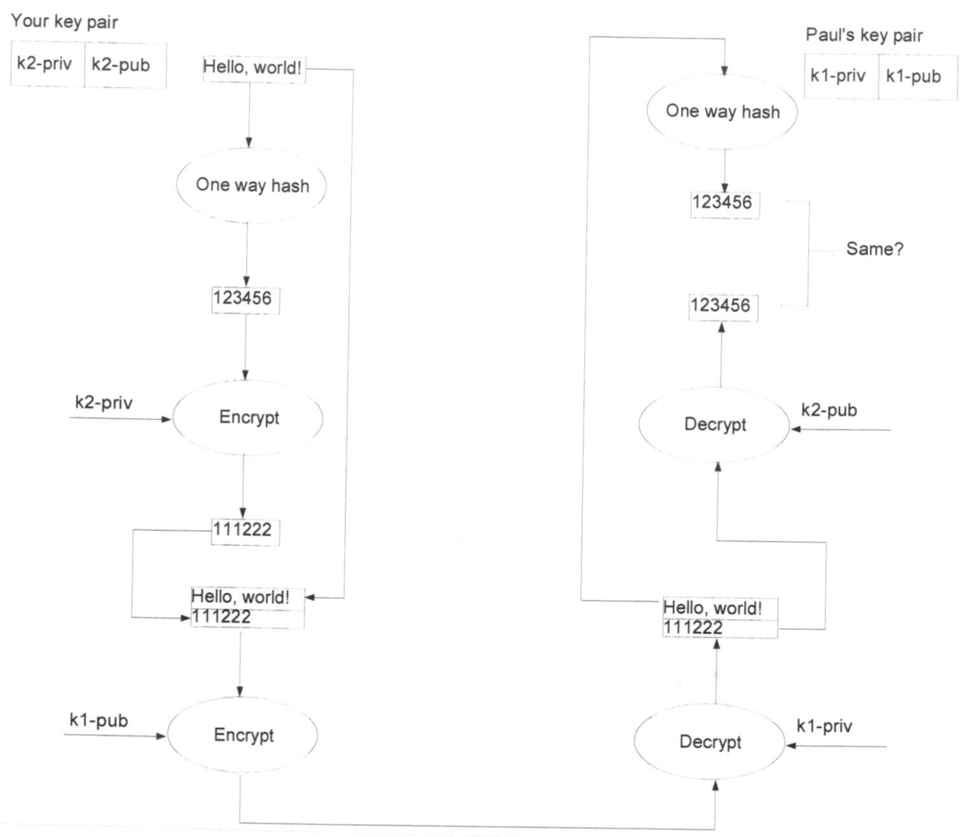

Certificate and CA

This seems to work very well. However, when you need to say send a confidential message to Paul, you'll need his public key. But how can you find out his public key? You can call him on the phone to ask him. But how can you be sure that the person on the phone is really Paul? If he is a hacker, he will tell you his public key. When you send the message to Paul using the hacker's public key, the hacker will be able to decrypt it using his private key.

If you need to communicate with many different individuals, this will get even more troublesome. To solve the problem, Paul may go to a government authority, show his ID card and etc and tell the authority his public key. Then the authority will generate an electronic message (like an email) stating Paul's public key. Finally, it signs that message using its own private key:

Name: Paul Public key: 666888
Signature

Such a signed message is called a "certificate". That authority is called a "certificate authority (CA)". Then Paul can put his certificate on his personal web site, email it to you directly or put it onto some 3rd party public web site. From where you get the certificate is unimportant. What is important is that if you can verify the signature of that CA and you trust what the CA says, then you can trust that public key in the certificate. In order to verify the signature, you will need the public key of that CA. What?! You're back to the origin of the problem. However, you only need to find out a single public key for a single entity (the CA), not a public key for everyone you need to communicate with. How to obtain that public key? Usually it is already configured in your browser or you can download it from a trusted web site, newspaper or other sources that you trust.

A CA doesn't really need to be a government authority. It can be well known commercial organizations such as VeriSign.

It means that in order to use asymmetric encryption and digital signature, people need private keys, public keys, a CA and certificates. All these elements combined together is called a “public key infrastructure (PKI)” because it provides a platform for us to use public keys.

Distinguished name

If you review the certificate:

Name: Paul
Public key: 666888
Signature

you will see that it is not that useful because there are probably millions of people named Paul in the world. Therefore, in a real certificate, usually the country, city and the company of that individual are also included like:

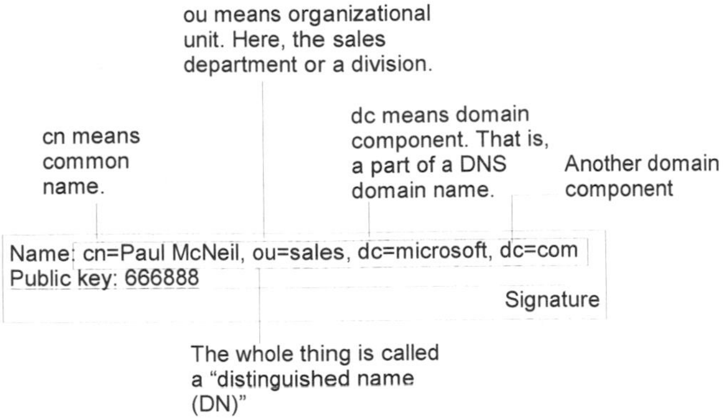

ou means organizational unit. Here, the sales department or a division.

cn means common name.

dc means domain component. That is, a part of a DNS domain name.

Another domain component

Name: cn=Paul McNeil, ou=sales, dc=microsoft, dc=com
Public key: 666888
Signature

The whole thing is called a “distinguished name (DN)”

Now if you're looking for the public key of Paul McNeil who works at IBM, you know that the certificate above should NOT be used.

Performance issue with asymmetric encryption

Suppose that you'd like to send an encrypted message to Paul. You can use Paul's public key to do that. However, in practice few people would do it this way, because asymmetric encryption is very slow. In contrast, symmetric encryption is a lot faster. To solve this problem, you can generate a random symmetric key, use it to encrypt the message, then use Paul's public key to encrypt that symmetric key and send it to Paul along with the encrypted message. Paul can use his private key to get back the symmetric key and then use it to decrypt the message:

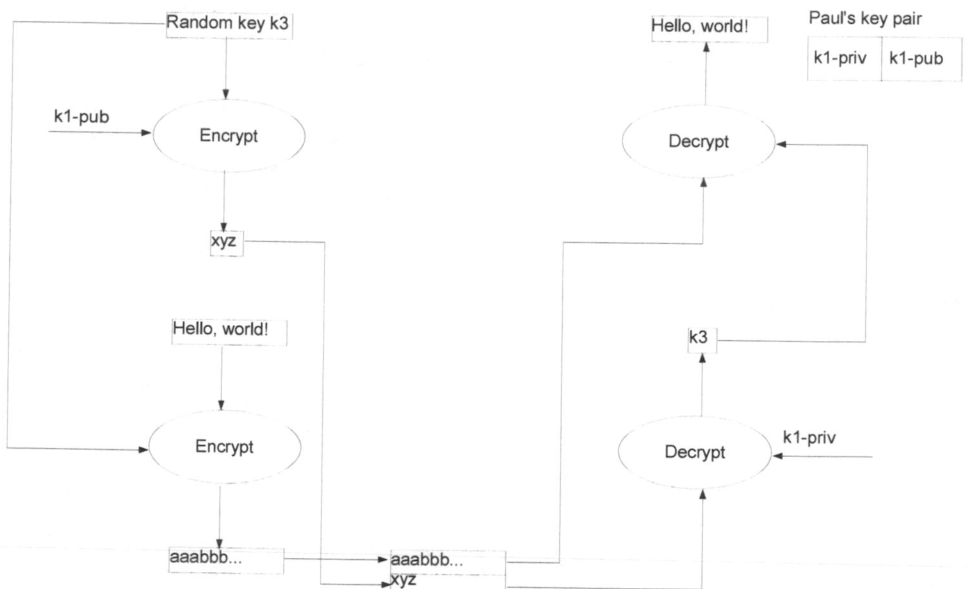

Keeping key pair and certificates in Java

In order to use PKI, typically you should have a private key for yourself (see the diagram below), a certificate for yourself so that you can send to others, a certificate for each person that you need to send something confidential to (e.g., Paul and Mary) and the public keys of the CA's that you trust. For the public key of the CA, you don't directly store its public key. Instead, you store its certificate which contains its public key. But who issued that certificate to it? It was issued by itself (signed by its own private key):

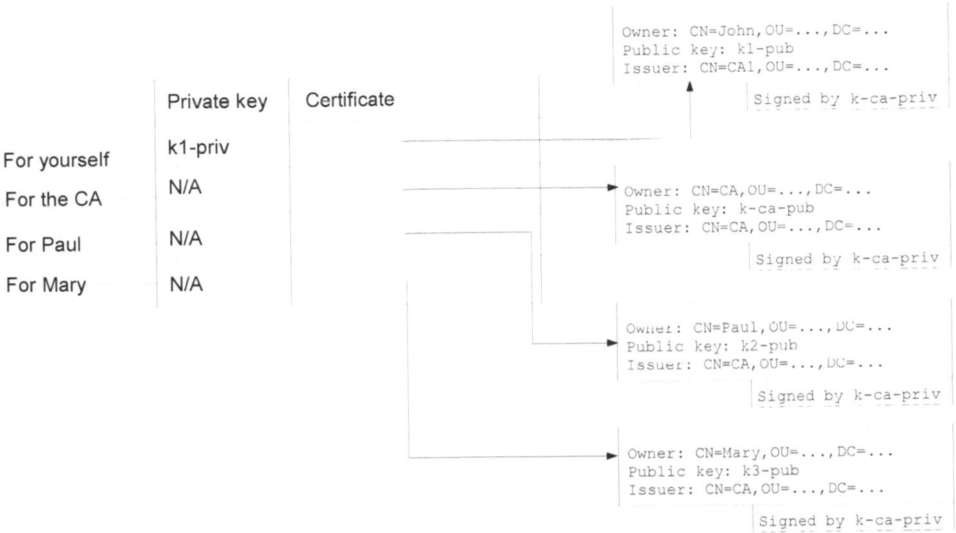

Such a table is called a keystore in Java (see the diagram below). A keystore is stored in a file. In addition, each entry in the table has a name called the alias of the entry. This way you can, e.g., tell the software to sign a particular message using the private key in the "john" entry (yourself), or encrypt the message using the public key in "paul" entry. Without the alias you will have to use the DN to refer to an entry:

keystore

Alias	Private key	Certificate
john	k1-priv	→
CA	N/A	→
paul	N/A	→
mary	N/A	→

Generating a key pair

In order to generate a key pair, you can use the keytool program in JDK. For example, if your JDK is in c:\Program Files\Java\jdk, then you can find keytool.exe in the bin sub-folder (i.e., c:\Program Files\Java\jdk\bin). For convenience, let's add c:\Program Files\Java\jdk\bin to the PATH:

Note that this PATH setting affects this command prompt only. If later you use a new command prompt, you'll need to set the PATH again. Next, create a folder named keys in your home folder to hold the keys and change into there.

Now, generate a key pair for your web service client:

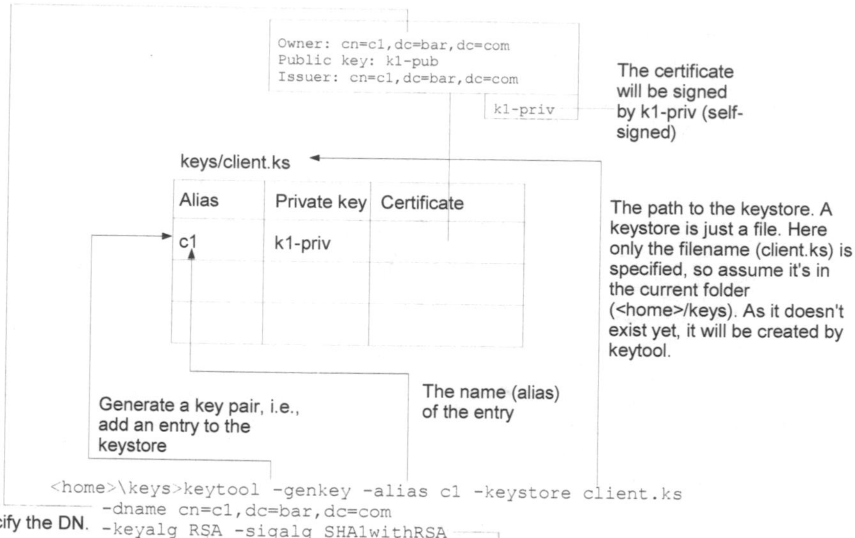

Let's run it:

```
keys\> keytool -genkey -alias c1 -keystore client.ks -keyalg RSA
   -dname cn=c1,dc=bar,dc=com
   -sigalg SHA1withRSA
Enter keystore password:
Re-enter new password:
Enter key password for <c1>
        (RETURN if same as keystore password):
Re-enter new password:
```

What is the purpose of it? You can consider that keytool will append this password to the content of the keystore and then generate a hash and store it into the keystore. If someone modifies the keystore without this password, he won't be able to update the hash. The next time you run keytool on this keystore, it will note the mismatch and warn you not to use this keystore anymore.

Let's enter "client-ks-pass" as the keystore password.

You need to provide an entry password to protect the entry for c1. You can consider that keytool will use this password to encrypt c1's private key. This way other people won't be able to read c1's private key.

Let's enter "c1-pass" as the entry password.

To verify that the entry has been added, you can list the entries:

```
keys\> keytool -list -keystore client.ks
Enter keystore password:

Keystore type: JKS
Keystore provider: SUN

Your keystore contains 1 entry

c1, Dec 21, 2009, PrivateKeyEntry,
Certificate fingerprint (MD5): D4:19:99:83:D9:EC:CC:79:11:9E:6E:8A:57:35:E7:FB
```

Note that it asks for the keystore password so that it can verify the hash. If you'd like to see more details in the entries, use the -v option:

```
keys\> keytool -list -v -keystore client.ks
Enter keystore password:

Keystore type: JKS
Keystore provider: SUN

Your keystore contains 1 entry

Alias name: c1
Creation date: Dec 21, 2009
Entry type: PrivateKeyEntry
Certificate chain length: 1
Certificate[1]:
Owner: CN=c1, DC=bar, DC=com
Issuer: CN=c1, DC=bar, DC=com
Serial number: 4b2f53d3
Valid from: Mon Dec 21 18:54:11 HKT 2009 until: Sun Mar 21 18:54:11 HKT 2010
Certificate fingerprints:
         MD5:  D4:19:99:83:D9:EC:CC:79:11:9E:6E:8A:57:35:E7:FB
         SHA1: D9:51:F8:68:11:08:FB:C7:D1:4B:7F:42:23:46:DD:8B:13:39:F6:00
         Signature algorithm name: SHA1withRSA
         Version: 3


*******************************************
*******************************************
```

You can see that both the Owner and the Issuer are set to the DN of c1. It shows that it is indeed a self-signed certificate. Having a self-signed certificate is not useful. You need to ask a CA to sign it. To do that, generate a certificate request first:

Generate a certificate request for the entry named "c1":

```
keys\>keytool -certreq -alias c1 -keystore client.ks -file c1.csr
```

Put the certificate request into this file

Run it:

```
keys\> keytool -certreq -alias c1 -keystore client.ks -file c1.csr
Enter keystore password:
Enter key password for <c1>
```

Now it has put the certificate request into the file c1.csr in the keys folder. You need to send to a CA. In real life, you should send it to VeriSign or some well known CA to get a certificate (of course a payment is required). Here you'll setup your own CA.

Setting up a CA

Go to http://www.openssl.org/related/binaries.html to download the Windows version of OpenSSL. Suppose the file is Win32OpenSSL-v0.9.8a.exe. Login as the Administrator and run it. Follow the instruction to complete the installation. Suppose that it has been installed into a folder named OpenSSL. To make it easier to run, add OpenSSL/bin to the PATH.

Next, create a folder named CA in your home folder to host the files of the CA. Then create a private key for the CA itself:

Some openssl commands need to save a random seed information to a file ("random file"). You need to tell it the path to that file. Here, just tell it to use a file named "rand" in the current folder.

```
c:\>cd CA

c:\CA>set RANDFILE=rand

c:\CA>openssl req -new -keyout cakey.pem -out careq.pem
```

Work on a request

Create a new private key and a certificate request

Put the private key into this file

Put the certificate request into this file

Run it and it will prompt you for the DN of the CA and a password to encrypt the private key (e.g., you may use "ca-pass"):

```
CA\> openssl req -new -keyout cakey.pem -out careq.pem
Generating a 1024 bit RSA private key
.............++++++
............................++++++
writing new private key to 'cakey.pem'
Enter PEM pass phrase:
Verifying - Enter PEM pass phrase:
-----
You are about to be asked to enter information that will be incorporated
into your certificate request.
What you are about to enter is what is called a Distinguished Name or a DN.
There are quite a few fields but you can leave some blank
For some fields there will be a default value,
If you enter '.', the field will be left blank.
-----
Country Name (2 letter code) [AU]:US
State or Province Name (full name) [Some-State]:
Locality Name (eg, city) []:
Organization Name (eg, company) [Internet Widgits Pty Ltd]:Test CA
Organizational Unit Name (eg, section) []:
Common Name (eg, YOUR name) []:CA
Email Address []:

Please enter the following 'extra' attributes
to be sent with your certificate request
A challenge password []:
An optional company name []:
```

In this example, the DC has been set to cn=CA,o=Test CA,c=US, in which o stands for organization and c stands for country. Next, generate a self-signed certificate for it:

Tell it actually the input is not a certificate, but a certificate request.

Self-sign a certificate using this private key.

Work on an (x509) certificate

The resulting self-signed certificate will be valid from now until 3650 days (10 years) later

```
CA\>openssl x509 -signkey cakey.pem -req -days 3650 -in careq.pem -out cacert.pem
-extfile c:\OpenSSL\bin\openssl.cnf -extensions v3_ca
```

Copy some "extension" settings from the openssl.cnf file in its v3_ca section. What you want is something like:

The input file (the certificate request)

The output file (the self-signed certificate)

```
Owner: ...
Issuer: ...
Extension 1 (Constraint): CA
Extension 2 (...) : ...
```

Run it and enter "ca-pass" as the password for the CA key:

```
CA\> openssl x509 -signkey cakey.pem -req -days 3650 -in careq.pem -out cacert.pem
-extfile c:\OpenSSL\bin\openssl.cnf -extensions v3_ca
Signature ok
subject=/C=US/ST=Some-State/O=Test CA/CN=CA
Getting Private key
Enter pass phrase for cakey.pem:
```

Now you're about to use this CA to sign the certificate request from John (john.csr). However, before that, you need to note that when a CA issues a new certificate, it will put a unique serial number into that certificate. So you need to tell OpenSSL what is the next serial number to use. To do that:

Store the string "02" into a file serial.txt. The file will be created. This way OpenSSL will use 02 as the next serial number. Then it will set it to 03 automatically.

```
CA\>echo 02 > serial.txt
```

Note that the "0" is necessary. Using "2" will NOT work because OpenSSL expects a hexadecimal number that contains an even number of digits.

To sign c1's certificate request:

Sign a certificate using this CA certificate. For example, it can find the DN of the CA here.

Actually the input is a certificate request, not a certificate.

Still working with x509 certificates.

The private key of the CA is in this file

The serial # is in this file.

```
CA\>openssl x509 -CA cacert.pem -CAkey cakey.pem -CAserial serial.txt -req
           -in ..\keys\c1.csr -out ..\keys\c1.cer -days 1095
```

The input file (certificate request for c1)

The output file (certificate for c1)

The certificate will be valid for 1095 days (3 years).

Run it and enter "ca-pass" as the password for the CA key:

```
CA\> openssl x509 -CA cacert.pem -CAkey cakey.pem -CAserial serial.txt -req
-in ../keys/c1.csr -out ../keys/c1.cer -days 1095
Signature ok
subject=/DC=com/DC=bar/CN=c1
Getting CA Private Key
Enter pass phrase for cakey.pem:
```

Importing the certificate into the keystore

Now you have got the certificate in c1.cer, you can import it into the keystore. However, before doing that, you must first import the certificate of the CA itself into your keystore as a trusted CA certificate, otherwise it will refuse to import John's certificate. To do that:

Change back to c:\keys

Import a certificate into the keystore.

Create a certificate entry named "testCA". You can use any name that you like and it won't make any difference.

```
CA\>cd ..\keys

keys\>keytool -import -alias testCA -file ..\CA\cacert.pem -keystore client.ks
```

The CA's certificate is in this file. In real world, when you receive your certificate from the CA (e.g., VeriSign), it will also give you its own certificate. Or you can probably download it from its web site.

Run it:

```
keys\> keytool -import -alias testCA -file ../CA/cacert.pem -keystore client.ks
Enter keystore password:
Owner: CN=CA, O=Test CA, ST=Some-State, C=US
Issuer: CN=CA, O=Test CA, ST=Some-State, C=US
Serial number: c896adcad015985e
Valid from: Mon Dec 21 19:48:29 HKT 2009 until: Thu Dec 19 19:48:29 HKT 2019
Certificate fingerprints:
         MD5:  BB:15:7D:0A:C4:5C:D7:58:C3:43:40:E0:FC:E3:87:E6
         SHA1: 47:7B:86:AF:52:A1:57:CD:83:03:AA:45:4A:B2:19:38:C1:2E:B8:5E
         Signature algorithm name: SHA1withRSA
         Version: 3

Extensions:

#1: ObjectId: 2.5.29.14 Criticality=false
SubjectKeyIdentifier [
KeyIdentifier [
0000: 23 F4 96 17 01 A4 54 84   FE B3 D8 C6 84 83 C8 65  #.....T........e
0010: 03 47 FC 3B                                        .G.;
]
]

#2: ObjectId: 2.5.29.19 Criticality=false
BasicConstraints:[
  CA:true
  PathLen:2147483647
]

#3: ObjectId: 2.5.29.35 Criticality=false
AuthorityKeyIdentifier [
KeyIdentifier [
0000: 23 F4 96 17 01 A4 54 84   FE B3 D8 C6 84 83 C8 65  #.....T........e
0010: 03 47 FC 3B                                        .G.;
]

[CN=CA, O=Test CA, ST=Some-State, C=US]
SerialNumber: [    c896adca d015985e]
]

Trust this certificate? [no]:  yes
Certificate was added to keystore
```

Note that it asked you to trust this certificate or not. This is a very important decision. If you trust this certificate as a CA certificate, you will trust all certificates issued by it. Next, add John's certificate to the keystore to replace his self-signed certificate. This is also done using the -import option:

When keytool finds an existing entry with the named "c1" in the keystore, it knows you're trying to replace a certificate issued by a CA for the existing self-signed one.

```
keys\>keytool -import -alias c1 -file c1.cer -keystore client.ks
```

The certificate is in this file.

Run it:

```
keys\> keytool -import -alias c1 -file c1.cer -keystore client.ks
Enter keystore password:
Enter key password for <c1>
Certificate reply was installed in keystore
```

To verify, you can list the entries in the keystore:

```
keys\>keytool -list -v -keystore client.ks
Keystore type: JKS
Keystore provider: SUN

Your keystore contains 2 entries

Alias name: testca
Creation date: Dec 21, 2009
Entry type: trustedCertEntry

Owner: CN=CA, O=Test CA, ST=Some-State, C=US
Issuer: CN=CA, O=Test CA, ST=Some-State, C=US
Serial number: c896adcad015985e
Valid from: Mon Dec 21 19:48:29 HKT 2009 until: Thu Dec 19 19:48:29 HKT 2019
Certificate fingerprints:
         MD5:  BB:15:7D:0A:C4:5C:D7:58:C3:43:40:E0:FC:E3:87:E6
         SHA1: 47:7B:86:AF:52:A1:57:CD:83:03:AA:45:4A:B2:19:38:C1:2E:B8:5E
         Signature algorithm name: SHA1withRSA
         Version: 3

*******************************************
*******************************************
```

There are 2 entries in the keystore.

Entry 1: It is a trusted certificate entry, i.e., a trusted CA certificate.

```
Alias name: c1
Creation date: Dec 21, 2009
Entry type: PrivateKeyEntry
Certificate chain length: 2
Certificate[1]:
Owner: CN=c1, DC=bar, DC=com
Issuer: CN=CA, O=Test CA, ST=Some-State, C=US
Serial number: 3
Valid from: Mon Dec 21 19:49:00 HKT 2009 until: Thu Dec 20 19:49:00 HKT 2012
Certificate fingerprints:
         MD5:  ED:0B:4A:D8:DD:0C:1C:E5:AF:06:8E:C8:F2:E7:C4:9C
         SHA1: DF:C5:4D:C0:5B:A4:8E:FD:00:EF:5E:AE:85:06:0F:20:91:B2:C8:E5
         Signature algorithm name: SHA1withRSA
         Version: 1
Certificate[2]:
Owner: CN=CA, O=Test CA, ST=Some-State, C=US
Issuer: CN=CA, O=Test CA, ST=Some-State, C=US
Serial number: c896adcad015985e
Valid from: Mon Dec 21 19:48:29 HKT 2009 until: Thu Dec 19 19:48:29 HKT 2019
Certificate fingerprints:
         MD5:  BB:15:7D:0A:C4:5C:D7:58:C3:43:40:E0:FC:E3:87:E6
         SHA1: 47:7B:86:AF:52:A1:57:CD:83:03:AA:45:4A:B2:19:38:C1:2E:B8:5E
         Signature algorithm name: SHA1withRSA

*******************************************
*******************************************
```

Entry 2

It is a key entry, i.e., a private key along with a certificate.

It means that there are two certificates in the entry.

The first certificate is c1's certificate. From the "Issuer" field you can see it is issued by the test CA, so the next certificate is that of the test CA.

The second certificate is the certificate of the test CA.

A certificate chain is also called a "certificate path". If the certificate of your test CA was issued by yet another CA, then the certificate path would contain the certificate of that other CA as the last certificate.

```
SecureService
   src
   repository
      modules
         rampart-1.3.mar
```

Just like the Axis server which has a repository, your Axis client can also have a repository.

Rename the WSDL to SecureService.wsdl and replace the word "Secure" for "Wrapped" in it. Update the build.xml file:

Signing SOAP messages

Now, let create a client that signs the SOAP messages. Copy the WrappedService and WrappedClient projects and paste them SecureService and SecureClient respectively. Rename the WSDL file in the service project as SecureService.wsdl and replace the word "Secure" for the word "Wrapped":

```
<?xml version="1.0" encoding="UTF-8" standalone="no"?>
<wsdl:definitions xmlns:soap="http://schemas.xmlsoap.org/wsdl/soap/"
  xmlns:tns="http://ttdev.com/ss" xmlns:wsdl="http://schemas.xmlsoap.org/wsdl/"
  xmlns:xsd="http://www.w3.org/2001/XMLSchema" name="SecureService"
  targetNamespace="http://ttdev.com/ss">
  <wsdl:types>
    <xsd:schema targetNamespace="http://ttdev.com/ss">
      <xsd:element name="concat">
        <xsd:complexType>
          <xsd:sequence>
            <xsd:element name="s1" type="xsd:string" />
            <xsd:element name="s2" type="xsd:string" />
          </xsd:sequence>
        </xsd:complexType>
      </xsd:element>
      <xsd:element name="concatResponse">
        <xsd:complexType>
          <xsd:sequence>
            <xsd:element name="r" type="xsd:string">
            </xsd:element>
          </xsd:sequence>
        </xsd:complexType>
      </xsd:element>
    </xsd:schema>
  </wsdl:types>
  <wsdl:message name="concatRequest">
    <wsdl:part element="tns:concat" name="parameters" />
  </wsdl:message>
  <wsdl:message name="concatResponse">
    <wsdl:part element="tns:concatResponse" name="parameters" />
  </wsdl:message>
  <wsdl:portType name="SecureService">
    <wsdl:operation name="concat">
      <wsdl:input message="tns:concatRequest" />
      <wsdl:output message="tns:concatResponse" />
    </wsdl:operation>
  </wsdl:portType>
  <wsdl:binding name="SecureServiceSOAP" type="tns:SecureService">
    <soap:binding style="document"
      transport="http://schemas.xmlsoap.org/soap/http" />
    <wsdl:operation name="concat">
      <soap:operation soapAction="http://ttdev.com/ss/NewOperation" />
```

```
      <wsdl:input>
        <soap:body use="literal" />
      </wsdl:input>
      <wsdl:output>
        <soap:body use="literal" />
      </wsdl:output>
    </wsdl:operation>
  </wsdl:binding>
  <wsdl:service name="SecureService">
    <wsdl:port binding="tns:SecureServiceSOAP" name="p1">
      <soap:address location="http://localhost:8080/ss/p1" />
    </wsdl:port>
  </wsdl:service>
</wsdl:definitions>
```

Then further modify it as:

It belongs to the web service policy namespace.

```
<wsdl:definitions xmlns:wsdl="http://schemas.xmlsoap.org/wsdl/"
   xmlns:soap="http://schemas.xmlsoap.org/wsdl/soap/"
   xmlns:tns="http://ttdev.com/ss"
   xmlns:xsd="http://www.w3.org/2001/XMLSchema"
   xmlns:sp="http://docs.oasis-open.org/ws-sx/ws-securitypolicy/200702"
   xmlns:wsp="http://www.w3.org/2006/07/ws-policy"
   xmlns:wsu="http://docs.oasis-open.org/wss/2004/01/oasis-200401-wss-
wssecurity-utility-1.0.xsd"
   name="SecureService"
   targetNamespace="http://ttdev.com/ss">
   <wsp:Policy wsu:Id="p1">
      <sp:SignedParts>
         <sp:Body />
      </sp:SignedParts>
   </wsp:Policy>
   <wsdl:types>
      ...
   </wsdl:types>
   <wsdl:message name="concatRequest">
      ...
   </wsdl:message>
   <wsdl:message name="concatResponse">
      ...
   </wsdl:message>
   <wsdl:portType name="SecureService">
      <wsdl:operation name="concat">
         <wsdl:input message="tns:concatRequest" />
         <wsdl:output message="tns:concatResponse" />
      </wsdl:operation>
   </wsdl:portType>
   <wsdl:binding name="SecureServiceSOAP" type="tns:SecureService">
      <soap:binding style="document"
         transport="http://schemas.xmlsoap.org/soap/http" />
      <wsdl:operation name="concat">
         <wsp:PolicyReference URI="#p1" wsdl:required="true" />
         <soap:operation .../>
         <wsdl:input>
            <soap:body use="literal" />
         </wsdl:input>
         <wsdl:output>
            <soap:body use="literal" />
         </wsdl:output>
      </wsdl:operation>
   </wsdl:binding>
   <wsdl:service name="SecureService">
      <wsdl:port binding="tns:SecureServiceSOAP" name="p1">
         <soap:address location="http://localhost:8080/ss/p1" />
      </wsdl:port>
   </wsdl:service>
</wsdl:definitions>
```

It belongs to the security policy namespace.

This is a "policy". A policy specifies non-functional requirements of the web service (e.g., security, quality of service). The syntax of specifying a policy is governed by the WS-Policy standard.

This is a "policy assertion". It requires certain parts of the SOAP message be signed.

The parts should be signed are listed here. Here, only the <Body> of the SOAP message should be signed.

As the <PolicyReference> element belongs to a foreign namespace (wsp), there is no guarantee that the program processing the WSDL file (e.g., WSDLToJava) understands it. This attribute requires that the program understand it, otherwise it should abort the processing.

Apply the policy "p1" to the SOAP binding of the concat operation. It means the <Body> of all the messages for the concat operation must be signed as long as they're using SOAP over HTTP. Without this the policy would be sitting there idle and would have no effect.

If you had multiple operations in the port type and they all required signed messages, you would move the <PolicyReference> to there so that it would apply to the SOAP binding of all the operations in that port type.

Saying that the <Body> should be signed is not enough. You still need to specify that asymmetric encryption should be used and what signature algorithms are supported and etc.:

This policy assertion states that asymmetric encryption should be used.

Why have an extra <Policy> element? It is used to AND the three child security assertions below. That is, they must be satisfied simultaneously.

```
<wsdl:definitions ...
  name="SecureService"
  targetNamespace="http://ttdev.com/ss">
  <wsp:Policy wsu:Id="p1">
    <sp:AsymmetricBinding>
      <wsp:Policy>
        <sp:InitiatorToken>
          ...
        </sp:InitiatorToken>
        <sp:RecipientToken>
          ...
        </sp:RecipientToken>
        <sp:AlgorithmSuite>
          ...
        </sp:AlgorithmSuite>
      </wsp:Policy>
    </sp:AsymmetricBinding>
    <sp:SignedParts>
      <sp:Body />
    </sp:SignedParts>
  </wsp:Policy>
  ...
</wsdl:definitions>
```

What kind of token (certificate here) should be used by the initiator (i.e., the client)?

What kind of token (certificate here) should be used by the recipient (i.e., the service)?

What kind of algorithm should be used?

Similarly, this <AsymmetricBinding> assertion and the <SignedParts> assertion are AND'ed together by the enclosing <Policy>.

You need to further specify the token types and the algorithm suite:

It modifies the meaning <Policy> to mean meeting any one of the child assertions is enough.

```
<wsp:Policy>
  <wsp:ExactlyOne>
    <sp:X509Token .../>
    <foo:FooToken .../>
    <bar:BarToken .../>
  </wsp:ExactlyOne>
</wsp:Policy>
```

Why use a <Policy> here? You could use it to require any one of the supported token formats such as:

```
<sp:AsymmetricBinding>
  <wsp:Policy>
    <sp:InitiatorToken>
      <wsp:Policy>
        <sp:X509Token
          sp:IncludeToken="http://docs.oasis-open.org/ws-sx/ws-
securitypolicy/200702/IncludeToken/AlwaysToRecipient">
          <wsp:Policy>
            <sp:WssX509V3Token10 />
          </wsp:Policy>
        </sp:X509Token>
      </wsp:Policy>
    </sp:InitiatorToken>
    <sp:RecipientToken>
      <wsp:Policy>
        <sp:X509Token
          sp:IncludeToken="http://docs.oasis-open.org/ws-sx/ws-
securitypolicy/200702/IncludeToken/Never">
          <wsp:Policy>
            <sp:WssX509V3Token10 />
          </wsp:Policy>
        </sp:X509Token>
      </wsp:Policy>
    </sp:RecipientToken>
    <sp:AlgorithmSuite>
      <wsp:Policy>
        <sp:TripleDesRsa15 />
      </wsp:Policy>
    </sp:AlgorithmSuite>
  </wsp:Policy>
</sp:AsymmetricBinding>
```

It should use an X509 token, which means an certificate. X509 is the official name.

The client should always include its token (certificate) in the message to the web service.

X509 certificates have different versions and presentations. Here use v3 and the XML presentation as specified in the web service security (WSS) X509 token profile 1.0.

Also use X509 v3 certificate for the web service.

The service should never send its certificate to the client. Instead, send enough information to the client so that the client can retrieve it. How? You'll see later.

Use 3DES for encryption and RSA 1.5 algorithm for digital signatures.

You could list other aspects of the algorithm suite here.

Finally, you still need to specify how to actually include the certificates in the messages (e.g., include them directly or just include their unique IDs). These options are specified by the Web Service Security (WSS) standard v1.0:

```
<wsdl:definitions ...
  name="SecureService"
  targetNamespace="http://ttdev.com/ss">
  <wsp:Policy wsu:Id="p1">
    <sp:AsymmetricBinding>
      ...
    </sp:AsymmetricBinding>
    <sp:Wss10>
      <wsp:Policy>
        <sp:MustSupportRefEmbeddedToken />
        <sp:MustSupportRefIssuerSerial />
      </wsp:Policy>
    </sp:Wss10>
    <sp:SignedParts>
      <sp:Body />
    </sp:SignedParts>
  </wsp:Policy>
  ...
</wsdl:definitions>
```

Supports WSS 1.0.

Both sides must be able deal with tokens (certificates) directly included in the messages.

Both sides must be able to use the issuer DN and serial number to look up the certificate.

Copy the WSDL to the client project. Update the CodeGenerator class in both projects. Delete the com.ttdev.ss package in both projects. Then generate the code in both projects. Create the SecureServiceImpl class:

```
@WebService(endpointInterface = "com.ttdev.ss.SecureService")
public class SecureServiceImpl implements SecureService {

  @Override
  public String concat(String s1, String s2) {
    return s1 + s2;
  }
}
```

In both projects, add the following dependencies in pom.xml:

```
<project ...>
  ...
  <dependencies>
    ...
    <dependency>
      <groupId>org.apache.rampart</groupId>
      <artifactId>rampart-policy</artifactId>
      <version>1.4</version>
    </dependency>
    <dependency>
      <groupId>org.apache.rampart</groupId>
      <artifactId>rampart-core</artifactId>
      <version>1.4</version>
    </dependency>
  </dependencies>
</project>
```

This Rampart package implements the WSS standard. Next, in the client project, modify the SecureService_P1_Client class to provide information needed by Rampart to perform the signing (e.g., the keystore alias to use):

```
...
import javax.security.auth.callback.Callback;
import javax.security.auth.callback.CallbackHandler;
import org.apache.cxf.ws.security.SecurityConstants;
import org.apache.ws.security.WSPasswordCallback;

public static void main(String args[]) throws Exception {
   ...
   SecureService_Service ss = new SecureService_Service(wsdlURL, SERVICE_NAME);
   SecureService port = ss.getP1();
   BindingProvider bp = (BindingProvider) port;
   Map<String, Object> context = bp.getRequestContext();
   context.put(SecurityConstants.SIGNATURE_USERNAME, "c1");
   context.put(SecurityConstants.CALLBACK_HANDLER, new CallbackHandler() {

      @Override
      public void handle(Callback[] callbacks) throws IOException,
            UnsupportedCallbackException {
         for (int i = 0; i < callbacks.length; i++) {
            WSPasswordCallback pwcb = (WSPasswordCallback) callbacks[i];
            String id = pwcb.getIdentifier();
            if (id.equals("c1")) {
               pwcb.setPassword("c1-pass");
            }
         }
      }
   });
   context.put(SecurityConstants.SIGNATURE_PROPERTIES, "crypto.properties");
   {
      System.out.println("Invoking concat...");
      java.lang.String _concat_s1 = "";
      java.lang.String _concat_s2 = "";
      java.lang.String _concat__return = ...;
      System.out.println(...);
   }
   System.exit(0);
}
```

The alias of the entry in the keystore. Use its private key to sign the message.

Rampart will need the password for the "c1" entry to sign the message. It will call this callback handler to retrieve the password.

Need the password for "c1"?

OK, tell you the password.

Rampart needs to more information such as the location of the keystore and etc. This kind of information will differ from site to site, so it is assumed to be in a properties file created by the operation team.

This is a classpath. So you'll create it in src/main/resources.

Create the crypto.properties file in src/main/resources:

Rampart uses a cryptographic provider to perform signing, encryption and etc. You specify the class of the provider to use this. Here you're telling it to use the Merlin provider which comes with rampart and uses the JDK to perform these tasks.

A Java keystore supports different formats. JKS is the default.

```
org.apache.ws.security.crypto.provider=org.apache.ws.security.components.crypto.Merlin
org.apache.ws.security.crypto.merlin.keystore.type=JKS
org.apache.ws.security.crypto.merlin.file=c:/Documents and Settings/kent/keys/client.ks
org.apache.ws.security.crypto.merlin.keystore.password=client-ks-pass
```

These properties are for the Merlin provider only. It has the concept of keystore (a Java concept) and etc.

The keystore password

The path to the keystore

Fill in the actual arguments for the concat() call and redirect it to the TCP Monitor so that you can observe the message:

```
public static void main(String args[]) throws Exception {
```

```
...
SecureService_Service ss = new SecureService_Service(wsdlURL, SERVICE_NAME);
SecureService port = ss.getP1();
BindingProvider bp = (BindingProvider) port;
Map<String, Object> context = bp.getRequestContext();
context.put(SecurityConstants.SIGNATURE_USERNAME, "c1");
context.put(SecurityConstants.CALLBACK_HANDLER, new CallbackHandler() {

  @Override
  public void handle(Callback[] callbacks) throws IOException,
      UnsupportedCallbackException {
    for (int i = 0; i < callbacks.length; i++) {
      WSPasswordCallback pwcb = (WSPasswordCallback) callbacks[i];
      String id = pwcb.getIdentifier();
      if (id.equals("c1")) {
        pwcb.setPassword("c1-pass");
      }
    }
  }
});
context.put(SecurityConstants.SIGNATURE_PROPERTIES, "crypto.properties");
context.put(BindingProvider.ENDPOINT_ADDRESS_PROPERTY,
    "http://localhost:1234/ss/p1");
{
  System.out.println("Invoking concat...");
  java.lang.String _concat_s1 = "abc";
  java.lang.String _concat_s2 = "123";
  java.lang.String _concat__return = port.concat(_concat_s1, _concat_s2);
  System.out.println("concat.result=" + _concat__return);
}
System.exit(0);
}
```

Launch TCP Monitor and let it listen on 1234. Run the service (even though it isn't prepared to the signed message yet). Run the client and you will see an error in the console. This is fine as the web service is not yet prepared to handle the digital signature. What is interesting is in the request message as shown in the TCP Monitor:

A <Security> element is added. It is a header entry. Everything about security is included here.

The "mustUnderstand" attribute is set to 1, meaning that the receiver (the service) must handle this header, otherwise it must return a SOAP fault (which is the case here).

```
<soap:Envelope xmlns:soap="http://schemas.xmlsoap.org/soap/envelope/">
  <soap:Header>
    <wsse:Security
      xmlns:wsse="..."
      soap:mustUnderstand="1">
      <wsse:BinarySecurityToken
        xmlns:wsse="..."
        xmlns:wsu="..."
        EncodingType="...200401-wss-soap-message-security-1.0#Base64Binary"
        ValueType="...oasis-200401-wss-x509-token-profile-1.0#X509v3"
        wsu:Id="CertId-88466A8D526A7838FF12614728119781">
          MIIB5zCCAVACAQMw...D4=
      </wsse:BinarySecurityToken>
      <ds:Signature xmlns:ds="http://www.w3.org/2000/09/xmldsig#"
        Id="Signature-1">
        <ds:SignedInfo>
          <ds:CanonicalizationMethod
            Algorithm="http://www.w3.org/2001/10/xml-exc-c14n#" />
          <ds:SignatureMethod Algorithm="...xmldsig#rsa-sha1" />
          <ds:Reference URI="#Id-9367927">
            <ds:Transforms>
              <ds:Transform Algorithm="http://www.w3.org/2001/10/xml-exc-c14n#" />
            </ds:Transforms>
            <ds:DigestMethod Algorithm="http://www.w3.org/2000/09/xmldsig#sha1" />
            <ds:DigestValue>lOs/bmu1cSoyQgIJ21wKaKGVqFQ=</ds:DigestValue>
          </ds:Reference>
        </ds:SignedInfo>
        <ds:SignatureValue>GbA6kZQ39Aw65xWc94TE/rbjwe....Jm4VudqALTU=</ds:SignatureValue>
        <ds:KeyInfo Id="KeyId-88466A8D526A7838FF12614728119882">
          <wsse:SecurityTokenReference
            xmlns:wsse="..."
            xmlns:wsu="..."
            wsu:Id="STRId-88466A8D526A7838FF12614728119913">
            <wsse:Reference
              xmlns:wsse="..."
              URI="#CertId-88466A8D526A7838FF12614728119781"
              ValueType="...oasis-200401-wss-x509-token-profile-1.0#X509v3" />
          </wsse:SecurityTokenReference>
        </ds:KeyInfo>
      </ds:Signature>
    </wsse:Security>
  </soap:Header>
  <soap:Body
    xmlns:wsu="..."
    wsu:Id="Id-9367927">
    <ns2:concat xmlns:ns2="http://ttdev.com/ss">
      <s1>abc</s1>
      <s2>123</s2>
    </ns2:concat>
  </soap:Body>
</soap:Envelope>
```

The token (certificate) is directly included here.

A <Signature> element represents a digital signature. You don't need to fully understand its details. If later you encrypt the message, there will be an <EncryptedData> element as its sibling.

The signature was created using this token (certificate).

The signature is signing over this element, i.e., the <Body> element.

The <Body> element is basically unchanged. The only exception is that an id has been added so that the signature can refer to it.

Supporting digital signatures in the web service

In the service project, modify the SecureService_P1_Server class as shown below:

Create the end point without publishing it yet.

The properties are like the request context in the client.

You'll create a keystore alias named "s1" for it later.

Provide the password for the "s1" entry.

You'll create this properties file later.

```
public class SecureService_P1_Server {

  protected SecureService_P1_Server() throws Exception {
    System.out.println("Starting Server");
    Object implementor = new SecureServiceImpl();
    String address = "http://localhost:8080/ss/p1";
    Endpoint endpoint = Endpoint.create(implementor);
    Map<String, Object> properties = endpoint.getProperties();
    properties.put(SecurityConstants.SIGNATURE_USERNAME, "s1");
    properties.put(SecurityConstants.CALLBACK_HANDLER,
        new CallbackHandler() {

          @Override
          public void handle(Callback[] callbacks)
              throws IOException, UnsupportedCallbackException {
            for (int i = 0; i < callbacks.length; i++) {
              WSPasswordCallback pwcb = (WSPasswordCallback) callbacks[i];
              String id = pwcb.getIdentifier();
              if (id.equals("s1")) {
                pwcb.setPassword("s1-pass");
              }
            }
          }
        });
    properties.put(SecurityConstants.SIGNATURE_PROPERTIES, "crypto.properties");
    endpoint.publish(address);
  }
  ...
}
```

Create the crypto.properites in src/main/resources:

```
org.apache.ws.security.crypto.provider=org.apache.ws.security.components.crypto.Me
rlin
org.apache.ws.security.crypto.merlin.keystore.type=JKS
org.apache.ws.security.crypto.merlin.file=c:/Documents and
Settings/kent/keys/service.ks
org.apache.ws.security.crypto.merlin.keystore.password=service-ks-pass
```

Next, you will create the keystore for the service (service.ks) and create the "s1" entry. So, open a command prompt, change into the "keys" folder and then:

```
keys\>keytool -genkey -alias s1 -keystore service.ks -dname cn=s1,dc=foo,dc=com
-keyalg RSA -sigalg SHA1withRSA
Enter keystore password:
Re-enter new password:
Enter key password for <s1>
        (RETURN if same as keystore password):
Re-enter new password:
```

Use "service-ks-pass" as the keystore password and "s1-pass" as the entry password for "s1". Then, generate a certificate request for it:

```
keys\>keytool -certreq -alias s1 -keystore service.ks -file s1.csr
Enter keystore password:
Enter key password for <s1>
```

Use your test CA to create a certificate for it (remember that "ca-pass" is the password for the CA key):

```
keys\>cd ..\CA

CA\>openssl x509 -CA cacert.pem -CAkey cakey.pem -CAserial serial.txt -req
```

```
-in ../keys/s1.csr -out ../keys/s1.cer -days 1095
Signature ok
subject=/DC=com/DC=foo/CN=s1
Getting CA Private Key
Enter pass phrase for cakey.pem:
```

Import the certificate of the CA:

```
CA\>cd ..\keys

keys\>keytool -import -alias testCA -keystore service.ks -file ../CA/cacert.pem
Enter keystore password:
Owner: CN=CA, O=Test CA, ST=Some-State, C=US
Issuer: CN=CA, O=Test CA, ST=Some-State, C=US
Serial number: c896adcad015985e
Valid from: Mon Dec 21 19:48:29 HKT 2009 until: Thu Dec 19 19:48:29 HKT 2019
Certificate fingerprints:
         MD5:  BB:15:7D:0A:C4:5C:D7:58:C3:43:40:E0:FC:E3:87:E6
         SHA1: 47:7B:86:AF:52:A1:57:CD:83:03:AA:45:4A:B2:19:38:C1:2E:B8:5E
         Signature algorithm name: SHA1withRSA
         Version: 3
...
Trust this certificate? [no]:  yes
Certificate was added to keystore
```

Import the certificate for the service into the keystore:

```
keys\>keytool -import -alias s1 -keystore service.ks -file s1.cer
Enter keystore password:
Enter key password for <s1>
Certificate reply was installed in keystore
```

Do you need to import c1's certificate? No. As the client will include it in the message, you don't need it in the keystore. On the other hand, do you need to import s1's certificate into the keystore for the client? Yes. This is because the web service will not send its certificate to the client, but just the issuer's DN and serial number of the certificate. So the client needs this certificate in its keystore. So, import it (recall that the client keystore password is "client-ks-pass"):

```
keys\>keytool -import -alias s1 -keystore client.ks -file s1.cer
Enter keystore password:
Certificate was added to keystore
```

Now, a very important step: For Rampart to take effect, it must have access to the policy information (in the WSDL file). However, for the moment, only the service stub (SecureService_Service) knows where the WSDL file is, but neither the SEI (SecureService) nor the implementation does:

```
@WebServiceClient(
  name = "SecureService",
  wsdlLocation = "file:src/main/resources/SecureService.wsdl",
  targetNamespace = "http://ttdev.com/ss")
public class SecureService_Service extends Service {
  ...
}

@WebService(
  targetNamespace = "http://ttdev.com/ss",
  name = "SecureService")
@XmlSeeAlso({ObjectFactory.class})
public interface SecureService {
  ...
}

@WebService(endpointInterface="com.ttdev.ss.SecureService")
public class SecureServiceImpl implements SecureService {
```

```
    @Override
    public String concat(String s1, String s2) {
      return s1 + s2;
    }
}
```

To fix the problem, either modify the SEI or the implementation class to add the information. As the the SEI is generated, it's better to modify the implementation class:

Specify the QName of the service. Why? If you don't, CXF will assume that it is the same as the class name (SecureServiceImpl) but there is no such service defined in the WSDL file. In the past it was fine because you didn't provide a WSDL file for it to check against

```
<wsdl:definitions>
  ...
  </wsdl:binding>
  <wsdl:service name="SecureService">
    <wsdl:port name="p1" ...>
      <soap:address .../>
    </wsdl:port>
  </wsdl:service>
</wsdl:definitions>
```

Specify the location of the WSDL file.

```
@WebService(
  endpointInterface="com.ttdev.ss.SecureService",
  wsdlLocation = "file:src/main/resources/SecureService.wsdl",
  targetNamespace = "http://ttdev.com/ss",
  serviceName = "SecureService")
public class SecureServiceImpl implements SecureService {

  @Override
  public String concat(String s1, String s2) {
    return s1 + s2;
  }
}
```

Now, run the service and then the client. This time it will work. If you check the SOAP response message in TCP Monitor, you'll see:

```
<soap:Envelope xmlns:soap="http://schemas.xmlsoap.org/soap/envelope/">
  <soap:Header>
    <wsse:Security
      xmlns:wsse="..."
      soap:mustUnderstand="1">
      <ds:Signature xmlns:ds="http://www.w3.org/2000/09/xmldsig#"
        Id="Signature-1">
        <ds:SignedInfo>
          <ds:CanonicalizationMethod
            Algorithm="http://www.w3.org/2001/10/xml-exc-c14n#" />
          <ds:SignatureMethod Algorithm="http://www.w3.org/2000/09/xmldsig#rsa-sha1" />
          <ds:Reference URI="#Id-22746539">
            <ds:Transforms>
              <ds:Transform Algorithm="http://www.w3.org/2001/10/xml-exc-c14n#" />
            </ds:Transforms>
            <ds:DigestMethod Algorithm="http://www.w3.org/2000/09/xmldsig#sha1" />
            <ds:DigestValue>XhWkOXyz2+OhnIeFFx4VHQTGeqg=</ds:DigestValue>
          </ds:Reference>
        </ds:SignedInfo>
        <ds:SignatureValue>
        bU2C...all/czvA=
        </ds:SignatureValue>
        <ds:KeyInfo Id="KeyId-B2DEEA4DF54BD8D8F712615434819612">
          <wsse:SecurityTokenReference
            xmlns:wsse="..."
            xmlns:wsu="..."
            wsu:Id="STRId-B2DEEA4DF54BD8D8F712615434819613">
            <ds:X509Data>
              <ds:X509IssuerSerial>
                <ds:X509IssuerName>CN=CA,O=Test
                  CA,ST=Some-State,C=US</ds:X509IssuerName>
                <ds:X509SerialNumber>4</ds:X509SerialNumber>
              </ds:X509IssuerSerial>
            </ds:X509Data>
          </wsse:SecurityTokenReference>
        </ds:KeyInfo>
      </ds:Signature>
    </wsse:Security>
  </soap:Header>
  <soap:Body
    xmlns:wsu="..."
    wsu:Id="Id-22746539">
    <ns2:concatResponse xmlns:ns2="http://ttdev.com/ss">
      <r>abc123</r>
    </ns2:concatResponse>
  </soap:Body>
</soap:Envelope>
```

There is no <BinarySecurityToken> here. It means the s1 certificate is not sent.

Use the issuer DN and certificate serial number (4 here) to identify the certificate. It is up to the client to look it up.

That is, it is telling the service that the certificate used to sign the message is issued by CN=CA,O=Test CA,ST=Some-State,C=US and the serial number of the certificate is 4. It is hoping that the client can use this information to locate the certificate and then use the public key in it to verify the signature. For this to work, the client may scan all the certificates in the keystore to try to find it. It means you must import s1's certificate into the keystore on the client.

Encrypting SOAP messages

At the moment the messages are signed, but they aren't encrypted and thus people on the Internet can see them. If the information is confidential, you should encrypt it. To do that, modify the policy in the WSDL files in both projects:

```
<?xml version="1.0" encoding="UTF-8"?>
<wsdl:definitions ...>
  <wsp:Policy wsu:Id="p1">
    <sp:AsymmetricBinding>
      ...
    </sp:AsymmetricBinding>
    <sp:Wss10>
      ...
    </sp:Wss10>
    <sp:SignedParts>
      <sp:Body />
    </sp:SignedParts>
    <sp:EncryptedParts>
      <sp:Body />
    </sp:EncryptedParts>
  </wsp:Policy>
  ...
</wsdl:definitions>
```

The <Body> element of the SOAP message should be encrypted. This assertion is AND'ed together with the others, so both signing and encryption must be done.

You're about to generate the code again, but this will overwrite your code in SecureService_P1_Server and SecureService_P1_Client. So, it's better to move the code into a your own classes. Move the server code into a SecureServer class:

```
public class SecureServer {
  public static void main(String[] args) {
    System.out.println("Starting Server");
    Object implementor = new SecureServiceImpl();
    String address = "http://localhost:8080/ss/p1";
    Endpoint endpoint = Endpoint.create(implementor);
    Map<String, Object> properties = endpoint.getProperties();
    properties.put(SecurityConstants.SIGNATURE_USERNAME, "s1");
    properties.put(SecurityConstants.CALLBACK_HANDLER,
        new CallbackHandler() {

          @Override
          public void handle(Callback[] callbacks)
              throws IOException, UnsupportedCallbackException {
            for (int i = 0; i < callbacks.length; i++) {
              WSPasswordCallback pwcb = (WSPasswordCallback) callbacks[i];
              String id = pwcb.getIdentifier();
              if (id.equals("s1")) {
                pwcb.setPassword("s1-pass");
              }
            }

          }
        });
    properties.put(SecurityConstants.SIGNATURE_PROPERTIES, "crypto.properties");
    endpoint.publish(address);
  }
}
```

Move the client code into a new SecureClient class:

```
public class SecureClient {

  public static void main(String[] args) {
    SecureService_Service ss = new SecureService_Service(
        SecureService_Service.WSDL_LOCATION,
        SecureService_Service.SERVICE);
    SecureService port = ss.getP1();
    BindingProvider bp = (BindingProvider) port;
    Map<String, Object> context = bp.getRequestContext();
```

```
      context.put(SecurityConstants.SIGNATURE_USERNAME, "c1");
      context.put(SecurityConstants.CALLBACK_HANDLER, new CallbackHandler() {

        @Override
        public void handle(Callback[] callbacks) throws IOException,
            UnsupportedCallbackException {
          for (int i = 0; i < callbacks.length; i++) {
            WSPasswordCallback pwcb = (WSPasswordCallback) callbacks[i];
            String id = pwcb.getIdentifier();
            if (id.equals("c1")) {
              pwcb.setPassword("c1-pass");
            }
          }
        }
      });
      context.put(SecurityConstants.SIGNATURE_PROPERTIES, "crypto.properties");
      context.put(BindingProvider.ENDPOINT_ADDRESS_PROPERTY,
          "http://localhost:1234/ss/p1");
      System.out.println("Invoking concat...");
      java.lang.String _concat_s1 = "abc";
      java.lang.String _concat_s2 = "123";
      java.lang.String _concat__return = port.concat(_concat_s1, _concat_s2);
      System.out.println("concat.result=" + _concat__return);
    }
  }
```

Generate the code again in both projects. Modify the SecureClient class:

```
public class SecureClient {

  public static void main(String[] args) {
    SecureService_Service ss = new SecureService_Service(
        SecureService_Service.WSDL_LOCATION,
        SecureService_Service.SERVICE);
    SecureService port = ss.getP1();
    BindingProvider bp = (BindingProvider) port;
    Map<String, Object> context = bp.getRequestContext();
    context.put(SecurityConstants.SIGNATURE_USERNAME, "c1");
    context.put(SecurityConstants.ENCRYPT_USERNAME, "s1");
    context.put(SecurityConstants.CALLBACK_HANDLER, new CallbackHandler() {

      @Override
      public void handle(Callback[] callbacks) throws IOException,
          UnsupportedCallbackException {
        for (int i = 0; i < callbacks.length; i++) {
          WSPasswordCallback pwcb = (WSPasswordCallback) callbacks[i];
          String id = pwcb.getIdentifier();
          if (id.equals("c1")) {
            pwcb.setPassword("c1-pass");
          }
        }
      }
    });
    context.put(SecurityConstants.SIGNATURE_PROPERTIES, "crypto.properties");
    context.put(SecurityConstants.ENCRYPT_PROPERTIES, "crypto.properties");
    context.put(BindingProvider.ENDPOINT_ADDRESS_PROPERTY,
        "http://localhost:1234/ss/p1");
    System.out.println("Invoking concat...");
    java.lang.String _concat_s1 = "abc";
    java.lang.String _concat_s2 = "123";
    java.lang.String _concat__return = port.concat(_concat_s1, _concat_s2);
    System.out.println("concat.result=" + _concat__return);
  }
}
```

Use this keystore alias to perform encryption. Here, get the certificate for the alias "s1" from the keystore and use the public key there to encrypt the message. Note that you don't need the password to get the public key.

Need to specify the keystore location and etc. for encryption purpose. Here, use the same thing for signing.

Make similar changes to the SecureServer class:

```
public class SecureServer {
  public static void main(String[] args) {
    System.out.println("Starting Server");
    Object implementor = new SecureServiceImpl();
    String address = "http://localhost:8080/ss/p1";
    Endpoint endpoint = Endpoint.create(implementor);
    Map<String, Object> properties = endpoint.getProperties();
    properties.put(SecurityConstants.SIGNATURE_USERNAME, "s1");
    properties.put(SecurityConstants.ENCRYPT_USERNAME, "c1");
    properties.put(SecurityConstants.CALLBACK_HANDLER,
        new CallbackHandler() {

          @Override
          public void handle(Callback[] callbacks)
              throws IOException, UnsupportedCallbackException {
            for (int i = 0; i < callbacks.length; i++) {
              WSPasswordCallback pwcb = (WSPasswordCallback) callbacks[i];
              String id = pwcb.getIdentifier();
              if (id.equals("s1")) {
                pwcb.setPassword("s1-pass");
              }
            }

          }
        });
    properties.put(SecurityConstants.SIGNATURE_PROPERTIES, "crypto.properties");
    properties.put(SecurityConstants.ENCRYPT_PROPERTIES, "crypto.properties");
    endpoint.publish(address);
  }

}
```

However, there is a problem here. As you're encrypting the response message using c1's public key, how can it find out c1's public key? You'll need to put c1's certificate in the keystore for the web service. In addition, this web service can only talk to a single client c1 (see the diagram below). If there is another client c2, it can encrypt the request using s1's public key, but s1 will encrypt the response using the public key of c1 (NOT c2), making c2 fail to decrypt it:

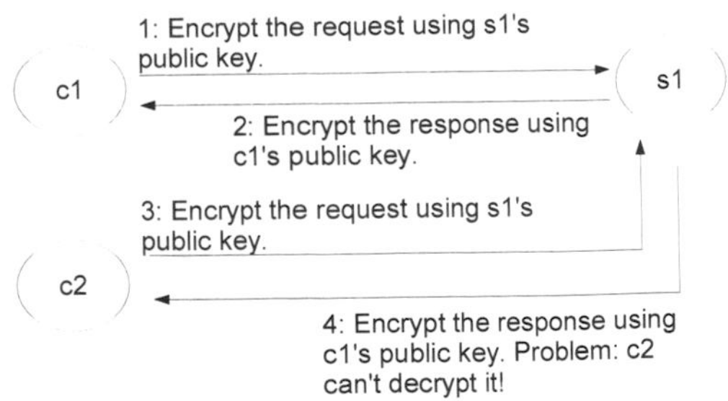

To solve this problem, Rampart supports a special way of operation. If c1 both signs and encrypts the request, it will sign it using its own private key (see the diagram below). If it also includes its certificate in the request, then Rampart on the server side can be instructed to look up this certificate in the request and use it to encrypt the response. Therefore, it will use c1's certificate to encrypt the response. If c2 sends it a request, it will encrypt the response using c2's certificate:

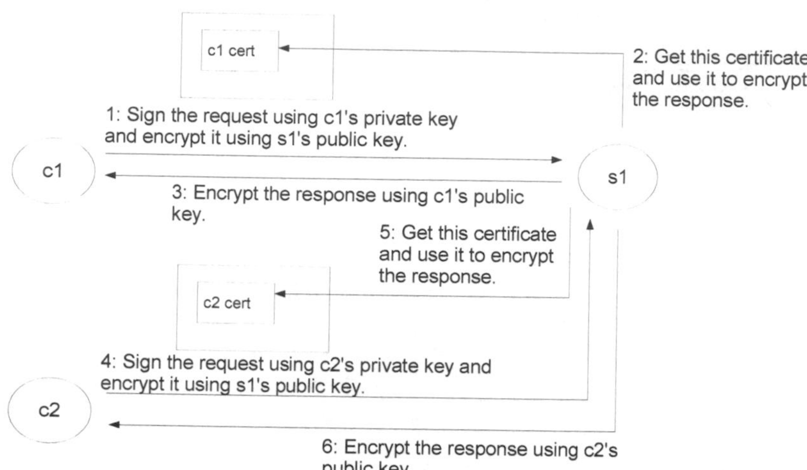

To enable this operation, put a special value "useReqSigCert" as the encryption username:

It stands for "use request signing certificate". That is, use the certificate that signed the request message.

```
public class SecureServer {
  public static void main(String[] args) {
    System.out.println("Starting Server");
    Object implementor = new SecureServiceImpl();
    String address = "http://localhost:8080/ss/p1";
    Endpoint endpoint = Endpoint.create(implementor);
    Map<String, Object> properties = endpoint.getProperties();
    properties.put(SecurityConstants.SIGNATURE_USERNAME, "s1");
    properties.put(SecurityConstants.ENCRYPT_USERNAME, "useReqSigCert");
    ...
  }
}
```

Now run the server and the client and they should continue to work. To verify that the messages are indeed encrypted, check them out in the TCP Monitor:

All encryption and signing information is included in the <Security> header.

This represents the encrypted symmetric key.

How the symmetric key was encrypted

Information about the private key that was used to encrypt this symmetric key. Here it refers to s1's certificate using the issuer DN and serial number.

The encrypted symmetric key

The certificate (c1's) and signature as before.

How was the content of the <Body> encrypted? It used 3DES.

The symmetric key used to encrypt the data

The encrypted content of the <Body>

The content of the <Body> has been encrypted.

```
<soap:Envelope xmlns:soap="http://schemas.xmlsoap.org/soap/envelope/"
   xmlns:xenc="http://www.w3.org/2001/04/xmlenc#">
   <soap:Header>
      <wsse:Security
         xmlns:wsse="..."
         soap:mustUnderstand="1">
         <xenc:EncryptedKey xmlns:xenc="http://www.w3.org/2001/04/xmlenc#"
            Id="EncKeyId-9B0F450EB808632604126154665090 75">
            <xenc:EncryptionMethod Algorithm="http://www.w3.org/2001/04/xmlenc#rsa-1_5" />
            <ds:KeyInfo xmlns:ds="http://www.w3.org/2000/09/xmldsig#">
               <wsse:SecurityTokenReference
                  xmlns:wsse="...">
                  <ds:X509Data>
                     <ds:X509IssuerSerial>
                        <ds:X509IssuerName>CN=CA,O=Test
                           CA,ST=Some-State,C=US</ds:X509IssuerName>
                        <ds:X509SerialNumber>4</ds:X509SerialNumber>
                     </ds:X509IssuerSerial>
                  </ds:X509Data>
               </wsse:SecurityTokenReference>
            </ds:KeyInfo>
            <xenc:CipherData>
               <xenc:CipherValue>PvaShUU...cpL4gIc=</xenc:CipherValue>
            </xenc:CipherData>
            <xenc:ReferenceList>
               <xenc:DataReference URI="#EncDataId-2" />
            </xenc:ReferenceList>
         </xenc:EncryptedKey>
         <wsse:BinarySecurityToken ...
            ValueType="...oasis-200401-wss-x509-token-profile-1.0#X509v3"
            wsu:Id="CertId-9B0F450EB80863260412615466499911">MIIB5zCCAVAC...TDWFD4=
         </wsse:BinarySecurityToken>
         <ds:Signature xmlns:ds="http://www.w3.org/2000/09/xmldsig#" Id="Signature-1">
            ...
         </ds:Signature>
      </wsse:Security>
   </soap:Header>
   <soap:Body
      xmlns:wsu="..."
      wsu:Id="Id-16874657">
      <xenc:EncryptedData xmlns:xenc="http://www.w3.org/2001/04/xmlenc#"
         Id="EncDataId-2" Type="http://www.w3.org/2001/04/xmlenc#Content">
         <xenc:Encr 3 cd yptionMethod
            Algorithm="http://www.w3.org/2001/04/xmlenc#tripledes-cbc" />
         <ds:KeyInfo xmlns:ds="http://www.w3.org/2000/09/xmldsig#">
            <wsse:SecurityTokenReference xmlns:wsse="...">
               <wsse:Reference
                  xmlns:wsse="..."
                  URI="#EncKeyId-9B0F450EB80863260412615466509075" />
            </wsse:SecurityTokenReference>
         </ds:KeyInfo>
         <xenc:CipherData>
            <xenc:CipherValue>tsfEY+S9tf...yk5H</xenc:CipherValue>
         </xenc:CipherData>
      </xenc:EncryptedData>
   </soap:Body>
</soap:Envelope>
```

Security issues when performing both signing and encrypting

When you're performing both signing and encryption, there are security issues. For example, if you sign the <Body> and then encrypt it, then the resulting message will be like:

```
<Header>
  <Security>
    <EncryptedKey>...</EncryptedKey>
    <Signature>
      <ds:SignedInfo>
        <ds:CanonicalizationMethod .../>
        <ds:SignatureMethod .../>
        <ds:Reference URI="#Id-26622782">
          ...
          <ds:DigestMethod .../>
          <ds:DigestValue>JOO/ATRze2p/BUBwlq1ZJ8xX9v4=</ds:DigestValue>
        </ds:Reference>
      </ds:SignedInfo>
      ...
    </Signature>
  </Security>
</Header>
<Body>
  encrypted data...
</Body>
```

The digest of the content of the <Body> element

The problem is that, if you run the client multiple times, the digest will be the same. This is the way it should be. Given some particular plain text, anyone can calculate the digest and it should be the same. This means that a hacker could calculate the digest of some common plain text to build a lookup table like:

Plain text

```
<ns1:concat xmlns:ns1="http://ttdev.com/ss">
  <s1>xyz</s1>
  <s2>111</s2>
</ns1:concat>
```

→ khg8fryfs37ufaeG

```
<ns1:concat xmlns:ns1="http://ttdev.com/ss">
  <s1>xyz</s1>
  <s2>abc</s2>
</ns1:concat>
```

→ HTsfjdiDFfhk

```
...
```

→ ...

Then he can capture your message, get the digest and use the lookup table above to recover the plain text, even though you've encrypted the content of the <Body> element. It means the digest is actually leaking the plain text.

You may wonder if the hacker can do the same thing using the encrypted content of the <Body> element?

```
<soapenv:Body ...>
  <xenc:EncryptedData Id="EncDataId-26622782" ...>
    <xenc:EncryptionMethod .../>
    <ds:KeyInfo ...>
      ...
    </ds:KeyInfo>
    <xenc:CipherData>
      <xenc:Ciph1f5erValue>
        dKeF1WLDqSV...
      </xenc:CipherValue>
    </xenc:CipherData>
  </xenc:EncryptedData>
</soapenv:Body>
```

The encrypted content of the <Body> element

If you run the client multiple times, you'll see that the encrypted content of the <Body> element will change every time. This is a basic requirement of encryption algorithms to prevent such a lookup attack (called "dictionary attack").

Now the question is how to prevent the digest from leaking information? There are three alternative solutions.

The first solution is to perform encryption first and then sign on the encrypted <Body> content. As the encrypted content changes every time, the digest will change every time. However, this is not a very good solution as digital signatures should be performed on what is seen by the users (i.e., plain text, not encrypted text). For the case on hand, as it is the client (not user) signing it, it may be good enough.

The second solution is to sign and then encrypt and finally also encrypt the signature.

The third solution is to include a random element (usually called "nonce" or "salt") into the plain text so that the digest changes every time. For example, you could add a third element to the request:

```
<ns1:concat xmlns:ns1="http://ttdev.com/ss">
  <s1>xyz</s1>
  <s2>111</s2>
  <salt>kguy8FDsfDFAfa389r</salt>
</ns1:concat>
```

This is the most flexible solution but it means a lot of extra work on you. Anyway, in order to implement the first solution (encrypt and then sign), modify the policy in both projects:

```
<wsp:Policy wsu:Id="p1">
  <sp:AsymmetricBinding>
    <wsp:Policy>
      <sp:InitiatorToken>
        ...
      </sp:InitiatorToken>
      <sp:RecipientToken>
        ...
      </sp:RecipientToken>
      <sp:AlgorithmSuite>
        ...
      </sp:AlgorithmSuite>
      <sp:EncryptBeforeSigning/>
```

```
    </wsp:Policy>
  </sp:AsymmetricBinding>
  ...
</wsp:Policy>
```

To implement the second solution, modify the policy:

```
<wsp:Policy wsu:Id="p1">
  <sp:AsymmetricBinding>
    ...
    <sp:EncryptBeforeSigning/>
    ...
  </sp:AsymmetricBinding>
  <sp:Wss10>
    ...
  </sp:Wss10>
  <sp:SignedParts>
    <sp:Body />
  </sp:SignedParts>
  <sp:EncryptedParts>
    <sp:Body />
  </sp:EncryptedParts>
  <sp:EncryptedElements>
    <sp:XPath>
      //*[local-name()='Signature']
    </sp:XPath>
  </sp:EncryptedElements>
</wsp:Policy>
```

Don't need this any more

It is like <EncryptedParts> but it is not using SOAP structures such as <Body> to refer the message. Instead, it uses something called XPath to refer to elements in the XML document.

Look for any descendant of XML root element (<Envelope> here)

Then select those whose element name (ignoring the namespace) is "Signature".

```
<soapenv:Envelope ...>
  <soapenv:Header>
    <wsse:Security ...>
      <xenc:EncryptedKey ...>...</xenc:EncryptedKey>
      <ds:Signature ...>
        ...
      </ds:Signature>
    </wsse:Security>
  </soapenv:Header>
</soapenv:Envelope>
```

Sending login information

Suppose that the web service will perform the requested operation only for selected users only. To do that, you can configure your client to send the user name and password to the web service. Such information is called a Username Token. To require a Username token in the request message, modify the policy:

```
<wsp:Policy wsu:Id="p1">
  <sp:AsymmetricBinding>
    ...
  </sp:AsymmetricBinding>
  <sp:Wss10>
    ...
  </sp:Wss10>
  <sp:SignedParts>
    ...
  </sp:SignedParts>
  <sp:EncryptedParts>
    ...
  </sp:EncryptedParts>
  <sp:SignedSupportingTokens>
      <wsp:Policy>
        <sp:UsernameToken
          sp:IncludeToken="http://docs.oasis-open.org/ws-sx/ws-
securitypolicy/200702/IncludeToken/AlwaysToRecipient"/>
      </wsp:Policy>
  </sp:SignedSupportingTokens>
</wsp:Policy>
```

A Username Token is not like the certificate token which is required for signing or encryption. Therefore it is just a supporting token. Here, you also require that it be signed to make sure that it has not been tampered with.

There can be other types of supporting tokens. Username token is just one possible type.

Always include it in the request message.

To specify the user name, modify the SecureClient class:

```
public class SecureClient {
  public static void main(String[] args) {
    SecureService_Service ss = new SecureService_Service(
        SecureService_Service.WSDL_LOCATION,
        SecureService_Service.SERVICE);
    SecureService port = ss.getP1();
    BindingProvider bp = (BindingProvider) port;
    Map<String, Object> context = bp.getRequestContext();
    context.put(SecurityConstants.USERNAME, "Paul");
    context.put(SecurityConstants.SIGNATURE_USERNAME, "c1");
    context.put(SecurityConstants.ENCRYPT_USERNAME, "s1");
    context.put(SecurityConstants.CALLBACK_HANDLER, new CallbackHandler() {
    ...
  }
}
```

So Rampart has the user name, but how does it know the password? It can use the password callback. So modify that class further:

```
public static void main(String[] args) {
  SecureService_Service ss = new SecureService_Service(
      SecureService_Service.WSDL_LOCATION,
      SecureService_Service.SERVICE);
  SecureService port = ss.getP1();
  BindingProvider bp = (BindingProvider) port;
  Map<String, Object> context = bp.getRequestContext();
  context.put(SecurityConstants.USERNAME, "Paul");
  context.put(SecurityConstants.SIGNATURE_USERNAME, "c1");
  context.put(SecurityConstants.ENCRYPT_USERNAME, "s1");
  context.put(SecurityConstants.CALLBACK_HANDLER, new CallbackHandler() {

    @Override
    public void handle(Callback[] callbacks) throws IOException,
        UnsupportedCallbackException {
      for (int i = 0; i < callbacks.length; i++) {
        WSPasswordCallback pwcb = (WSPasswordCallback) callbacks[i];
        String id = pwcb.getIdentifier();
        switch (pwcb.getUsage()) {
        case WSPasswordCallback.DECRYPT:
        case WSPasswordCallback.SIGNATURE: {
          if (id.equals("c1")) {
            pwcb.setPassword("c1-pass");
          }
          break;
        }
        case WSPasswordCallback.USERNAME_TOKEN: {
          if (id.equals("Paul")) {
            pwcb.setPassword("paul-pass");
          }
          break;
        }
        }
      }
    }

  });
  ...
}
```

When Rampart needs to sign or decrypt...

When Rampart needs to send a Username token...

Tell Rampart the password for Paul. In a real application, you may prompt the user (presumably Paul) for his password.

How can the web service verify the password? Again, Rampart replies on the password callback to get the correct password for comparison. So, modify the SecureServer class:

```
public class SecureServer {
  public static void main(String[] args) {
    System.out.println("Starting Server");
    Object implementor = new SecureServiceImpl();
    String address = "http://localhost:8080/ss/p1";
    Endpoint endpoint = Endpoint.create(implementor);
    Map<String, Object> properties = endpoint.getProperties();
    properties.put(SecurityConstants.SIGNATURE_USERNAME, "s1");
    properties.put(SecurityConstants.ENCRYPT_USERNAME, "useReqSigCert");
    properties.put(SecurityConstants.CALLBACK_HANDLER,
        new CallbackHandler() {

          @Override
          public void handle(Callback[] callbacks)
              throws IOException, UnsupportedCallbackException {
            for (int i = 0; i < callbacks.length; i++) {
              WSPasswordCallback pwcb = (WSPasswordCallback) callbacks[i];
```

```
            String id = pwcb.getIdentifier();
            switch (pwcb.getUsage()) {
            case WSPasswordCallback.DECRYPT:
            case WSPasswordCallback.SIGNATURE:
              if (id.equals("s1")) {
                      pwcb.setPassword("s1-pass");
              }
              break;
            case WSPasswordCallback.USERNAME_TOKEN:
              if (id.equals("Paul")) {
                      pwcb.setPassword("paul-pass");
              }
              break;
            }
          }
        }
      });
    ...
  }
}
```

In a real service you'll probably look up the user and the password from a database or LDAP, instead of hard coding it in the source code.

Now run the server and then the client. You should see the Username token in the TCP Monitor:

```
<soapenv:Envelope ...>
  <soapenv:Header>
    <wsse:Security ...>
      <xenc:EncryptedKey Id="EncKeyId-29857804">
        ...
      </xenc:EncryptedKey>
      <wsse:UsernameToken
        xmlns:wsu="..."
        wsu:Id="UsernameToken-6659511">
        <wsse:Username>Paul</wsse:Username>
        <wsse:Password
          Type="http://docs.oasis-open.org/wss/
2004/01/oasis-200401-wss-username-token-profile-1.0#PasswordDigest">
          6GW32nj7XJ0sTyIjDZrcQWn3X0E=
        </wsse:Password>
        <wsse:Nonce>/D2oMduF226uzRd4Rs3Bkw==</wsse:Nonce>
        <wsu:Created>2007-12-15T06:16:55.765Z</wsu:Created>
      </wsse:UsernameToken>
      ...
      <ds:Signature xmlns:ds="http://www.w3.org/2000/09/xmldsig#"
        Id="Signature-25421790">
        <ds:SignedInfo>
          ...
          <ds:Reference URI="#UsernameToken-6659511">
              Algorithm="http://www.w3.org/2000/09/xmldsig#sha1" />
            <ds:DigestValue>
              Ht4ubB6JdHcLyaJUxYiwdnSQVj0=
            </ds:DigestValue>
          </ds:Reference>
        </ds:SignedInfo>
        ...
      </ds:Signature>
    </wsse:Security>
    ...
</soapenv:Envelope>
```

The Username token

Paul is the user name.

For security, the password is not sent as clear text but as a digest.

The token is signed.

To fight against dictionary attack, a nonce and a time stamp are included when calculating the digest:

password + nonce + time stamp

digest

In addition, the web service can remember the nonces seen in a short recent period. If the same nonce is used again, it is a replay attack.

If you don't want others to even see the user name of "c1", you can encrypt the Username token. All that is required is to change <SignedSupportingTokens> to <SignedEncryptedSupportingTokens> in the policy.

What if different users have different permissions? You can retrieve the user name in your own code and decide what permissions he has. To do that, you need to understand the data structure created by Rampart after processing the request message. There could be multiple Rampart handlers running. Each will store its result into an element of a Vector (see the diagram below). Each Rampart handler instance may perform multiple actions, e.g., verify its signature, verify a Username token or decrypt a message. Therefore, for each action it will create a WSSecurityEngineResult to represent the result of that action. So, each handler creates a vector-like structure to store all such results. This is the WSHandlerResult. For example, in the diagram, the first action is SIGN, which means verifying a signature, the result contains the certificate used and etc. The second action is UT, which means verifying a Username token, the result contains the user name:

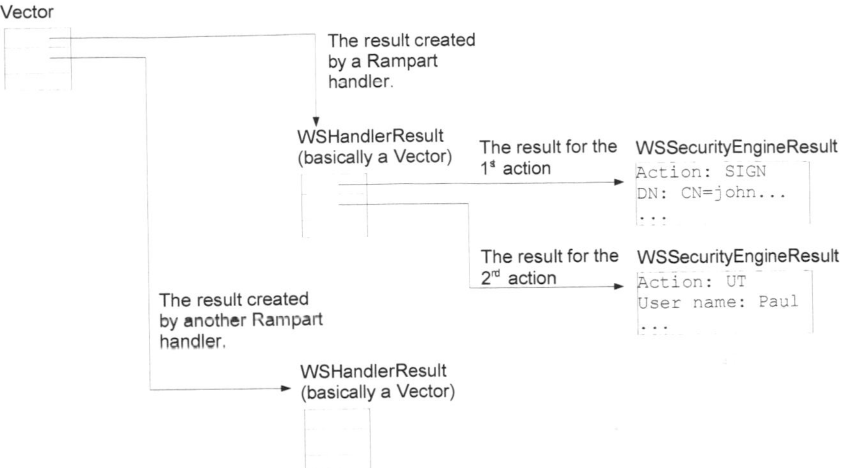

Now, to retrieve the user name in the implementation object, modify SecureServiceImpl.java:

```
...
import java.security.Principal;
import java.util.Vector;
import javax.annotation.Resource;
import javax.xml.ws.WebServiceContext;
import javax.xml.ws.handler.MessageContext;
import org.apache.ws.security.WSConstants;
import org.apache.ws.security.WSSecurityEngineResult;
import org.apache.ws.security.handler.WSHandlerConstants;
import org.apache.ws.security.handler.WSHandlerResult;

@WebService(...)
public class SecureServiceImpl implements SecureService {
  @Resource
  WebServiceContext context;

  @Override
  public String concat(String s1, String s2) {
    checkUser();
    return s1 + s2;
  }

  @SuppressWarnings("unchecked")
  private void checkUser() {
    MessageContext msgContext = context.getMessageContext();
    Vector<WSHandlerResult> handlersResults = (Vector<WSHandlerResult>) msgContext
        .get(WSHandlerConstants.RECV_RESULTS);
    for (WSHandlerResult handlerResult : handlersResults) {
      Vector<WSSecurityEngineResult> actionsResults = handlerResult.getResults();
      for (WSSecurityEngineResult actionResult : actionsResults) {
        int action = ((Integer) actionResult
            .get(WSSecurityEngineResult.TAG_ACTION)).intValue();
        if (action == WSConstants.UT) {
          Principal p = (Principal) actionResult
              .get(WSSecurityEngineResult.TAG_PRINCIPAL);
          if (p != null) {
            System.out.println("Checking " + p.getName());
            return; // return if the user has the required permission
          }
        }
      }
    }
    throw new RuntimeException("Unable to find a user");
  }
}
```

When CXF sees this annotation, it will inject the context into it.

The web service context provides information regarding this web service.

The message context provides information regarding this request message.

Get the results for a all Rampart handlers.

Get the action results for a single Rampart handler.

For testing, just print out the name.

Get the user principal. A Principal object represents a user id. It only has a "name" field.

Get the action and check if it is UT (verify a Username token).

Now run the service and then the client. You should see the output in the console:

```
...
Checking Paul
...
```

Installing Rampart into Axis2

In order to use Rampart with Axis2, you need to install Rampart into Axis2. So, go to http://ws.apache.org/axis2/modules to download it. Suppose that it is rampart-1.4.zip. Unzip it into a folder, say, rampart. Rampart needs another library xalan 2.7.0. If you're using JDK 5 or earlier, you probably has only an old version. So, in that case, download xalan-2.7.0.jar from http://www.apache.org/dist/java-repository/xalan/jars and put it into rampart/lib.

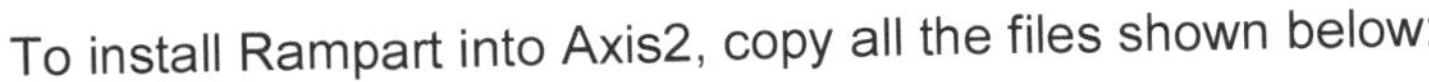

To install Rampart into Axis2, copy all the files shown below:

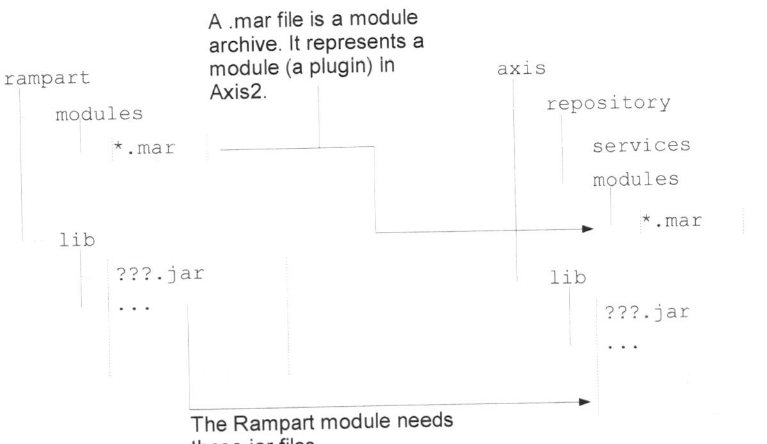

Creating a secure client in Axis2

Copy the Axis2WrappedClient and paste it as Axis2SecureClient. Copy the WSDL file from the SecureClient project into it (and delete the existing WSDL file). Add the Rampart dependencies to the pom.xml file.

Next, modify the CodeGenerator class to use the right WSDL file. Modify it to use an older version of WS Policy and WS Security Policy:

```
<?xml version="1.0" encoding="UTF-8" standalone="no"?>
<wsdl:definitions xmlns:soap="http://schemas.xmlsoap.org/wsdl/soap/"
  xmlns:tns="http://ttdev.com/ss" xmlns:wsdl="http://schemas.xmlsoap.org/wsdl/"
  xmlns:sp="http://schemas.xmlsoap.org/ws/2005/07/securitypolicy"
  xmlns:wsp="http://schemas.xmlsoap.org/ws/2004/09/policy"
  xmlns:wsu="http://docs.oasis-open.org/wss/2004/01/oasis-200401-wss-wssecurity-
utility-1.0.xsd"
  xmlns:xsd="http://www.w3.org/2001/XMLSchema" name="SecureService"
  targetNamespace="http://ttdev.com/ss">
  <wsp:Policy wsu:Id="p1">
    <sp:AsymmetricBinding>
      <wsp:Policy>
        <sp:InitiatorToken>
          <wsp:Policy>
            <sp:X509Token
              sp:IncludeToken="http://schemas.xmlsoap.org/ws/2005/07/
securitypolicy/IncludeToken/AlwaysToRecipient">
              <wsp:Policy>
                <sp:WssX509V3Token10 />
              </wsp:Policy>
            </sp:X509Token>
          </wsp:Policy>
        </sp:InitiatorToken>
        <sp:RecipientToken>
          <wsp:Policy>
            <sp:X509Token
              sp:IncludeToken="http://schemas.xmlsoap.org/ws/2005/07/
securitypolicy/IncludeToken/Never">
              <wsp:Policy>
                <sp:WssX509V3Token10 />
              </wsp:Policy>
```

```
            </sp:X509Token>
          </wsp:Policy>
        </sp:RecipientToken>
        <sp:AlgorithmSuite>
          <wsp:Policy>
            <sp:TripleDesRsa15 />
          </wsp:Policy>
        </sp:AlgorithmSuite>
      </wsp:Policy>
    </sp:AsymmetricBinding>
    <sp:Wss10>
      <wsp:Policy>
        <sp:MustSupportRefEmbeddedToken />
        <sp:MustSupportRefIssuerSerial />
      </wsp:Policy>
    </sp:Wss10>
    <sp:SignedParts>
      <sp:Body />
    </sp:SignedParts>
    <sp:EncryptedParts>
      <sp:Body />
    </sp:EncryptedParts>
    <sp:EncryptedElements>
      <sp:XPath>
        //*[local-name()='Signature']
      </sp:XPath>
    </sp:EncryptedElements>
    <sp:SignedSupportingTokens>
      <wsp:Policy>
        <sp:UsernameToken
          sp:IncludeToken="http://schemas.xmlsoap.org/ws/2005/07/
securitypolicy/IncludeToken/AlwaysToRecipient" />
      </wsp:Policy>
    </sp:SignedSupportingTokens>
  </wsp:Policy>
  <wsdl:types>
    <xsd:schema targetNamespace="http://ttdev.com/ss">
      <xsd:element name="concat">
        <xsd:complexType>
          <xsd:sequence>
            <xsd:element name="s1" type="xsd:string" />
            <xsd:element name="s2" type="xsd:string" />
          </xsd:sequence>
        </xsd:complexType>
      </xsd:element>
      <xsd:element name="concatResponse">
        <xsd:complexType>
          <xsd:sequence>
            <xsd:element name="r" type="xsd:string">
            </xsd:element>
          </xsd:sequence>
        </xsd:complexType>
      </xsd:element>
    </xsd:schema>
  </wsdl:types>
  <wsdl:message name="concatRequest">
    <wsdl:part element="tns:concat" name="parameters" />
  </wsdl:message>
  <wsdl:message name="concatResponse">
    <wsdl:part element="tns:concatResponse" name="parameters" />
  </wsdl:message>
  <wsdl:portType name="SecureService">
    <wsdl:operation name="concat">
      <wsdl:input message="tns:concatRequest" />
      <wsdl:output message="tns:concatResponse" />
    </wsdl:operation>
  </wsdl:portType>
  <wsdl:binding name="SecureServiceSOAP" type="tns:SecureService">
```

```
      <wsp:PolicyReference URI="#p1" wsdl:required="true" />
      <soap:binding style="document"
        transport="http://schemas.xmlsoap.org/soap/http" />
      <wsdl:operation name="concat">
        <soap:operation soapAction="http://ttdev.com/ss/NewOperation" />
        <wsdl:input>
          <soap:body use="literal" />
        </wsdl:input>
        <wsdl:output>
          <soap:body use="literal" />
        </wsdl:output>
      </wsdl:operation>
    </wsdl:binding>
    <wsdl:service name="SecureService">
      <wsdl:port binding="tns:SecureServiceSOAP" name="p1">
        <soap:address location="http://localhost:8080/ss/p1" />
      </wsdl:port>
    </wsdl:service>
  </wsdl:definitions>
```

BUG ALERT: In Axis2 1.5.1 and Rampart 1.4 there is a bug preventing the Username Token from working with signing/encryption. So, you may need to comment out the <SignedSupportingTokens> from the policy.

Delete the com.ttdev.ss package and the src/main/resources/META-INF folder. Then run the CodeGenerator class.

To make Rampart available to your client, copy rampart.mar into your client project in such a folder structure:

```
SecureClient
  src
  repository
    modules
      rampart.mar
```

Just like the Axis2 server which has a repository, your Axis2 client can also have a repository.

In the client project, create a SecureClient class:

```
package com.ttdev.ss;
...
import org.apache.axiom.om.OMElement;
import org.apache.axiom.om.impl.builder.StAXOMBuilder;
import org.apache.axis2.client.Options;
import org.apache.axis2.context.ConfigurationContext;
import org.apache.axis2.context.ConfigurationContextFactory;
import org.apache.neethi.Policy;
import org.apache.neethi.PolicyEngine;
import org.apache.rampart.RampartMessageData;

public class SecureClient {
  public static void main(String[] args) throws FileNotFoundException,
      XMLStreamException, RemoteException {
    ConfigurationContext context = ConfigurationContextFactory
        .createConfigurationContextFromFileSystem("repository");
    SecureServiceStub stub = new SecureServiceStub(context,
                "http://localhost:1234/axis2/services/SecureService");
    stub._getServiceClient().engageModule("rampart");
    StAXOMBuilder builder = new StAXOMBuilder(
                         "src/main/resources/rampart-config.xml");
    OMElement configElement = builder.getDocumentElement();
    Policy rampartConfig = PolicyEngine.getPolicy(configElement);
    stub._getServiceClient().getAxisService().getPolicySubject().
      attachPolicy(rampartConfig);
    String result = stub.concat("xyz", "111");
    System.out.println(result);
  }
}
```

Having rampart available is not enough, you must "engage" it, which means enable it.

Tell the Axis2 client to load configurations from the "repository" folder in the current folder (project root). Here it will find the module archive for Rampart.

Load the rampart-config.xml file and get its root element. You'll create this file next to provide information such as the signing alias.

Convert the <Policy> XML element into a Policy Java object.

Internally the service stub uses a service client to invoke the service.

Get the service description and then add the policy object to it.

Create the rampart-config.xml in the src/main/resources folder:

The rampart configuration happens to be also in the form of a policy.

All the other elements here are in the rampart namespace

The user name for the UsernameToken

The aliases of the keystore entries for signing and encryption respectively.

Rampart will create an instance of this class and ask it for the password.

Security provider and keystore information for signing

Security provider and keystore information for encryption

```
<?xml version="1.0" encoding="UTF-8"?>
<wsp:Policy xmlns:wsp="http://schemas.xmlsoap.org/ws/2004/09/policy"
  xmlns="http://ws.apache.org/rampart/policy">
  <RampartConfig>
    <user>Paul</user>
    <userCertAlias>c1</userCertAlias>
    <encryptionUser>s1</encryptionUser>
    <passwordCallbackClass>
      com.ttdev.ss.PasswordCallbackHandler
    </passwordCallbackClass>
    <signatureCrypto>
      <crypto provider="org.apache.ws.security.components.crypto.Merlin">
        <property name="org.apache.ws.security.crypto.merlin.keystore.type">
          JKS
        </property>
        <property name="org.apache.ws.security.crypto.merlin.file">
          ../../keys/client.ks
        </property>
        <property name="org.apache.ws.security.crypto.merlin.keystore.password">
          client-ks-pass
        </property>
      </crypto>
    </signatureCrypto>
    <encryptionCrypto>
      <crypto provider="org.apache.ws.security.components.crypto.Merlin">
        <property name="org.apache.ws.security.crypto.merlin.keystore.type">
          JKS
        </property>
        <property name="org.apache.ws.security.crypto.merlin.file">
          ../../keys/client.ks
        </property>
        <property name="org.apache.ws.security.crypto.merlin.keystore.password">
          client-ks-pass
        </property>
      </crypto>
    </encryptionCrypto>
  </RampartConfig>
</wsp:Policy>
```

Create the PasswordCallbackHandler class in the com.ttdev.ss package:

```
package com.ttdev.ss;
...
import javax.security.auth.callback.Callback;
import javax.security.auth.callback.CallbackHandler;
import javax.security.auth.callback.UnsupportedCallbackException;
import org.apache.ws.security.WSPasswordCallback;

public class PasswordCallbackHandler implements CallbackHandler {
  @Override
  public void handle(Callback[] callbacks) throws IOException,
      UnsupportedCallbackException {
    for (int i = 0; i < callbacks.length; i++) {
      WSPasswordCallback pwcb = (WSPasswordCallback) callbacks[i];
      String id = pwcb.getIdentifer();
      switch (pwcb.getUsage()) {
      case WSPasswordCallback.DECRYPT:
      case WSPasswordCallback.SIGNATURE: {
        if (id.equals("c1")) {
          pwcb.setPassword("c1-pass");
        }
        break;
      }
      case WSPasswordCallback.USERNAME_TOKEN: {
```

```
          if (id.equals("Paul")) {
            pwcb.setPassword("paul-pass");
          }
          break;
        }
      }
    }
  }
}
```

Creating a secure service in Axis2

Copy the Axis2WrappedService and paste it as Axis2SecureService. Copy the WSDL file from the SecureService project into it (and delete the existing WSDL file). Add the Rampart dependencies to the pom.xml file.

Next, modify the CodeGenerator class to use the right WSDL file. Delete the com.ttdev.ss package and the src/main/resources/META-INF folder. Then run the CodeGenerator class. Fill in the code in the SecureServiceSkeleton class:

```
package com.ttdev.ss;

import java.security.Principal;
import java.util.Vector;
import org.apache.axis2.context.MessageContext;
import org.apache.ws.security.WSConstants;
import org.apache.ws.security.WSSecurityEngineResult;
import org.apache.ws.security.handler.WSHandlerConstants;
import org.apache.ws.security.handler.WSHandlerResult;

public class SecureServiceSkeleton {
  public java.lang.String concat(java.lang.String s1, java.lang.String s2) {
    checkUser();
    return s1 + s2;
  }

  @SuppressWarnings("unchecked")
  private void checkUser() {
    MessageContext msgContext = MessageContext.getCurrentMessageContext();
    Vector<WSHandlerResult> handlersResults = (Vector<WSHandlerResult>) msgContext
        .getProperty(WSHandlerConstants.RECV_RESULTS);
    for (WSHandlerResult handlerResult : handlersResults) {
      Vector<WSSecurityEngineResult> actionsResults = handlerResult
          .getResults();
      for (WSSecurityEngineResult actionResult : actionsResults) {
        int action = ((Integer) actionResult
            .get(WSSecurityEngineResult.TAG_ACTION)).intValue();
        if (action == WSConstants.UT) {
          Principal p = (Principal) actionResult
              .get(WSSecurityEngineResult.TAG_PRINCIPAL);
          if (p != null) {
            System.out.println("Checking " + p.getName());
            return; // return if the user has the required permission
          }
        }
      }
    }
    throw new RuntimeException("Unable to find a user");
  }
}
```

It is very similar to the CXF version except that the MessageContext class is NOT the one defined in JAXWS; it is a class provided by Axis2.

To engage the Rampart module, modify the src/main/resources/META-INF/services.xml file:

```
<serviceGroup>
  <service name="SecureService">
    <messageReceivers>
      <messageReceiver mep="http://www.w3.org/ns/wsdl/in-out"
        class="com.ttdev.ss.SecureServiceMessageReceiverInOut" />
    </messageReceivers>
    <parameter name="ServiceClass">com.ttdev.ss.SecureServiceSkeleton
    </parameter>
    <parameter name="useOriginalwsdl">true</parameter>
    <parameter name="modifyUserWSDLPortAddress">true</parameter>
    <operation name="concat" mep="http://www.w3.org/ns/wsdl/in-out"
      namespace="http://ttdev.com/ss">
      <actionMapping>http://ttdev.com/ss/NewOperation
      </actionMapping>
      <outputActionMapping>
        http://ttdev.com/ss/SecureService/concatResponse
      </outputActionMapping>
    </operation>
    <module ref="rampart" />
  </service>
</serviceGroup>
```

To make the policy available to it, copy the policy from the WSDL into the services.xml file. Make sure you copy the definitions for the wsp, wsu and sp prefixes into the <Policy> element:

```
<serviceGroup>
  <service name="SecureService">
    <messageReceivers>
      <messageReceiver mep="http://www.w3.org/ns/wsdl/in-out"
        class="com.ttdev.ss.SecureServiceMessageReceiverInOut" />
    </messageReceivers>
    <parameter name="ServiceClass">com.ttdev.ss.SecureServiceSkeleton
    </parameter>
    <parameter name="useOriginalwsdl">true</parameter>
    <parameter name="modifyUserWSDLPortAddress">true</parameter>
    <operation name="concat" mep="http://www.w3.org/ns/wsdl/in-out"
      namespace="http://ttdev.com/ss">
      <actionMapping>http://ttdev.com/ss/NewOperation
      </actionMapping>
      <outputActionMapping>
        http://ttdev.com/ss/SecureService/concatResponse
      </outputActionMapping>
    </operation>
    <module ref="rampart" />
    <wsp:Policy
      xmlns:sp="http://schemas.xmlsoap.org/ws/2005/07/securitypolicy"
      xmlns:wsp="http://schemas.xmlsoap.org/ws/2004/09/policy"
      xmlns:wsu="http://docs.oasis-open.org/wss/2004/01/oasis-200401-wss-
wssecurity-utility-1.0.xsd"
      wsu:Id="p1">
      <sp:AsymmetricBinding>
        ...
      </sp:AsymmetricBinding>
      <sp:Wss10>
        <wsp:Policy>
          <sp:MustSupportRefEmbeddedToken />
          <sp:MustSupportRefIssuerSerial />
        </wsp:Policy>
      </sp:Wss10>
      <sp:SignedParts>
        <sp:Body />
      </sp:SignedParts>
      <sp:EncryptedParts>
```

```
        <sp:Body />
      </sp:EncryptedParts>
      <sp:EncryptedElements>
        <sp:XPath>
          //*[local-name()='Signature']
        </sp:XPath>
      </sp:EncryptedElements>
      <sp:SignedSupportingTokens>
        ...
      </sp:SignedSupportingTokens>
    </wsp:Policy>
  </service>
</serviceGroup>
```

To make the configuration available to Rampart, add it as a policy assertion inside the <Policy> element:

```
<serviceGroup>
  <service name="SecureService">
    <messageReceivers>
      <messageReceiver mep="http://www.w3.org/ns/wsdl/in-out"
        class="com.ttdev.ss.SecureServiceMessageReceiverInOut" />
    </messageReceivers>
    <parameter name="ServiceClass">com.ttdev.ss.SecureServiceSkeleton
    </parameter>
    <parameter name="useOriginalwsdl">true</parameter>
    <parameter name="modifyUserWSDLPortAddress">true</parameter>
    <operation name="concat" mep="http://www.w3.org/ns/wsdl/in-out"
      namespace="http://ttdev.com/ss">
      <actionMapping>http://ttdev.com/ss/NewOperation
      </actionMapping>
      <outputActionMapping>
        http://ttdev.com/ss/SecureService/concatResponse
      </outputActionMapping>
    </operation>
    <module ref="rampart" />
    <wsp:Policy ...
      wsu:Id="p1">
      <sp:AsymmetricBinding>
        ...
      </sp:AsymmetricBinding>
      <sp:Wss10>
        <wsp:Policy>
          <sp:MustSupportRefEmbeddedToken />
          <sp:MustSupportRefIssuerSerial />
        </wsp:Policy>
      </sp:Wss10>
      <sp:SignedParts>
        <sp:Body />
      </sp:SignedParts>
      <sp:EncryptedParts>
        <sp:Body />
      </sp:EncryptedParts>
      <sp:EncryptedElements>
        <sp:XPath>
          //*[local-name()='Signature']
        </sp:XPath>
      </sp:EncryptedElements>
      <sp:SignedSupportingTokens>
        ...
      </sp:SignedSupportingTokens>
      <RampartConfig xmlns="http://ws.apache.org/rampart/policy">
        <userCertAlias>s1</userCertAlias>
        <encryptionUser>useReqSigCert</encryptionUser>
        <passwordCallbackClass>
          com.ttdev.ss.PasswordCallbackHandler
        </passwordCallbackClass>
        <signatureCrypto>
```

```
          <crypto provider="org.apache.ws.security.components.crypto.Merlin">
            <property name="org.apache.ws.security.crypto.merlin.keystore.type">
              JKS
            </property>
            <property name="org.apache.ws.security.crypto.merlin.file">
              c:/Documents and Settings/kent/keys/service.ks
            </property>
            <property
              name="org.apache.ws.security.crypto.merlin.keystore.password">
              service-ks-pass
            </property>
          </crypto>
        </signatureCrypto>
        <encryptionCrypto>
          <crypto provider="org.apache.ws.security.components.crypto.Merlin">
            <property name="org.apache.ws.security.crypto.merlin.keystore.type">
              JKS
            </property>
            <property name="org.apache.ws.security.crypto.merlin.file">
              c:/Documents and Settings/kent/keys/service.ks
            </property>
            <property
              name="org.apache.ws.security.crypto.merlin.keystore.password">
              service-ks-pass
            </property>
          </crypto>
        </encryptionCrypto>
      </RampartConfig>
    </wsp:Policy>
  </service>
</serviceGroup>
```

Create the PasswordCallbackHandler class in the com.ttdev.ss package:

```
package com.ttdev.ss;
...
import javax.security.auth.callback.Callback;
import javax.security.auth.callback.CallbackHandler;
import javax.security.auth.callback.UnsupportedCallbackException;
import org.apache.ws.security.WSPasswordCallback;

public class PasswordCallbackHandler implements CallbackHandler {
  @Override
  public void handle(Callback[] callbacks) throws IOException,
      UnsupportedCallbackException {
    for (int i = 0; i < callbacks.length; i++) {
      WSPasswordCallback pwcb = (WSPasswordCallback) callbacks[i];
      String id = pwcb.getIdentifer();
      switch (pwcb.getUsage()) {
      case WSPasswordCallback.DECRYPT:
      case WSPasswordCallback.SIGNATURE:
        if (id.equals("s1")) {
          pwcb.setPassword("s1-pass");
        }
        break;
      case WSPasswordCallback.USERNAME_TOKEN:
        if (id.equals("Paul")) {
          pwcb.setPassword("paul-pass");
        }
        break;
      }
    }
  }
}
```

Set the artifact ID to SecureService in pom.xml and then run it as Maven package. Deploy it into Axis2 as service.

However, Axis2 needs a couple of jar files in order to do the work: copy the following files into to the axis2/lib folder:

- <home>/.m2/repository/backport-util-concurrent/backport-util-concurrent/3.1/backport-util-concurrent-3.1.jar
- <home>/.m2/repository/bouncycastle/bcprov-jdk13/132/bcprov-jdk13-132.jar

Then restart the Axis2 server. Finally, run the TCP Monitor, let it listen on port 1234 and run the client. It should work.

Summary

WS-Policy allows you to specify non-functional requirements such as security on web services.

For a policy to influence the runtime behavior, the client and the service need access to it at runtime. For CXF, the service stub will refer to the WSDL file by path to access the policies. For the service, you need to do the same thing (specify the path to the WSDL file) with @WebService attached to your implementation class. For Axis2, the policies will be "compiled" into the service stub for the client. For the service, you need to copy them into the services.xml file.

To sign or encrypt a message, specify in the policy the configuration settings such as algorithms to use, whether to include the certificate (token) and how (direct include or issuer DN plus serial number and etc.). You also specify which parts should be signed and which parts should be encrypted.

Rampart implements the WS-Security standard and can be used to satisfy security requirements expressed in policies. It gets information from the policy. In addition, you also need to provide further configurations by passing them as properties or as an extra policy. Such configurations include the user name alias, password callback class, what cryptographic provider to use (e.g., JDK), the location of the keystore and the keystore password.

When performing both signing and encrypting, to fight against dictionary attacks, you should encrypt the signature, encrypt before signing or include a nonce into the digest.

To send authentication information, you can use a Username token. This is also specified in a policy. Your password callback class should provide the password. The Username token should be signed and probably also be encrypted. You can retrieve the user name in your web service to perform authorization.

Chapter 9

Creating scalable web services with REST

What's in this chapter?

In this chapter you'll learn how to create web services that can handle a huge number of requests by adopting the REST architecture.

Scalability difficulty with SOAP

Suppose that you'd like to create a web service like what's offered by Amazon to allow clients to query information of books. Definitely this can be done with SOAP over HTTP:

```
POST /books HTTP/1.1

<Envelope>
   <Body>
      <bookQuery isbn="1234-5678-9"/>
   </Body>
</Envelope>
```

Server

```
HTTP/1.1 200 OK

<Envelope>
   <Body>
      <book>
         <isbn>1234-5678-9</isbn>
         <title>Java programming</title>
         ...
      </book>
   </Body>
</Envelope>
```

However, if there are a huge number of such clients or a huge number of such requests, a single server may be unable to handle it. So, you may add more servers (see below). But where do they get the book information from? They have to get it from a single database. This incurs two problems: First, even if you could set up a database cluster, the scalability is limited. Second, the web service servers probably need to stay close to the database and thus can't be located near the clients:

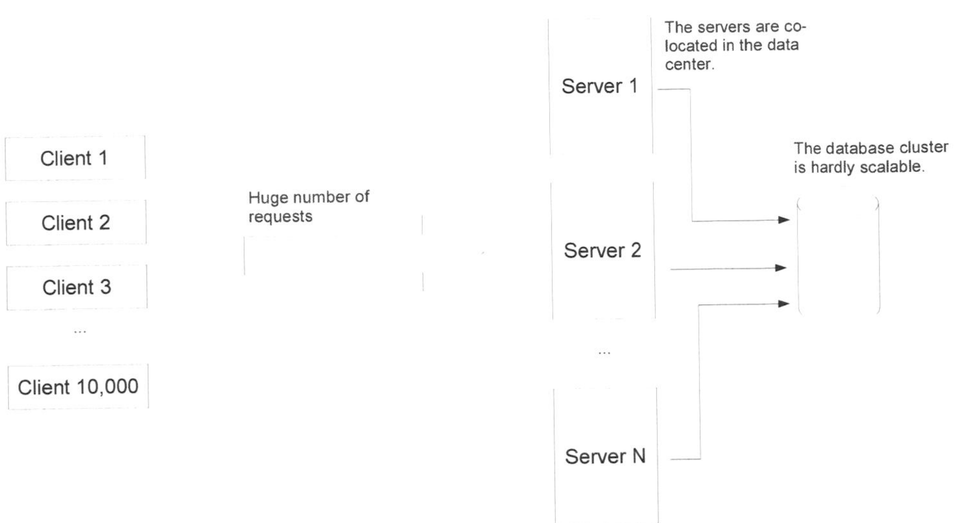

This is not a very scalable solution. Instead, note that this query operation is a read-only operation, then why hit the database at all? It is possible to set up cache proxies as shown below. Then, if a client in Europe queries for the book 1234, the proxy in Europe only needs to contact the main server only once to get the data. For subsequent queries on the same book from other European clients, it can return the result to the clients without contacting the main server at all and therefore the proxies will have shifted the load away from the main server. In addition, as the proxy and the clients are all in Europe, the response will be very fast:

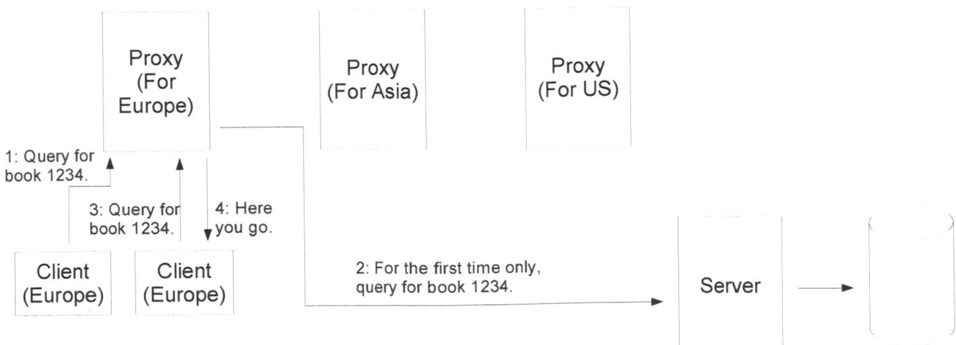

To scale it even further, you could even, say, set up a child proxy for each country in Europe, forming a hierarchy of proxies:

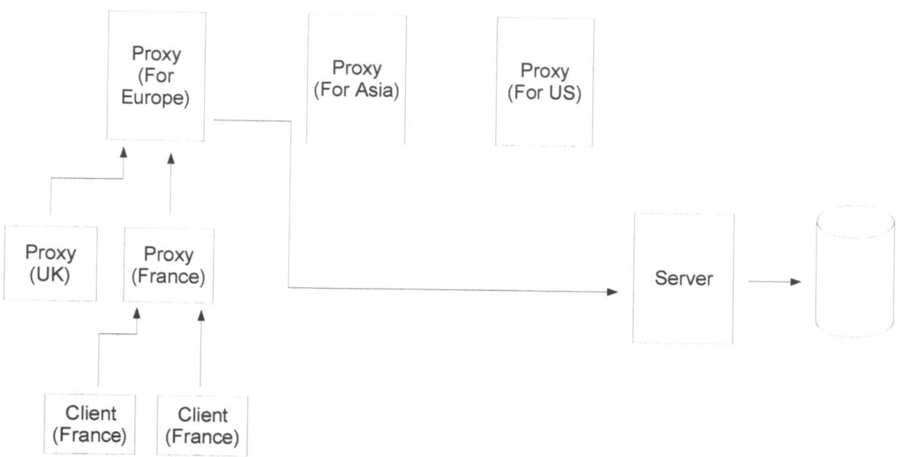

This is a highly scalable architecture. Of course, a proxy shouldn't cache the information forever as sometimes the book's information is updated. But let's handle this issue later.

For now, consider how to set up such a proxy? The proxy needs to check if the HTTP request is a SOAP message and then check if it is the <bookQuery> operation. If so, extract the isbn attribute from the <bookQuery> element and use it as the key to look up its cache. It means that this proxy is completely tailor-made for this particular web service. If you had 100 operations, you would need to develop 100 proxy programs. This is a serious problem. You need a generic proxy that works for all operations.

Using a generic proxy

In order to use a generic proxy, all web service operations must state if they are read-only or not in a standard way (see below). In addition, they must indicate their target objects (the book in the example) being operated on in a standard way so that the proxy can look up the result with the target as the key:

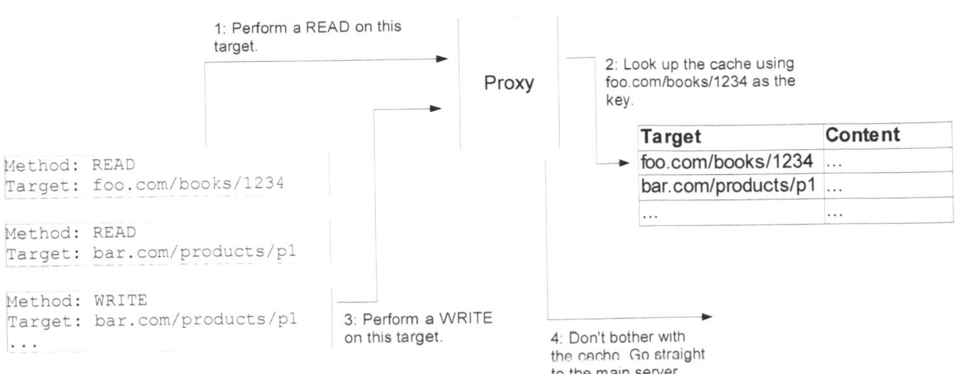

If you look carefully at the requests, they look exactly like standard HTTP requests:

```
Method: READ                          GET /books/1234
Target: foo.com/books/1234            Host: foo.com

Method: READ                          GET /products/p1
Target: bar.com/products/p1           Host: bar.com

Method: WRITE                         PUT /products/p1
Target: bar.com/products/p1           Host: bar.com
...
                                      ...
```

Therefore, as long as you represent web service operations as standard HTTP requests, standard HTTP proxies can be used to cache the results of read-only operations (GET requests) and thus achieving extreme scalability. This is not a co-incident: HTTP was designed to be highly scalable in day one.

What about the response? As you aren't using SOAP, you don't need the <Envelope>, but you still would like it to remain language neutral, so you may probably continue to use XML (see below). Of course, XML is just one of the possible representations of the book, not the book itself. For example, you could represent it as HTML or even image showing the cover of the book.

```
GET /books/1234
Host: foo.com
```

```
HTTP/1.1 200 OK

<book>
   <isbn>1234-5678-9</isbn>
   <title>Java programming</title>
   ...
</book>
```

This style/architecture of network computing system is called REST

(REpresentative State Transfer): the representation state (e.g., an XML document) of a target, or rather, a resource in the official terms (e.g., the book) is transferred from one host to another (e.g., server to proxy to client). A web service using this style is called a RESTful web service.

Creating a RESTful web service

Let's implement this book query operation in a RESTful web service. Copy the SimpleService project and paste it as BookService. Delete the WSDL file as it is not required for a RESTful web service. Instead, create an XSD file named BookService.xsd (the name is unimportant) in its place:

```
<?xml version="1.0" encoding="UTF-8"?>
<schema xmlns="http://www.w3.org/2001/XMLSchema"
targetNamespace="http://ttdev.com/bs"
  xmlns:tns="http://ttdev.com/bs" elementFormDefault="qualified">
    <element name="book">
    <complexType>
      <sequence>
        <element name="isbn" type="string"></element>
        <element name="title" type="string"></element>
      </sequence>
    </complexType>
    </element>
</schema>
```

You can create it visually or just input the text by hand. This XSD file defines the schema for the <book> element used as the response. Next, modify the CodeGenerator class:

XJC stands for XML-Java compiler. It generates Java classes corresponding to XML elements or types.

Put the generated .java files into this folder.

```
package com.ttdev;

import com.sun.tools.xjc.XJCFacade;

public class CodeGenerator {
   public static void main(String[] args) throws Throwable {
      XJCFacade.main(new String[] {
            "-d", "src/main/java",
            "src/main/resources/BookService.xsd" });
   }
}
```

The path to the XSD file to be read by the compiler.

Delete the com.ttdev.ss package. Run the CodeGenerator class. You should see messages like below in the console:

```
parsing a schema...
compiling a schema...
com/ttdev/bs/Book.java
com/ttdev/bs/ObjectFactory.java
com/ttdev/bs/package-info.java
```

Refresh the project and you should see those new files in the com.ttdev.bs package. Next, proceed to create a class named BookResource in that package:

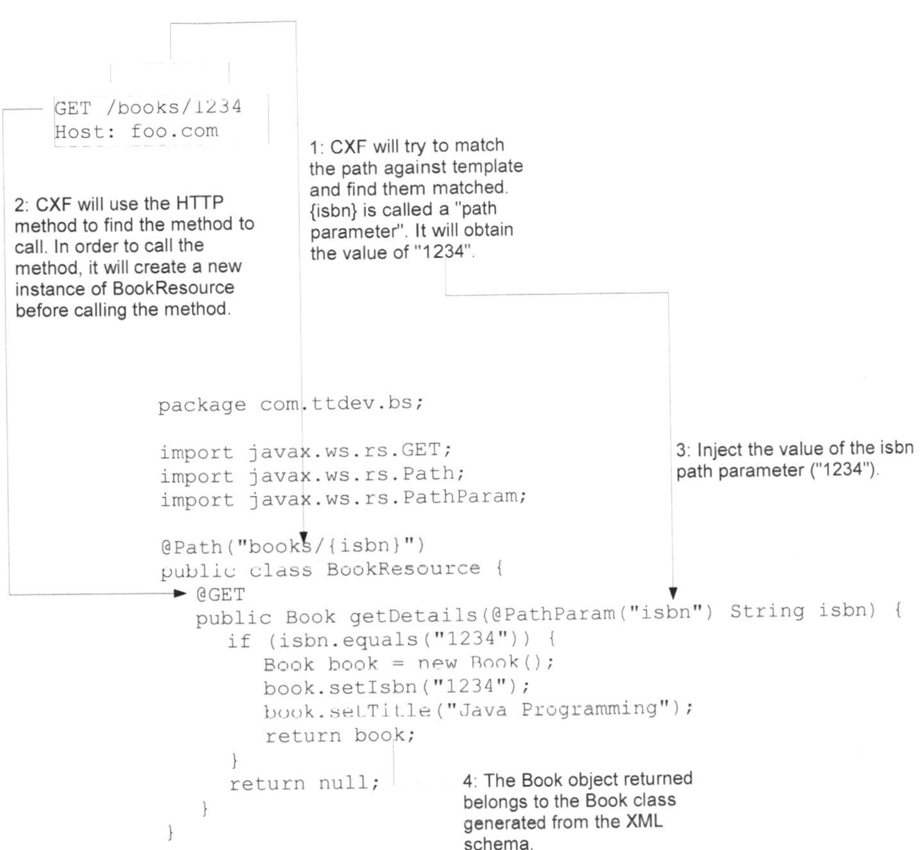
GET /books/1234
Host: foo.com
1: CXF will try to match the path against template and find them matched. {isbn} is called a "path parameter". It will obtain the value of "1234".
2: CXF will use the HTTP method to find the method to call. In order to call the method, it will create a new instance of BookResource before calling the method.
3: Inject the value of the isbn path parameter ("1234").
4: The Book object returned belongs to the Book class generated from the XML schema.

```
package com.ttdev.bs;

import javax.ws.rs.GET;
import javax.ws.rs.Path;
import javax.ws.rs.PathParam;

@Path("books/{isbn}")
public class BookResource {
  @GET
  public Book getDetails(@PathParam("isbn") String isbn) {
    if (isbn.equals("1234")) {
      Book book = new Book();
      book.setIsbn("1234");
      book.setTitle("Java Programming");
      return book;
    }
    return null;
  }
}
```

Note that the annotations used such as @Path and @GET are all defined in the javax.ws.rs package. They are standardized in the JAX-RS (Java API for XML for RESTful web services) specification.

Create a BookServer class in the com.ttdev.bs package to publish the book resource:

```
package com.ttdev.bs;

import org.apache.cxf.jaxrs.JAXRSServerFactoryBean;

public class BookServer {
   public static void main(String[] args) throws InterruptedException {
      JAXRSServerFactoryBean sf = new JAXRSServerFactoryBean();
      sf.setResourceClasses(BookResource.class);
      sf.setAddress("http://localhost:8080/bs");
      sf.create();
      System.out.println("Started");
      Thread.sleep(5 * 60 * 1000);
      System.out.println("ended");
      System.exit(0);
   }
}
```

This factory can create JAX-RS server objects.

Tell it the resource classes available.

Create and launch the server.

Tell it the address to listen on. This is the base address for the whole server.

Combining the base address and the resource path, you get the full URL for that resource.

(+) → http://localhost:8080/bs/books/1234

```
@Path("books/{isbn}")
public class BookResource {
   ...
}
```

Note that the way to publish JAX-RS resources in a console application is not standardized (you'll learn how to do it in a web container using a standard method). The method above is specific to Apache CXF.

To test it quickly, go to the browser to try to access http://localhost:8080/bs/books/1234. You should get the <book> element returned.

To test it with a client, copy the BookService project and paste it as a BookClient project. Delete the BookResource and BookServer classes as the client isn't supposed to have access to them. Run the CodeGenerator to generate the classes representing the XML elements.

Next, create a BookClient class in the com.ttdev.bs package:

```
package com.ttdev.bs;

import org.apache.cxf.jaxrs.client.WebClient;

public class BookClient {
   public static void main(String[] args) throws InterruptedException {
      WebClient client = WebClient.create("http://localhost:8080/bs");
      client.path("books/1234");
      Book book = client.get(Book.class);
      System.out.println(book.getTitle());
   }
}
```

Create a web client and use this URL as the base URL.

Append books/1234 to the base URL and get http://localhost:8080/bs/books/1234.

Send a GET request. Parse the response as a <book> element to get back a Book object.

Run the server and the client. The client should print the book title "Java

Programming" successfully.

Enabling caching by a proxy

Suppose that you will update your book information only once every day at 10:00am (see below). If a proxy performs a GET on book 1234 at 11:00am, the server can tell it that the information will remain valid for the next 23 hours. In that period, if a client asks the proxy for book 1234 in that period, the proxy can simply return the cached information without asking the server again:

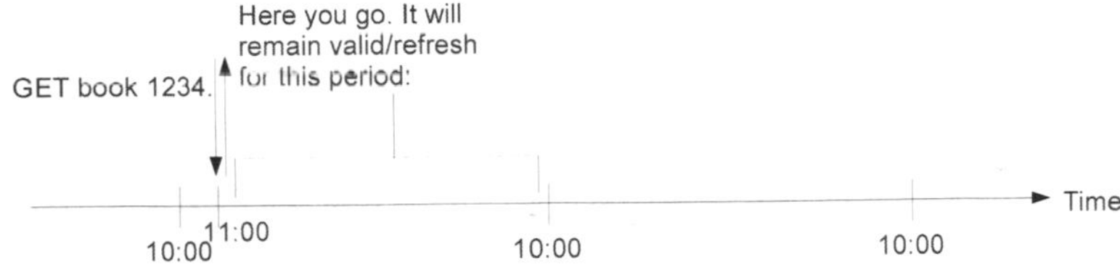

To implement this idea, modify the BookResource class:

```
...
import javax.ws.rs.core.CacheControl;
import javax.ws.rs.core.Response;
import javax.ws.rs.core.Response.ResponseBuilder;

@Path("books/{isbn}")
public class BookResource {
   @GET
   public Response getDetails(@PathParam("isbn") String isbn) {
      if (isbn.equals("1234")) {
         Book book = new Book();
         book.setIsbn("1234");
         book.setTitle("Java Programming");
         ResponseBuilder builder = Response.ok(book);
         GregorianCalendar now = new GregorianCalendar();
         GregorianCalendar nextUpdate = getNextUpdateTime(now);
         int maxAge = (int) ((nextUpdate.getTimeInMillis() - now
               .getTimeInMillis()) / 1000L);
         CacheControl cacheControl = new CacheControl();
         cacheControl.setMaxAge(maxAge);
         builder.cacheControl(cacheControl);
         builder.expires(nextUpdate.getTime());
         return builder.build();
      }
      return null;
   }

   private GregorianCalendar getNextUpdateTime(GregorianCalendar now) {
      GregorianCalendar nextUpdate = new GregorianCalendar();
      nextUpdate.setTime(now.getTime());
      nextUpdate.set(Calendar.HOUR_OF_DAY, 10);
      nextUpdate.set(Calendar.MINUTE, 0);
      nextUpdate.set(Calendar.SECOND, 0);
      nextUpdate.set(Calendar.MILLISECOND, 0);
      if (now.get(Calendar.HOUR_OF_DAY) >= 10) {
         nextUpdate.add(Calendar.DAY_OF_YEAR, 1);
      }
      return nextUpdate;
   }
}
```

Create an HTTP response builder that will create a response with the OK status code (200). In addition, convert the book object into XML and use it as the body (content) of the response.

For how long the response will remain valid (in seconds).

Calculate the time when the next update should occur (10:00am today if the current hour is < 10 or 10:00am tomorrow otherwise).

Set the Cache-Control header in the response.

Only HTTP 1.1 proxies understand the Cache-Control header. For HTTP 1.0 proxies, set the expiry date and time using the Expires header.

Build the response.

Run the server. To view the headers generated, use telnet as shown below:

```
> telnet localhost 8080
Trying 127.0.0.1...
Connected to localhost.
Escape character is '^]'.
GET /bs/books/1234 HTTP/1.1
Host: localhost
Accept: text/xml

HTTP/1.1 200 OK
Content-Type: text/xml
Cache-Control: no-transform;max-age=65027
Expires: Sat, 26 Dec 2009 02:00:00 GMT
Date: Fri, 25 Dec 2009 07:56:12 GMT
Content-Length: 144
Server: Jetty(6.1.21)

<?xml version="1.0" encoding="UTF-8" standalone="yes"?><book
xmlns="http://ttdev.com/bs"><isbn>1234</isbn><title>Java
Programming</title></book>
```

Why the expiry date and time has been set 2:00 of 10:00? This is because the time zone on my computer is GMT+8. So the local 10:00 is 2:00 in GMT.

Validating the cached response after expiry

What happens when it has passed 10:00am tomorrow (see below)? If the proxy needs to GET the book 1234 again, as the cached response has expired, does it need to ask the server again? Yes. But has the book definitely be updated? Maybe or maybe not. So, a better way is that the proxy should tell the version of its copy to the server for checking. If the version in the server is the same, the server can tell the proxy to continue to use its existing copy and extend its expiry date:

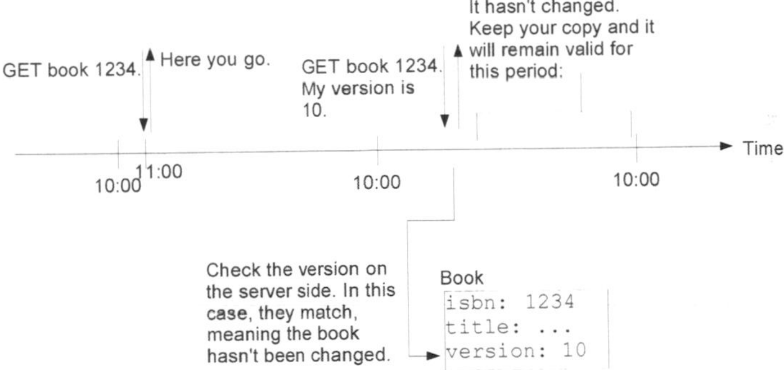

If the book has the version aren't the same (see below), the server can then send the new copy, with the new version number and new expiry date:

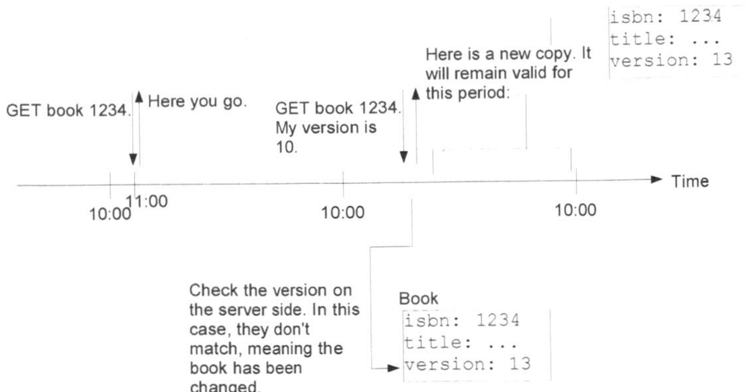

This process is called "cache validation" and the GET operation with a version number is called a "conditional GET". The benefit of a conditional GET is that the state of the book may not need to be transferred if the versions match. This saves computing resources on the server and the bandwidth.

To implement this idea, let's keep a last-modified timestamp for each book as the version. As a first attempt, you may try to modify the Book class:

```
@XmlAccessorType(XmlAccessType.FIELD)
@XmlType(name = "", propOrder = { "isbn", "title" })
@XmlRootElement(name = "book")
public class Book {
```

```
    @XmlElement(required = true)
    protected String isbn;
    @XmlElement(required = true)
    protected String title;

    private Date lastModified;
    ...
}
```

The problem is that this class was generated from the XML schema. If the schema changes, you will generate it again and overwrite your changes. As this Book class is only used to transfer the state of the book to the client, technically it belongs to the I/O layer. Therefore, it's better to rename it as BookState (without adding a timestamp to it). Then create a Book class to represent the book in the business domain layer.

However, as this Book class was generated by the from the XML schema, renaming it manually is no good and won't stick. A better way is to tell the XJC tool to always map the <Book> element to the BookState class. To do that, create a bindings.xml file (the name is unimportant) in the src/main/resources folder:

A JAXB binding is used to further specify Java meaning to the XML elements to override the default mapping.

You're specifying Java meaning to stuff in this XSD file.

Attach Java meaning to which XML element? Starts from <schema>, then go into an <element> whose name attribute is "book":

```
<?xml version="1.0" encoding="UTF-8"?>
<jaxb:bindings
   xmlns:jaxb="http://java.sun.com/xml/ns/jaxb"
   xmlns:xsd="http://www.w3.org/2001/XMLSchema"
   schemaLocation="BookService.xsd"
   jaxb:version="2.0">
   <jaxb:bindings node="/xsd:schema/xsd:element[@name='book']">
      <jaxb:class
         name="BookState">
      </jaxb:class>
   </jaxb:bindings>
</jaxb:bindings>
```

You must define the namespace for the XPath to match.

This is the key part: Map the <book> element to BookState class.

```
<?xml version="1.0" encoding="UTF-8"?>
<schema
   xmlns="http://www.w3.org/2001/XMLSchema" ...>
   <element name="book">
      <complexType>
         <sequence>
            <element name="isbn" type="string"></element>
            <element name="title" type="string"></element>
         </sequence>
      </complexType>
   </element>
</schema>
```

To enable auto-completion, you can choose Window | Preferences, choose XML | XML Catalog and add a new user entry:

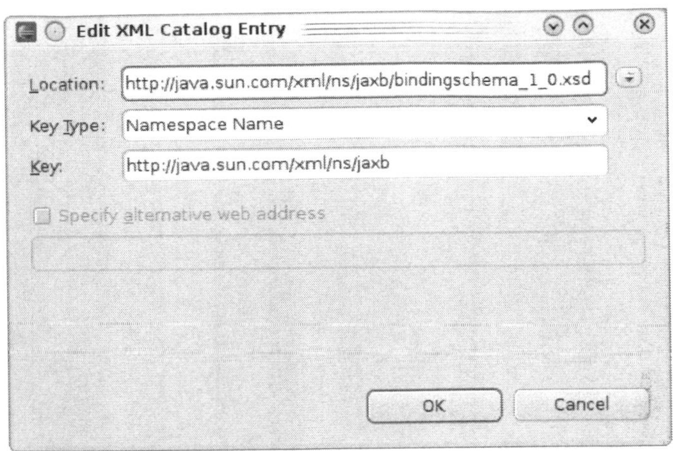

Tell the code generator to use this bindings.xml file:

```
public class CodeGenerator {
  public static void main(String[] args) throws Throwable {
    XJCFacade.main(new String[] {
        "-b", "src/main/resources/bindings.xml",
        "-d", "src/main/java",
        "src/main/resources/BookService.xsd" });
  }
}
```

Run it again it should generate a BookState class. Then proceed to define your own Book class (in the domain layer):

```
package com.ttdev.bs;

import java.util.Date;

public class Book {
  private String isbn;
  private String title;
  private Date lastModified;

  public Book(String isbn, String title) {
    this.isbn = isbn;
    this.title = title;
    this.lastModified = new Date();
  }
  public String getIsbn() {
    return isbn;
  }
  public String getTitle() {
    return title;
  }
  public Date getLastModified() {
    return lastModified;
  }
  public void setIsbn(String isbn) {
    this.isbn = isbn;
  }
  public void setTitle(String title) {
    this.title = title;
  }
  public void setLastModified(Date lastModified) {
    this.lastModified = lastModified;
```

```
    }
  }
```

Create a BookDB class to represent a database of books:

```
package com.ttdev.bs;

public class BookDB {
  private Book book1234;

  public BookDB() {
    book1234 = new Book("1234", "Java Programming");
  }
  public Book getBook1234() {
    return book1234;
  }
  public static BookDB instance = new BookDB();
}
```

Modify the BookResource class to use the BookDB and convert a Book to a BookState:

```
@Path("books/{isbn}")
public class BookResource {
  @GET
  public Response getDetails(@PathParam("isbn") String isbn) {
    BookDB bookDB = BookDB.instance;
    if (isbn.equals("1234")) {
      Book book = bookDB.getBook1234();
      BookState st = getBookState(book);
      ResponseBuilder builder = Response.ok(st);
      GregorianCalendar now = new GregorianCalendar();
      GregorianCalendar nextUpdate = getNextUpdateTime(now);
      int maxAge = (int) ((nextUpdate.getTimeInMillis() - now
          .getTimeInMillis()) / 1000L);
      CacheControl cacheControl = new CacheControl();
      cacheControl.setMaxAge(maxAge);
      builder.cacheControl(cacheControl);
      builder.expires(nextUpdate.getTime());
      return builder.build();
    }
    return null;
  }
  public static BookState getBookState(Book book) {
    BookState st = new BookState();
    st.setIsbn(book.getIsbn());
    st.setTitle(book.getTitle());
    return st;
  }
  private GregorianCalendar getNextUpdateTime(GregorianCalendar now) {
    GregorianCalendar nextUpdate = new GregorianCalendar();
    nextUpdate.setTime(now.getTime());
    nextUpdate.set(Calendar.HOUR_OF_DAY, 10);
    nextUpdate.set(Calendar.MINUTE, 0);
    nextUpdate.set(Calendar.SECOND, 0);
    nextUpdate.set(Calendar.MILLISECOND, 0);
    if (now.get(Calendar.HOUR_OF_DAY) >= 10) {
      nextUpdate.add(Calendar.DAY_OF_YEAR, 1);
    }
    return nextUpdate;
  }
}
```

Modify the BookResource class further to handle conditional GETs:

```
...
import javax.ws.rs.core.Context;
import javax.ws.rs.core.Request;

@Path("books/{isbn}")
public class BookResource {
   @GET
   public Response getDetails(@Context Request request,
         @PathParam("isbn") String isbn) {
      BookDB bookDB = BookDB.instance;
      if (isbn.equals("1234")) {
         Book book = bookDB.getBook1234();
         ResponseBuilder builder = request.evaluatePreconditions(
               book.getLastModified());
         if (builder != null) {
            setExpiry(builder);
         } else {
            BookState st = getBookState(book);
            builder = Response.ok(st);
            builder.lastModified(book.getLastModified());
            setExpiry(builder);
         }
         return builder.build();
      }
      return null;
   }
   private void setExpiry(ResponseBuilder builder) {
      GregorianCalendar now = new GregorianCalendar();
      GregorianCalendar nextUpdate = getNextUpdateTime(now);
      int maxAge = (int) ((nextUpdate.getTimeInMillis() - now
            .getTimeInMillis()) / 1000L);
      CacheControl cacheControl = new CacheControl();
      cacheControl.setMaxAge(maxAge);
      builder.cacheControl(cacheControl);
      builder.expires(nextUpdate.getTime());
   }
   ...
}
```

@Context can be used to inject some contextual objects into an argument. Here, you use it to inject the current HTTP request.

This is the key part: You provide the current last-modified timestamp of the book to check against that in the request. If they match, CXF will create a response builder that says "Keep your current copy" with an empty body. If they don't match, it will return null to indicate that you need to build a new response yourself.

Even if the proxy gets to keep its local copy, you should still tell it the next expiry date and time.

The timestamps don't match. Need to send a new copy.

Make sure to send the last-modified timestamp so that it can quote it later.

However, there is still a slight glitch: When HTTP uses the last-modified timestamp as the version, it has precision to the second only but the java.util.Date class in Java has precision to the millisecond. It means when the proxy quotes the truncated timestamp to the server, they won't match due to the milliseconds. To fix the problem, you must truncate the timestamp from the Book before using it:

```
public class BookResource {
   @GET
   public Response getDetails(@Context Request request,
         @PathParam("isbn") String isbn) {
      BookDB bookDB = BookDB.instance;
      if (isbn.equals("1234")) {
         Book book = bookDB.getBook1234();
         ResponseBuilder builder = request.evaluatePreconditions(getVersion(book));
         if (builder != null) {
            setExpiry(builder);
         } else {
            BookState st = getBookState(book);
            builder = Response.ok(st);
```

```
        builder.lastModified(getVersion(book));
        setExpiry(builder);
      }
      return builder.build();
    }
    return null;
  }
  private Date getVersion(Book book) {
    Date lastModified = book.getLastModified();
    GregorianCalendar calendar = new GregorianCalendar();
    calendar.setTime(lastModified);
    calendar.set(Calendar.MILLISECOND, 0);
    return calendar.getTime();
  }
  ...
}
```

To test it, you need a way to modify the book. So, do it in the BookServer class:

```
public class BookServer {
  public static void main(String[] args) throws InterruptedException,
      IOException {
    JAXRSServerFactoryBean sf = new JAXRSServerFactoryBean();
    sf.setResourceClasses(BookResource.class);
    sf.setAddress("http://localhost:8080/bs");
    sf.create();
    System.out.println("Started");
    BufferedReader br = new BufferedReader(new InputStreamReader(System.in));
    for (;;) {
      System.out.println("Enter command: u--update. q--quit");
      String cmd = br.readLine();
      if (cmd.equals("u")) {
        BookDB.instance.getBook1234().setLastModified(new Date());
      } else if (cmd.equals("q")) {
        System.exit(0);
      }
    }
  }
}
```

Now, run the server, use telnet to GET the book (see below). You should get the last-modified timestamp as the version:

```
GET /bs/books/1234 HTTP/1.1
Host: localhost
Accept: text/xml

HTTP/1.1 200 OK
Content-Type: text/xml
Last-Modified: Sat, 26 Dec 2009 04:07:09 GMT
Cache-Control: no-transform;max-age=78770
Expires: Sun, 27 Dec 2009 02:00:00 GMT
Date: Sat, 26 Dec 2009 04:07:09 GMT
Content-Length: 144
Server: Jetty(6.1.21)

<?xml version="1.0" encoding="UTF-8" standalone="yes"?><book
xmlns="http://ttdev.com/bs"><isbn>1234</isbn><title>Java
Programming</title></book>
```

Next, use telnet to perform a conditional GET. As the book hasn't been modified, it should tell you to keep using the local copy, with a new expiry date and time but no body content:

```
GET /bs/books/1234 HTTP/1.1
Host: localhost
Accept: text/xml
If-Modified-Since: Sat, 26 Dec 2009 04:07:09 GMT
```

```
HTTP/1.1 304 Not Modified
Content-Type: text/xml
Cache-Control: no-transform;max-age=78748
Expires: Sun, 27 Dec 2009 02:00:00 GMT
Date: Sat, 26 Dec 2009 04:07:31 GMT
Server: Jetty(6.1.21)
```

Next, in the console enter "u" to update the book. Use telnet to perform a conditional GET again. This way, it should send you a new copy with a new timestamp (version) and a new expiry date and time:

```
GET /bs/books/1234 HTTP/1.1
Host: localhost
Accept: text/xml
If-Modified-Since: Sat, 26 Dec 2009 04:07:09 GMT

HTTP/1.1 200 OK
Content-Type: text/xml
Last-Modified: Sat, 26 Dec 2009 04:09:48 GMT
Cache-Control: no-transform;max-age=78571
Expires: Sun, 27 Dec 2009 02:00:00 GMT
Date: Sat, 26 Dec 2009 04:10:28 GMT
Content-Length: 144
Server: Jetty(6.1.21)

<?xml version="1.0" encoding="UTF-8" standalone="yes"?><book
xmlns="http://ttdev.com/bs"><isbn>1234</isbn><title>Java
Programming</title></book>
```

Using other kinds of versions

You don't have to use a timestamp as the version. For example, you could use a long integer as the version number. To do that, modify the Book class:

```
public class Book {
  private String isbn;
  private String title;
  private Date lastModified;
  private long version;

  public Book(String isbn, String title) {
    this.isbn = isbn;
    this.title = title;
    this.lastModified = new Date();
    this.version = 0;
  }
  public long getVersion() {
    return version;
  }
  public String getIsbn() {
    return isbn;
  }
  public String getTitle() {
    return title;
  }
  public Date getLastModified() {
    return lastModified;
  }
  public void setIsbn(String isbn) {
    this.isbn = isbn;
    version++;
  }
  public void setTitle(String title) {
    this.title = title;
    version++;
```

```
    }
    public void setLastModified(Date lastModified) {
      this.lastModified = lastModified;
      version++;
    }
  }
```

Here you're using both a long version number and a timestamp. You could simply use one of them. However, HTTP 1.0 clients will only understand a timestamp, so when you're in the process of transitioning from HTTP 1.0 to 1.1, you may use both.

Modify the BookResource class to use the long version number:

```
...
import javax.ws.rs.core.EntityTag;

@Path("books/{isbn}")
public class BookResource {
   @GET
   public Response getDetails(@Context Request request,
         @PathParam("isbn") String isbn) {
      BookDB bookDB = BookDB.instance;
      if (isbn.equals("1234")) {
         Book book = bookDB.getBook1234();
         EntityTag entityTag = new EntityTag(Long.toString(book.getVersion()));
         ResponseBuilder builder = request.evaluatePreconditions(
               getVersion(book), entityTag);
         if (builder != null) {
            setExpiry(builder);
         } else {
            BookState st = getBookState(book);
            builder = Response.ok(st);
            builder.lastModified(getVersion(book));
            builder.tag(Long.toString(book.getVersion()));
            setExpiry(builder);
         }
         return builder.build();
      }
      return null;
   }
   ...
}
```

The generic version is called an "entity tag" or "ETag". For HTTP, it is only a string. The meaning is up to you to interpret.

Here you're providing both a ETag and a timestamp. It will return a response builder (304 Not Motified) only if all the versions in the request match the values you provide.

If you only use an ETag but not a timestamp, you can call it like request.evaluatePreconditions(entityTag).

Hand out the ETag, along with the timestamp.

Run the server and use telnet to test it again:

```
GET /bs/books/1234 HTTP/1.1
Host: localhost
Accept: text/xml

HTTP/1.1 200 OK
Content-Type: text/xml
Last-Modified: Sat, 26 Dec 2009 04:40:43 GMT
ETag: 0
Cache-Control: no-transform;max-age=76756
Expires: Sun, 27 Dec 2009 02:00:00 GMT
Date: Sat, 26 Dec 2009 04:40:43 GMT
Content-Length: 144
Server: Jetty(6.1.21)

<?xml version="1.0" encoding="UTF-8" standalone="yes"?><book
xmlns="http://ttdev.com/bs"><isbn>1234</isbn><title>Java
Programming</title></book>
```

Quote the same timestamp and ETag and it should tell not "Not Modified":

```
GET /bs/books/1234 HTTP/1.1
Host: localhost
Accept: text/xml
If-Modified-Since: Sat, 26 Dec 2009 04:40:43 GMT
If-None-Match: 0

HTTP/1.1 304 Not Modified
Content-Type: text/xml
Cache-Control: no-transform;max-age=74378
Expires: Sun, 27 Dec 2009 02:00:00 GMT
Date: Sat, 26 Dec 2009 05:20:21 GMT
Server: Jetty(6.1.21)
```

Update the book with the "u" command. Then trying it again will result in a new copy with a new timestamp and a new ETag:

```
GET /bs/books/1234 HTTP/1.1
Host: localhost
Accept: text/xml
If-Modified-Since: Sat, 26 Dec 2009 04:40:43 GMT
If-None-Match: 0

HTTP/1.1 200 OK
Content-Type: text/xml
Cache-Control: no-transform;max-age=74298
Expires: Sun, 27 Dec 2009 02:00:00 GMT
Date: Sat, 26 Dec 2009 05:21:41 GMT
Last-Modified: Sat, 26 Dec 2009 05:21:32 GMT
ETag: 1
Content-Length: 144
Server: Jetty(6.1.21)

<?xml version="1.0" encoding="UTF-8" standalone="yes"?><book
xmlns="http://ttdev.com/bs"><isbn>1234</isbn><title>Java
Programming</title></book>
```

BUG ALERT: CXF 2.2.5 is not checking the If-None-Match header at all. The above worked due to the timestamp only.

What if books can be updated at any time?

If books can be updated at any time, you may decide that it is still OK for clients (and proxies) to use the response for, say, one hour or 10 minutes or whatever. Of course, then a client may be seeing outdated result.

If this is unacceptable, that is, you need the clients to always see the updated result, you may set max-age to 0 and set the Expires header to a timestamp in the past. This way, the proxy will need to validate the cached response every time it wants to use it.

In summary, you should always set the version (ETag or timestamp). You may then decide the max-age according to your business needs.

Performing an update

Now you have implemented the read operation (HTTP GET method), how to update a book? For example, you can use an HTTP PUT method like:

Update book 1234.

```
PUT /books/1234 HTTP/1.1

<book>
   <isbn>1234</isbn>
   <title>C# programming</title>
   ...
</book>
```

The new content is specified in the body.

Note that it is not the POST method which means "add", not "update". To implement this idea, modify the BookResource class:

```
PUT /books/1234 HTTP/1.1

<book>
   <isbn>1234</isbn>
   <title>C# programming</title>
   ...
</book>
```

This method will handle PUT requests.

CXF notes that there is only one argument that has no annotation, so it will try to convert the body into Java and inject it into here.

```
...
import javax.ws.rs.PUT;

@Path("books/{isbn}")
public class BookResource {
   ...
   @PUT
   public Response update(@PathParam("isbn") String isbn, BookState st) {
      ResponseBuilder builder;
      BookDB bookDB = BookDB.instance;
      if (isbn.equals("1234")) {
         Book book = bookDB.getBook1234();
         book.setIsbn(st.getIsbn());
         book.setTitle(st.getTitle());
         book.setLastModified(new Date());
         builder = Response.noContent();
      } else {
         builder = Response.status(Status.NOT_FOUND);
      }
      return builder.build();
   }
}
```

This will return the status code 204, meaning that it was successful but no content is returned.

The book the request is trying to update doesn't exist, so tell it that it was not found (status code 404).

To test it, you can't use a browser as most browsers only implement GET and POST, but not PUT. So, you need to modify the BookClient class. Before that, copy the bindings.xml file and CodeGenerator class to it. Run the CodeGenerator class. Delete the existing Book class. Modify the BookClient class to use the BookState class:

```
public class BookClient {
   public static void main(String[] args) throws InterruptedException {
      WebClient client = WebClient.create("http://localhost:8080/bs");
      client.path("books/1234");
      BookState book = client.get(BookState.class);
      System.out.println(book.getTitle());
   }
}
```

Next, further modify it to test the update operation:

```
public class BookClient {
```

```
  public static void main(String[] args) throws InterruptedException {
    WebClient client = WebClient.create("http://localhost:8080/bs");
    client.path("books/1234");
    BookState book = client.get(BookState.class);
    System.out.println(book.getTitle());
    book.setTitle("C# Programming");
    client.put(book);
    book = client.get(BookState.class);
    System.out.println(book.getTitle());
  }
}
```

Run the server and then run the client. The client should print:

```
Java Programming
C# Programming
```

If you'd like, you can use TCP Monitor to view the messages. Let it listen on port 1234 as usual and then modify the client:

```
public class BookClient {
  public static void main(String[] args) throws InterruptedException {
    WebClient client = WebClient.create("http://localhost:1234/bs");
    client.path("books/1234");
    BookState book = client.get(BookState.class);
    System.out.println(book.getTitle());
    book.setTitle("C# Programming");
    client.put(book);
    book = client.get(BookState.class);
    System.out.println(book.getTitle());
  }
}
```

Implementing add

To add a book, you should use the POST method. But POST to where? POST to the collections of books as identified by the /books URL:

```
POST /books HTTP/1.1

<book>
  ...
</book>
```

To do that, create a BooksResource class (note that it is plural. Not BookResource):

```
...
import java.net.URI;
import java.net.URISyntaxException;
import javax.ws.rs.POST;

@Path("books")
public class BooksResource {
   @POST
   public Response add(@Context Request request, BookState st) {
      BookDB.instance.addBook(new Book(st.getIsbn(), st.getTitle()));
      try {
         ResponseBuilder builder = Response.created(new URI(
               "http://localhost:8080/bs/books/" + st.getIsbn()));
         return builder.build();
      } catch (URISyntaxException e) {
         throw new RuntimeException(e);
      }
   }
}
```

You'll create this method next.

Return a 201 (Created) status code. You must provide the URL to the new object. It will be sent to the client using a Location header.

Implement the addBook() method in the BookDB class:

```
public class BookDB {
   private Book book1234;
   private Map<String, Book> books;

   public BookDB() {
      books = new HashMap<String, Book>();
      Book book1234 = new Book("1234", "Java Programming");
      addBook(book1234);
   }
   public Book getBook1234() {
      return books.get("1234");
   }
   public void addBook(Book book) {
      books.put(book.getIsbn(), book);
   }
   public static BookDB instance = new BookDB();
}
```

Add the resource class to the server and delete the code to modify a book:

```
public class BookServer {
   public static void main(String[] args) throws InterruptedException,
         IOException {
      JAXRSServerFactoryBean sf = new JAXRSServerFactoryBean();
      sf.setResourceClasses(BooksResource.class, BookResource.class);
      sf.setAddress("http://localhost:8080/bs");
      sf.create();
      System.out.println("Started");
      ...
   }
}
```

Modify the client to test it:

```
public class BookClient {
  public static void main(String[] args) throws InterruptedException {
    WebClient client = WebClient.create("http://localhost:8080/bs");
    BookState st = new BookState();
    st.setIsbn("5678");
    st.setTitle("Design Patterns");
    client.path("books");
    client.post(st);
    client.back(true);
    client.path("books/5678");
    BookState book = client.get(BookState.class);
    System.out.println(book.getTitle());
  }
}
```

Reset to the base URL. If you don't do that, the path below (books/5678) will be appended to the existing URL (http://localhost:8080/bs/books) and will end up as http://localhost:8080/bs/books/books/5678.

If you specify false, it will back up just one level instead of going to the base URL. In this case, it will go from http://localhost:8080/bs/books back to http://localhost:8080/bs. That will also work.

As you are trying to retrieve a book other than book 1234, you need to enhance the GET method:

```
@Path("books/{isbn}")
public class BookResource {
  @GET
  public Response getDetails(@Context Request request,
      @PathParam("isbn") String isbn) {
    BookDB bookDB = BookDB.instance;
    if (bookDB.contains(isbn)) {
      Book book = bookDB.getBook(isbn);
      EntityTag entityTag = new EntityTag(Long
          .toString(book.getVersion()));
      ResponseBuilder builder = request.evaluatePreconditions(
          getVersion(book), entityTag);
      if (builder != null) {
        setExpiry(builder);
      } else {
        BookState st = getBookState(book);
        builder = Response.ok(st);
        builder.lastModified(getVersion(book));
        builder.tag(Long.toString(book.getVersion()));
        setExpiry(builder);
      }
      return builder.build();
    } else {
      return Response.status(Status.NOT_FOUND).build();
    }
  }
  ...
}
```

Define the contains() and getBook() methods:

```
public class BookDB {
  private Map<String, Book> books;

  public BookDB() {
    books = new HashMap<String, Book>();
    Book book1234 = new Book("1234", "Java Programming");
    addBook(book1234);
  }
  public Book getBook1234() {
    return books.get("1234");
  }
  public void addBook(Book book) {
    books.put(book.getIsbn(), book);
```

```
  }
  public boolean contains(String isbn) {
    return books.containsKey(isbn);
  }
  public Book getBook(String isbn) {
    return books.get(isbn);
  }
  public static BookDB instance = new BookDB();
}
```

Even though it is working, hard-coding the URL in the source code is no good as you just don't know in advance in which host(s) the service will be deployed to:

```
@Path("books")
public class BooksResource {
  @POST
  public Response add(@Context Request request, BookState st) {
    BookDB.instance.addBook(new Book(st.getIsbn(), st.getTitle()));
    try {
      ResponseBuilder builder = Response.created(new URI(
          "http://localhost:8080/bs/books/" + st.getIsbn()));
      return builder.build();
    } catch (URISyntaxException e) {
      throw new RuntimeException(e);
    }

  }
}
```

To solve this problem, JAX-RS provides a class to help you create URLs:

```
...
import javax.ws.rs.core.UriBuilder;
import javax.ws.rs.core.UriInfo;

@Path("books")
public class BooksResource {
  @POST
  public Response add(@Context Request request, @Context UriInfo uriInfo,
       BookState st) {
    BookDB.instance.addBook(new Book(st.getIsbn(), st.getTitle()));
    UriBuilder uriBuilder = uriInfo.getBaseUriBuilder();
    uriBuilder.path(BookResource.class);
    ResponseBuilder builder = Response.created(uriBuilder.build(st.getIsbn()));
    return builder.build();
  }
}
```

Create a "URI builder". You can use it to build a URI. Here, you set the initial URI to the base URI (http://localhost:8080/bs).

Inject information regarding the URI.

Look into this resource class to find the path and append it to the URI so far. So, you'll get http://localhost:8080/bs/book/{isbn}.

Fill the value (e.g., 5678) into the first path parameter:

```
@Path("book/{isbn}")
public class BookResource {
  ...
}
```

View the response in TCP Monitor and the Location header should be set properly:

```
HTTP/1.1 201 Created
Content-Type: text/xml
Location: http://localhost:8080/bs/books/5678
Date: Sat, 26 Dec 2009 09:54:13 GMT
Content-Length: 0
Server: Jetty(6.1.21)
```

Implementing delete

To implement delete, use the HTTP DELETE method:

```
@Path("books/{isbn}")
public class BookResource {
  ...
  @DELETE
  public Response delete(@PathParam("isbn") String isbn) {
    ResponseBuilder builder;
    BookDB bookDB = BookDB.instance;
    if (bookDB.contains(isbn)) {
      bookDB.delete(isbn);
      builder = Response.noContent();
    } else {
      builder = Response.status(Status.NOT_FOUND);
    }
    return builder.build();
  }
}
```

Implement the delete():

```
public class BookDB {
  private Map<String, Book> books;

  public BookDB() {
    books = new HashMap<String, Book>();
    Book book1234 = new Book("1234", "Java Programming");
    addBook(book1234);
  }
  public Book getBook1234() {
    return books.get("1234");
  }
  public void addBook(Book book) {
    books.put(book.getIsbn(), book);
  }
  public boolean contains(String isbn) {
    return books.containsKey(isbn);
  }
  public Book getBook(String isbn) {
    return books.get(isbn);
  }
  public void delete(String isbn) {
    books.remove(isbn);
  }
  public static BookDB instance = new BookDB();
}
```

Modify the client to test it:

```
public class BookClient {
  public static void main(String[] args) throws InterruptedException {
    WebClient client = WebClient.create("http://localhost:8080/bs");
    client.path("books/1234");
    client.delete();
    Response response = client.get();
    System.out.println(response.getStatus());
  }
}
```

Run the server and then the client. The client should print 404 as the status code. Note that CXF will also print an exception to warn you that something is wrong. That is fine and harmless.

Listing the reviews on a book

Suppose that a book may have zero or more reviews given by readers. In order to retrieve the reviews, what URL should you use? You may try http://localhost:8080/bs/reviews but it is not saying which book is concerned.

A next attempt may be http://localhost:8080/bs/reviews?book=1234. This works. However, some older proxies were configured by default to not cache containing query parameters because in the past a lot of dynamically generated HTTP responses did not include Cache-Control headers, so the proxy developers decided to ignore them completely.

Another alternative is http://localhost:8080/bs/books/1234/reviews, which can be interpret as getting to the books, get the book 1234, get its reviews. This looks nice because there is a parent-child relationship.

What should the response be like? It could be:

```
<reviews>
  <review>
    <by>John Doe</by>
    <text>I like this book...</text>
  </review>
  <review>
    <by>...</by>
    <text>...</text>
  </review>
</reviews>
```

To implement this idea, modify the XSD file:

```
<?xml version="1.0" encoding="UTF-8"?>
<schema xmlns="http://www.w3.org/2001/XMLSchema"
targetNamespace="http://ttdev.com/bs"
  xmlns:tns="http://ttdev.com/bs" elementFormDefault="qualified">
  <element name="book">
    <complexType>
      <sequence>
        <element name="isbn" type="string"></element>
        <element name="title" type="string"></element>
      </sequence>
    </complexType>
  </element>
  <element name="reviews">
    <complexType>
      <sequence>
        <element ref="tns:review" minOccurs="0" maxOccurs="unbounded">
        </element>
      </sequence>
    </complexType>
  </element>
  <element name="review">
    <complexType>
      <sequence>
        <element name="by" type="string"></element>
        <element name="text" type="string"></element>
      </sequence>
    </complexType>
  </element>
</schema>
```

Modify the bindings.xml file to map <reviews> and <review> to Java classes named ReviewsState and ReviewState respectively:

```
<?xml version="1.0" encoding="UTF-8"?>
<jaxb:bindings
  xmlns:jaxb="http://java.sun.com/xml/ns/jaxb"
  xmlns:xsd="http://www.w3.org/2001/XMLSchema"
  schemaLocation="BookService.xsd"
  jaxb:version="2.0">
  <jaxb:bindings node="/xsd:schema/xsd:element[@name='book']">
    <jaxb:class name="BookState"></jaxb:class>
  </jaxb:bindings>
  <jaxb:bindings node="/xsd:schema/xsd:element[@name='reviews']">
    <jaxb:class name="ReviewsState"></jaxb:class>
  </jaxb:bindings>
  <jaxb:bindings node="/xsd:schema/xsd:element[@name='review']">
    <jaxb:class name="ReviewState"></jaxb:class>
  </jaxb:bindings>
</jaxb:bindings>
```

Run the CodeGenerator class to generate the code. Then, modify the BookResource class:

+ → books/{isbn}/reviews

The @Path specified by the method is appended to the @Path specified by the class to get the full path for the method.

```
@Path("books/{isbn}")
public class BookResource {
  @Path("reviews")
  @GET
  public Response getReviews(@PathParam("isbn") String isbn) {
    BookDB bookDB = BookDB.instance;
    if (bookDB.contains(isbn)) {
      Book book = bookDB.getBook(isbn);
      ReviewsState result = new ReviewsState();
      for (Review r : book.getReviews()) {
        ReviewState st = new ReviewState();
        st.setBy(r.getBy());
        st.setText(r.getText());
        result.getReview().add(st);
      }
      ResponseBuilder builder = Response.ok(result);
      setExpiry(builder);
      return builder.build();
    } else {
      return Response.status(Status.NOT_FOUND).build();
    }
  }
  ...
}
```

It's a GET request.

You'll create this method next.

Don't forget to set the expiry headers in order for it to be cached.

Create the getReviews() method in the Book class:

```
public class Book {
  private String isbn;
  private String title;
  private Date lastModified;
  private long version;
  private List<Review> reviews;

  public Book(String isbn, String title) {
    this.isbn = isbn;
    this.title = title;
    this.lastModified = new Date();
    this.version = 0;
    this.reviews = new ArrayList<Review>();
  }
  ...
```

```
    public List<Review> getReviews() {
      return reviews;
    }
  }
```

Create the Review class:

```
public class Review {
  private String by;
  private String text;

  public Review(String by, String text) {
    this.by = by;
    this.text = text;
  }
  public String getBy() {
    return by;
  }
  public void setBy(String by) {
    this.by = by;
  }
  public String getText() {
    return text;
  }
  public void setText(String text) {
    this.text = text;
  }
}
```

Modify the BookDB class to hard code some reviews:

```
public class BookDB {
  private Map<String, Book> books;

  public BookDB() {
    books = new HashMap<String, Book>();
    Book book1234 = new Book("1234", "Java Programming");
    List<Review> reviews = book1234.getReviews();
    reviews.add(new Review("John", "Great book!"));
    reviews.add(new Review("Judy", "Excellent!"));
    addBook(book1234);
  }
  ...
}
```

Run the server and try to access http://localhost:8080/bs/books/1234/reviews. You should get:

```
<?xml version="1.0" encoding="UTF-8" standalone="yes"?>
<reviews xmlns="http://ttdev.com/bs">
  <review>
    <by>John</by>
    <text>Great book!</text>
  </review>
  <review>
    <by>Judy</by>
    <text>Excellent!</text>
  </review>
</reviews>
```

Even though it is working, currently it is the book resource handling the request for the reviews. This is not ideal. Instead, you should have a reviews resource handling the request.

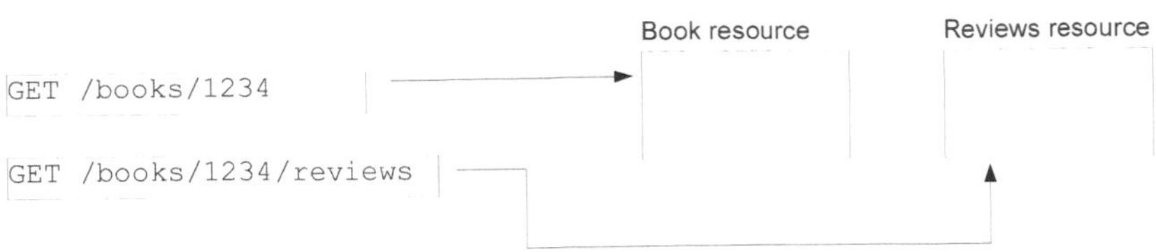

The question is how to write the Reviews resource. Let's try as shown below. You can see that this will duplicate the logic of locating a book already done in the BookResource class.

```
@Path("books/{isbn}/review")
public class ReviewsResource {
    @GET
    public Response getReviews(@PathParam("isbn") String isbn) {
        BookDB bookDB = BookDB.instance;
        if (bookDB.contains(isbn)) {
            Book book = bookDB.getBook(isbn);
            ...
        } else {
            ...
        }
    }
}
```

```
@Path("books/{isbn}")
public class BookResource {
    ...
    @GET
    public Response getDetails(@Context Request request,
            @PathParam("isbn") String isbn) {
        BookDB bookDB = BookDB.instance;
        if (bookDB.contains(isbn)) {
            Book book = bookDB.getBook(isbn);
            ...
        } else {
            ...
        }
    }
}
```

To avoid duplicating the logic, you should use the BookResource to locate the book and then ask it to give you a ReviewsResource. For example, see the diagram below, for a path like /books/1234/xyz, CXF first locates and creates the book resource. Then it finds that foo() method has a matching path (/books/{isbn}/xyz) and a matching HTTP method, so it calls that foo() method and get the response. If the path is /books/1234/reviews, as before, CXF first locates and creates the book resource. Then it finds that the bar() method has matching path (/books/{isbn}/reviews) but it doesn't indicate the HTTP method. This is telling CXF that this method will create a child resource. So, it calls that bar() method to get another resource (a book reviews resource). Then it traces into that resource and look for a method annotated with @GET. In this case it will find the baz() method. So it calls that baz() method and get the response:

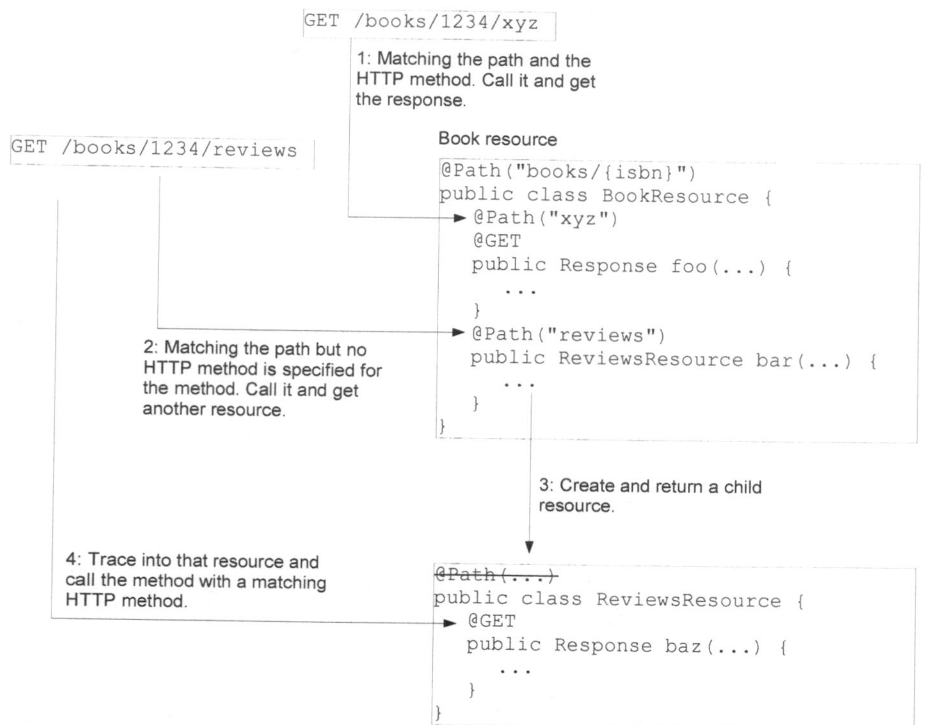

Note that the child resource (ReviewsResource) doesn't need to be annotated with @Path as it is already done with a method in its parent (the bar() method above).

To implement this idea, modify the BookResource class to give it such a child resource returning method:

```
@Path("books/{isbn}")
public class BookResource {
   @Path("reviews")
   @GET
   public ReviewsResource getReviewsResource(@PathParam("isbn") String isbn) {
      BookDB bookDB = BookDB.instance;
      if (bookDB.contains(isbn)) {
         Book book = bookDB.getBook(isbn);
         return new ReviewsResource(book);
      } else {
         Response response = Response.status(Status.NOT_FOUND).build();
         throw new WebApplicationException(response);
      }
   }
   ...
}
```

Create such a resource and provide the book to it.

If the book is not found, you'd like to return a 404 (Not Found) status code. However, as you're now supposed to return a resource, not a response. The solution is to throw a WebApplicationException wrapping a response. When CXF receives this exception, it will return the response included in it.

Very important: Do not indicate any HTTP method here. You're delegating the request to the child resource, so let that child resource handle the various HTTP methods (GET, PUT or whatever).

Create the ReviewsResource class:

Note that it has no @Path annotation because this is already done by the method in the parent resource.

This resource represents the reviews for this book only, not for all books.

Once CXF reaches this resource through a book resource, it will find the method with a matching HTTP method as usual.

the setExpiry() method is defined in the BookResource class. Can't access it for now. You'll fix it later.

```
@Path(...)
public class ReviewsResource {
   private Book book;

   public ReviewsResource(Book book) {
      this.book = book;
   }
   @GET
   public Response getReviews() {
      ReviewsState result = new ReviewsState();
      for (Review r : book.getReviews()) {
         ReviewState st = new ReviewState();
         st.setBy(r.getBy());
         st.setText(r.getText());
         result.getReview().add(st);
      }
      ResponseBuilder builder = Response.ok(result);
      // setExpiry(builder);
      return builder.build();
   }
}
```

To make the setExpiry() method available to it, put it into a new class and name it, say, CacheController:

```
public class CacheController {
  public static void setExpiry(ResponseBuilder builder) {
    GregorianCalendar now = new GregorianCalendar();
    GregorianCalendar nextUpdate = getNextUpdateTime(now);
    int maxAge = (int) ((nextUpdate.getTimeInMillis() - now
         .getTimeInMillis()) / 1000L);
    CacheControl cacheControl = new CacheControl();
    cacheControl.setMaxAge(maxAge);
    builder.cacheControl(cacheControl);
    builder.expires(nextUpdate.getTime());
  }
  private static GregorianCalendar getNextUpdateTime(GregorianCalendar now) {
    GregorianCalendar nextUpdate = new GregorianCalendar();
    nextUpdate.setTime(now.getTime());
    nextUpdate.set(Calendar.HOUR_OF_DAY, 10);
    nextUpdate.set(Calendar.MINUTE, 0);
    nextUpdate.set(Calendar.SECOND, 0);
    nextUpdate.set(Calendar.MILLISECOND, 0);
    if (now.get(Calendar.HOUR_OF_DAY) >= 10) {
      nextUpdate.add(Calendar.DAY_OF_YEAR, 1);
    }
    return nextUpdate;
  }
}
```

Let both the BookResource and ReviewsResource classes use it:

```
@Path("books/{isbn}")
public class BookResource {
   ...
   @GET
   public Response getDetails(@Context Request request,
        @PathParam("isbn") String isbn) {
     BookDB bookDB = BookDB.instance;
```

```
      if (bookDB.contains(isbn)) {
        Book book = bookDB.getBook(isbn);
        EntityTag entityTag = new EntityTag(Long
            .toString(book.getVersion()));
        ResponseBuilder builder = request.evaluatePreconditions(
            getVersion(book), entityTag);
        if (builder != null) {
          CacheController.setExpiry(builder);
        } else {
          BookState st = getBookState(book);
          builder = Response.ok(st);
          builder.lastModified(getVersion(book));
          builder.tag(Long.toString(book.getVersion()));
          CacheController.setExpiry(builder);
        }
        return builder.build();
      } else {
        return Response.status(Status.NOT_FOUND).build();
      }
    }
  }

  public class ReviewsResource {
    ...
    @GET
    public Response getReviews() {
      ReviewsState result = new ReviewsState();
      for (Review r : book.getReviews()) {
        ReviewState st = new ReviewState();
        st.setBy(r.getBy());
        st.setText(r.getText());
        result.getReview().add(st);
      }
      ResponseBuilder builder = Response.ok(result);
      CacheController.setExpiry(builder);
      return builder.build();
    }
  }
```

Run the service and access the reviews again at http://localhost:8080/bs/books/1234/reviews. It should continue to work.

Providing the full review text on demand

Suppose that the client may only want to display a brief summary of each review to the user. If the user would like to see the full review, he can click on a link to display the full review. To do that, the initial response may be like:

Now it is not a review but just a reference to a review.

Just a little summary text

The URL to GET the full review. Here, 0 is the index (first review for that book) and used as an unique ID.

```
<reviews>
   <reviewRef>
      <summary>Great...</summary>
      <url>http://localhost:8080/bs/books/1234/reviews/0
   </review>
   <review>
      <summary>Execellent...</summary>
      <url>http://localhost:8080/bs/books/1234/reviews/1
   </review>
</reviews>
```

To implement this idea, modify the XSD file:

```
<schema xmlns="http://www.w3.org/2001/XMLSchema"
targetNamespace="http://ttdev.com/bs"
  xmlns:tns="http://ttdev.com/bs" elementFormDefault="qualified">
  <element name="book">
    <complexType>
      <sequence>
        <element name="isbn" type="string"></element>
        <element name="title" type="string"></element>
      </sequence>
    </complexType>
  </element>
  <element name="reviews">
    <complexType>
      <sequence>
        <element ref="tns:reviewRef" minOccurs="0" maxOccurs="unbounded">
        </element>
      </sequence>
    </complexType>
  </element>
  <element name="reviewRef">
    <complexType>
      <sequence>
        <element name="summary" type="string"></element>
        <element name="url" type="anyURI"></element>
      </sequence>
    </complexType>
  </element>
  <element name="review">
    <complexType>
      <sequence>
        <element name="by" type="string"></element>
        <element name="text" type="string"></element>
      </sequence>
    </complexType>
  </element>
</schema>
```

Generate the code again. Then modify the ReviewsResource class to return a list of review references:

```
public class ReviewsResource {
  private Book book;

  public ReviewsResource(Book book) {
    this.book = book;
  }
  @GET
  public Response getReviews(@Context UriInfo uriInfo) {
    ReviewsState result = new ReviewsState();
    int index = 0;
    for (Review r : book.getReviews()) {
      ReviewRef ref = new ReviewRef();
      ref.setSummary(r.getText().split(" ")[0]);
      UriBuilder builder = uriInfo.getAbsolutePathBuilder();
      builder.path(ReviewsResource.class, "getReview");
      ref.setUrl(builder.build(index).toString());
      result.getReviewRef().add(ref);
      index++;
    }
    ResponseBuilder builder = Response.ok(result);
    CacheController.setExpiry(builder);
    return builder.build();
  }
  @Path("{index}")
  @GET
  public Response getReview(@PathParam("index") int index) {
    try {
      Review review = book.getReviews().get(index);
      ReviewState st = new ReviewState();
      st.setBy(review.getBy());
      st.setText(review.getText());
      ResponseBuilder builder = Response.ok(st);
      CacheController.setExpiry(builder);
      return builder.build();
    } catch (IndexOutOfBoundsException e) {
      return Response.status(Status.NOT_FOUND).build();
    }
  }
}
```

Use the first word of review text as the summary.

Use the current full path (books/1234/reviews) as the initial path in the URI builder.

Find the @Path value attached to this method and append it to the path so far. So you will get books/1234/reviews/{index}.

Fill in the index value to get something like books/1234/reviews/0.

Even though it is not written in this class, this resource class will handle paths like books/1234/reviews. So, this method will handle paths like books/1234/reviews/{index}.

Run the service and try to access http://localhost:8080/bs/books/1234/reviews in the browser. You should get the links:

```
<?xml version="1.0" encoding="UTF-8" standalone="yes"?>
<reviews xmlns="http://ttdev.com/bs">
  <reviewRef>
    <summary>Great</summary>
    <url>http://localhost:8080/bs/books/1234/reviews/0</url>
  </reviewRef>
  <reviewRef>
    <summary>Excellent!/summary>
    <url>http://localhost:8080/bs/books/1234/reviews/1</url>
  </reviewRef>
</reviews>
```

Accessing a particular review by http://localhost:8080/bs/books/1234/reviews/0 will also work.

Implementing search

Suppose that you'd like to allow clients to search for books. They can specify a keyword such as "Java" to match books whose titles contain the word "Java". They can also specify, say, a date to match books that were published after that date. Furthermore, both conditions can be specified simultaneously.

Obviously this operation is a GET operation, but what is the resource being read? It is a certain selection of books that meet the search criteria. The URL could be http://localhost:8080/bs/bookselections/keyword/java/pubdate/12-26-2009. However, this doesn't look very natural as it is not a true parent-child relationship between "bookselections" and "keyword", and between "keyword" and "java".

An alternative is to use query parameters such as http://localhost:8080/bs/bookselections?keyword=java&pubdate=12-26-2009. This is a better when you aren't following a parent-child hierarchy.

To implement this function, modify the XSD file to define the structure of the response:

```
<schema xmlns="http://www.w3.org/2001/XMLSchema"
targetNamespace="http://ttdev.com/bs"
  xmlns:tns="http://ttdev.com/bs" elementFormDefault="qualified">
  <element name="book">
    <complexType>
      <sequence>
        <element name="isbn" type="string"></element>
        <element name="title" type="string"></element>
      </sequence>
    </complexType>
  </element>
  <element name="books">
    <complexType>
      <sequence>
        <element ref="tns:book" minOccurs="0" maxOccurs="unbounded">
        </element>
      </sequence>
    </complexType>
  </element>
  <element name="reviews">
    <complexType>
      <sequence>
        <element ref="tns:reviewRef" minOccurs="0" maxOccurs="unbounded">
        </element>
      </sequence>
    </complexType>
  </element>
  <element name="reviewRef">
    <complexType>
      <sequence>
        <element name="summary" type="string"></element>
        <element name="url" type="anyURI"></element>
      </sequence>
    </complexType>
  </element>
  <element name="review">
    <complexType>
      <sequence>
        <element name="by" type="string"></element>
        <element name="text" type="string"></element>
```

```
      </sequence>
    </complexType>
  </element>
</schema>
```

Modify the bindings.xml file:

```
<jaxb:bindings
  xmlns:jaxb="http://java.sun.com/xml/ns/jaxb"
  xmlns:xsd="http://www.w3.org/2001/XMLSchema"
  schemaLocation="BookService.xsd"
  jaxb:version="2.0">
  <jaxb:bindings node="/xsd:schema/xsd:element[@name='book']">
    <jaxb:class name="BookState"></jaxb:class>
  </jaxb:bindings>
  <jaxb:bindings node="/xsd:schema/xsd:element[@name='books']">
    <jaxb:class name="BooksState"></jaxb:class>
  </jaxb:bindings>
  <jaxb:bindings node="/xsd:schema/xsd:element[@name='reviews']">
    <jaxb:class name="ReviewsState"></jaxb:class>
  </jaxb:bindings>
  <jaxb:bindings node="/xsd:schema/xsd:element[@name='review']">
    <jaxb:class name="ReviewState"></jaxb:class>
  </jaxb:bindings>
</jaxb:bindings>
```

Generate the code again. Then create a BookSelectionsResource class:

```
http://localhost:8080/bs/books/selections?keyword=java&pubdate=12-26-2009
```

Inject the value of the query parameter into the argument.

```
@Path("bookselections")
public class BookSelectionsResource {
  @GET
  public Response select(@QueryParam("keyword") String keyword,
      @QueryParam("pubdate") String pubDate) {
    List<Book> books = BookDB.instance.searchBooks(keyword, pubDate);
    BooksState result = new BooksState();
    for (Book book : books) {
      BookState st = new BookState();
      st.setIsbn(book.getIsbn());
      st.setTitle(book.getTitle());
      result.getBook().add(st);
    }
    ResponseBuilder builder = Response.ok(result);
    CacheController.setExpiry(builder);
    return builder.build();
  }
}
```

You'll create this method next.

What you get is a string, but you need a Date. In that case, CXF will try two things:

1: Try a constructor taking a String (the Date class does have this constructor).

2: Try a static method named "valueOf" or "fromString".

```
public class Date {
  public Date(String s) {
    ...
  }
  public static Object valueOf(String s) {
    ...
  }
  public static Object fromString(String s) {
    ...
  }
}
```

Create the searchBooks() method in the BookDB class as shown below. Here, you simply return all the books.

```
public class BookDB {
  private Map<String, Book> books;
  ...
  public List<Book> searchBooks(String keyword, String pubDate) {
    return new ArrayList<Book>(books.values());
  }
}
```

Register the resource class with the server:

```
public class BookServer {
  public static void main(String[] args) throws InterruptedException,
      IOException {
    JAXRSServerFactoryBean sf = new JAXRSServerFactoryBean();
    sf.setResourceClasses(BooksResource.class, BookResource.class,
        BookSelectionsResource.class);
    sf.setAddress("http://localhost:8080/bs");
    sf.create();
    ...
  }
}
```

Now run the server and try to access http://localhost:8080/bs/bookselections?keyword=java&pubdate=12-26-2009. You should get the book listing:

```
<?xml version="1.0" encoding="UTF-8" standalone="yes"?>
<books xmlns="http://ttdev.com/bs">
  <book>
    <isbn>1234</isbn>
    <title>Java Programming</title>
  </book>
</books>
```

What if the client specifies only, say, the keyword but not the pubdate? Then null will be injected as the value as the pubdate. Therefore, In a real web service you will probably need to check like:

```
@Path("bookselections")
public class BookSelectionsResource {
  @GET
  public Response select(@QueryParam("keyword") String keyword,
      @QueryParam("pubdate") String pubDate) {
    if (keyword == null) {
      ...
    }
    if (pubDate == null) {
      ...
    }
    List<Book> books = BookDB.instance.searchBooks(keyword, pubDate);
    ...
  }
}
```

How to send query parameters using the CXF web client? It can be done like this:

```
public class BookClient {
  public static void main(String[] args) throws InterruptedException {
    WebClient client = WebClient.create("http://localhost:8080/bs");
    client.path("bookselections");
    client.query("keyword", "Java");
    client.query("pubdate", new GregorianCalendar(2009, 11, 26).getTime());
    BooksState st = client.get(BooksState.class);
    for (BookState st : books.getBook()) {
      System.out.println(st.getTitle());
    }
  }
```

```
}
```

To have the BooksState class, copy the XSD file and bindings.xml file to the client project and generate the code again. Run the client and it should print:

```
Java Programming
```

Doing it in Axis2

The REST support in Axis2 is quite complicated and difficult to use. So, I will not cover it here.

Summary

If you need to create a highly scalable web service, definitely consider the REST architecture. It means standardizing on the way the methods (GET, PUT, etc.) and the resources are specified (URI). This way proxies will be able to cache the responses.

To truly support caching, you should set the expiry date and time. Then you should support conditional GETs (validations) using a timestamp or an ETag (or both).

Usually the path in the URI is designed to reflect a parent-child hierarchy. For other relationships, you may use query parameters.

The response body is usually XML to remain platform and language neutral. To generate such XML or to read it, you will use JAXB to convert between Java and XML. In particular, you should start from XML schema and generate the corresponding Java classes. You can use JAXB bindings file to customize the mapping.

Using JAX-RS, the runtime will use the path (or its initial portion) to locate the resource class, create an instance and use the remaining of the path to locate the method. The method may return a response or may return a child resource for it to trace into. For the former case, the method must be annotated with the HTTP method it can handle. For the latter case, it must not have such an annotation.

You can use parameters in the @Path annotation so that you can handle multiple paths.

You can inject various types information from the request into the arguments of your resource methods such as path parameters, query parameters, the request itself or the body of the request (converted to a Java object).

Commonly you may need to include URIs to related resources in a response. To build such URLs, it's easier to use the UriBuilder which can be injected.

Chapter 10

Deploying your services and integrating them with Spring

What's in this chapter?

In this chapter you'll learn how to deploy your web services in a web container such as Tomcat and let them invoke business logic in Spring beans.

Deploying the simple service

Up until now you've been running your web services from console applications. Behind your back CXF has been running a web server called Jetty to route the HTTP requests to your services. In production, you're likely already running a web server such as Tomcat and therefore you probably want to deploy your services there.

To do that, let's take the SimpleService project as an example. Copy it and paste it as SimpleWebApp. Modify the pom.xml file:

```
<project ...>
  <modelVersion>4.0.0</modelVersion>
  <groupId>SimpleWebApp</groupId>
  <artifactId>SimpleWebApp</artifactId>
  <version>0.0.1-SNAPSHOT</version>
  <packaging>war</packaging>
  ...
</project>
```

The <packaging> element tells the Eclipse Maven plugin that it is a web application. Right click the project and choose Maven | Update Project Configuration for the change to take effect.

Then create a servlet named SimpleServlet in the com.ttdev.ss package:

```
package com.ttdev.ss;

import javax.servlet.ServletConfig;
import javax.servlet.ServletException;
import javax.xml.ws.Endpoint;
import org.apache.cxf.BusFactory;
import org.apache.cxf.transport.servlet.CXFNonSpringServlet;

public class SimpleServlet extends CXFNonSpringServlet {

  private static final long serialVersionUID = 1L;

  @Override
  public void loadBus(ServletConfig servletConfig) throws ServletException {
    super.loadBus(servletConfig);
    BusFactory.setDefaultBus(getBus());
    Object implementor = new SimpleServiceImpl();
    Endpoint.publish("/p1", implementor);
  }
}
```

Extend this servlet class. It is provided by CXF to handle the HTTP requests.

On initialization, the super class will create a "bus" by reading configuration files. The bus is the central place for all endpoints.

Use that bus as the default bus.

Publish an endpoint. It will attach itself to the default bus.

Use a relative path. If you deploy your web application as http://localhost:8080/ss, then the full URL will be http://localhost:8080/ss/p1.

Modify the src/main/webapp/WEB-INF/web.xml file to register the servlet:

```
<?xml version="1.0" encoding="UTF-8"?>
```

```
<web-app ...>
  <display-name>SimpleService</display-name>
  <welcome-file-list>
    <welcome-file>index.html</welcome-file>
    <welcome-file>index.htm</welcome-file>
    <welcome-file>index.jsp</welcome-file>
    <welcome-file>default.html</welcome-file>
    <welcome-file>default.htm</welcome-file>
    <welcome-file>default.jsp</welcome-file>
  </welcome-file-list>
  <servlet>
    <servlet-name>s1</servlet-name>
    <servlet-class>com.ttdev.ss.SimpleServlet</servlet-class>
  </servlet>
  <servlet-mapping>
    <servlet-name>s1</servlet-name>
    <url-pattern>/services/*</url-pattern>
  </servlet-mapping>
</web-app>
```

Right click the project and choose Run As | Maven package. It will create a SimpleWebApp-0.0.1-SNAPSHOT.war in the target folder. You're ready to deploy it into Tomcat.

Installing Tomcat

If you already have Tomcat installed, skip to the next section. Otherwise, go to http://tomcat.apache.org to download a binary package of Tomcat. Download the zip version instead of the Windows exe version. Suppose that it is apache-tomcat-6.0.16.zip. Unzip it into a folder, say tomcat. Note that Tomcat 6.x works with JDK 5 or above.

Before you can run it, make sure the environment variable JAVA_HOME is defined to point to your JDK folder (e.g., C:\Program Files\Java\jdk1.5.0_02). If you don't have it, define it now.

Now, open a command prompt, change to tomcat/bin and then run startup.bat. If it is working, you should see:

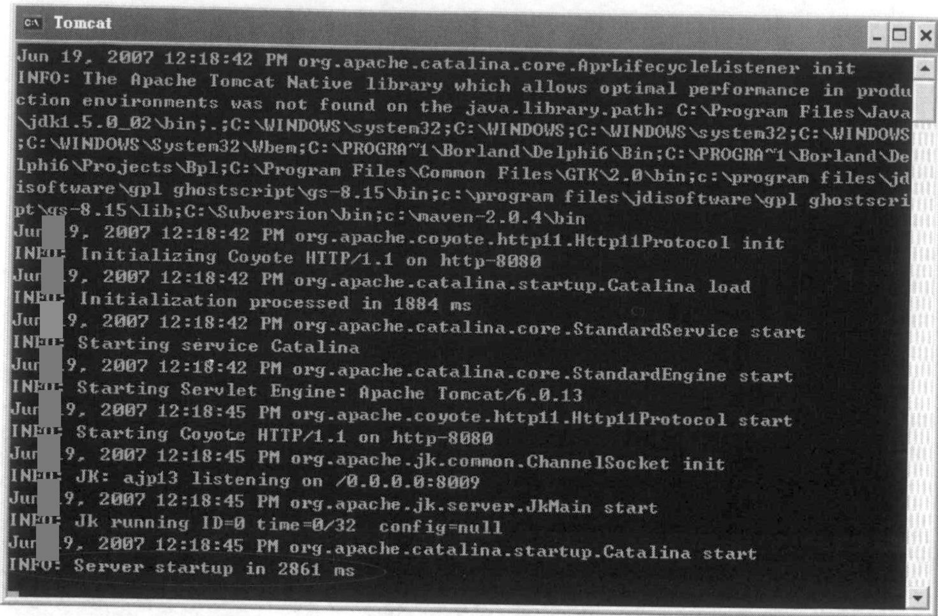

Open a browser and go to http://localhost:8080 and you should see:

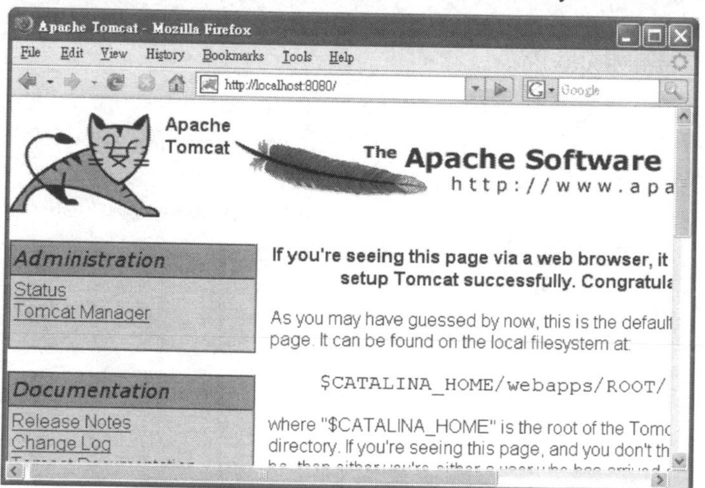

Let's shut it down by changing to tomcat/bin and running shutdown.bat.

To deploy the SimpleWebApp-0.0.1-SNAPSHOT.war file into Tomcat, simply copy it into tomcat/webapps folder (create it if it doesn't exist yet). You can copy it as ss.war so that it will be available http://localhost:8080/ss. Then start Tomcat and try to access http://localhost:8080/ss/services/p1?wsdl. You should see the WSDL file.

To access it from the client, copy the SimpleClient project and paste it as SimpleWebAppClient. Then modify the SimpleService_P1_Client class to use the right address:

```
public final class SimpleService_P1_Client {
  ...
  public static void main(String args[]) throws Exception {
    ...
    SimpleService_Service ss = new SimpleService_Service(wsdlURL,
        SERVICE_NAME);
    SimpleService port = ss.getP1();
    BindingProvider bp = (BindingProvider) port;
    Map<String, Object> context = bp.getRequestContext();
    context.put(BindingProvider.ENDPOINT_ADDRESS_PROPERTY,
        "http://localhost:8080/ss/services/p1");
    {
      System.out.println("Invoking concat...");
      com.ttdev.ss.ConcatRequest _concat_parameters = new ConcatRequest();
      _concat_parameters.setS1("abc");
      _concat_parameters.setS2("123");
      java.lang.String _concat__return = port.concat(_concat_parameters);
      System.out.println("concat.result=" + _concat__return);

    }
    System.exit(0);
  }
}
```

Run it and it should print:

```
Invoking concat...
concat.result=abc123
```

Invoking Spring beans from your implementation object

Up until now all your web services perform very simple operations such as concatenating two strings. In practice, they should really invoke business logic such as placing an order for some goods. Typically such business logic may have been implemented as Spring beans. Let's work on such an example. If you don't use Spring, skip this section.

Suppose that the business logic is implemented in the SimpleBean class:

```
package com.ttdev.ss;

public class SimpleBean {
  public String concat(String s1, String s2) {
    return s1 + s2;
  }
}
```

Define the Spring bean in a file named beans.xml in the src/main/webapp/WEB-INF folder:

```
<beans xmlns="http://www.springframework.org/schema/beans"
  xmlns:xsi="http://www.w3.org/2001/XMLSchema-instance"
  xsi:schemaLocation="
http://www.springframework.org/schema/beans
http://www.springframework.org/schema/beans/spring-beans-2.5.xsd">
  <bean id="simpleBean" class="com.ttdev.ss.SimpleBean">
  </bean>
</beans>
```

In order to let your implementation object access this simpleBean, the easiest way is to turn it into a Spring bean. So, modify the beans.xml file:

```
<beans ...>
  <bean id="simpleBean" class="com.ttdev.ss.SimpleBean">
  </bean>
  <bean id="simpleImpl" class="com.ttdev.ss.SimpleServiceImpl">
    <property name="simpleBean" ref="simpleBean" />
  </bean>
</beans>
```

Modify the SimpleServiceImpl class to have a property named "simpleBean" and use it to perform the business operation:

```
package com.ttdev.ss;

@WebService(endpointInterface = "com.ttdev.ss.SimpleService")
public class SimpleServiceImpl implements SimpleService {
  private SimpleBean simpleBean;

  public void setSimpleBean(SimpleBean simpleBean) {
    this.simpleBean = simpleBean;
  }
  @Override
  public String concat(ConcatRequest parameters) {
    return simpleBean.concat(parameters.getS1(), parameters.getS2());
  }
}
```

As it is now a Spring bean, you can just new it yourself when creating the endpoint:

```
public class SimpleServlet extends CXFNonSpringServlet {

  private static final long serialVersionUID = 1L;

  @Override
  public void loadBus(ServletConfig servletConfig) throws ServletException {
    super.loadBus(servletConfig);
    BusFactory.setDefaultBus(getBus());
    Object implementor = new SimpleServiceImpl();
    Endpoint.publish("/p1", implementor);
  }
}
```

Instead, tell CXF to create an endpoint from the simpleImpl bean:

```
<beans xmlns="http://www.springframework.org/schema/beans"
   xmlns:xsi="http://www.w3.org/2001/XMLSchema-instance"
   xmlns:jaxws="http://cxf.apache.org/jaxws"
   xsi:schemaLocation="
http://www.springframework.org/schema/beans
http://www.springframework.org/schema/beans/spring-beans-2.5.xsd
http://cxf.apache.org/jaxws http://cxf.apache.org/schemas/jaxws.xsd">
   <bean id="simpleBean" class="com.ttdev.ss.SimpleBean">
   </bean>
   <bean id="simpleImpl" class="com.ttdev.ss.SimpleServiceImpl">
      <property name="simpleBean" ref="simpleBean" />
   </bean>
   <jaxws:endpoint id="endPoint1" address="/p1" implementor="#simpleImpl">
   </jaxws:endpoint>
</beans>
```

Use this bean as the implementation object.

To initialize Spring file, use CXFServlet in place of your SimpleServlet which will load Spring automatically:

```
<web-app ...>
   <display-name>SimpleWebApp</display-name>
   <welcome-file-list>
      <welcome-file>index.html</welcome-file>
      <welcome-file>index.htm</welcome-file>
      <welcome-file>index.jsp</welcome-file>
      <welcome-file>default.html</welcome-file>
      <welcome-file>default.htm</welcome-file>
      <welcome-file>default.jsp</welcome-file>
   </welcome-file-list>
   <servlet>
      <servlet-name>s1</servlet-name>
      <servlet-class>org.apache.cxf.transport.servlet.CXFServlet</servlet-class>
   </servlet>
   <servlet-mapping>
      <servlet-name>s1</servlet-name>
      <url-pattern>/services/*</url-pattern>
   </servlet-mapping>
</web-app>
```

But how to provide your beans.xml file to Spring? The easiest way is to rename it as cxf-servlet.xml. By default the CXFServlet will try to load such a bean definition file.

Now, package the project again and restart Tomcat. Run the client and it should continue to work.

Deploying RESTful web services

Copy the BookService project and paste it as BookWebApp. Modify the pom.xml file:

```
<project ...>
   <modelVersion>4.0.0</modelVersion>
   <groupId>BookWebApp</groupId>
   <artifactId>BookWebApp</artifactId>
   <version>0.0.1-SNAPSHOT</version>
   <packaging>war</packaging>
   ...
</project>
```

Right click the project and choose Maven | Update Project Configuration for the change to take effect. Assuming that your resource classes aren't using Spring, modify the src/main/webapp/WEB-INF/web.xml file to register a servlet and specify the resource classes:

```
<web-app xmlns:xsi="http://www.w3.org/2001/XMLSchema-instance"
   xmlns="http://java.sun.com/xml/ns/javaee"
xmlns:web="http://java.sun.com/xml/ns/javaee/web-app_2_5.xsd"
   xsi:schemaLocation="http://java.sun.com/xml/ns/javaee
http://java.sun.com/xml/ns/javaee/web-app_2_5.xsd"
   id="WebApp_ID" version="2.5">
   <display-name>BookWebApp</display-name>
   <welcome-file-list>
      <welcome-file>index.html</welcome-file>
      <welcome-file>index.htm</welcome-file>
      <welcome-file>index.jsp</welcome-file>
      <welcome-file>default.html</welcome-file>
      <welcome-file>default.htm</welcome-file>
      <welcome-file>default.jsp</welcome-file>
   </welcome-file-list>
   <servlet>
      <servlet-name>s1</servlet-name>
      <servlet-class>
         org.apache.cxf.jaxrs.servlet.CXFNonSpringJaxrsServlet
      </servlet-class>
      <init-param>
         <param-name>jaxrs.serviceClasses</param-name>
         <param-value>
         com.ttdev.bs.BooksResource com.ttdev.bs.BookResource
com.ttdev.bs.BookSelectionsResource
         </param-value>
      </init-param>
   </servlet>
   <servlet-mapping>
      <servlet-name>s1</servlet-name>
      <url-pattern>/services/*</url-pattern>
   </servlet-mapping>
</web-app>
```

This servlet will register the resource classes listed below:

The class names are separated by a space, not newline and not anything else.

The resources will be available under this path (/services).

Right click the project and choose Run As | Maven package. It will create a BookWebApp-0.0.1-SNAPSHOT.war in the target folder. Copy it into tomcat/webapps as bs.war to deploy it. Then you should be able to access the resources like http://localhost:8080/bs/services/books/1234 or http://localhost:8080/bs/services/books/1234/reviews.

Invoking Spring beans from your resource objects

In the BookWebApp project, assume that the business logic is implemented in a BooksService class:

```
package com.ttdev.bs;

public class BooksService {

  public boolean contains(String isbn) {
    return BookDB.instance.contains(isbn);
  }
  public Book getBook(String isbn) {
    return BookDB.instance.getBook(isbn);
  }
}
```

In order for, say, the BookResource object to get access to this Spring bean, it's best to let the BookResource object become a Spring bean itself. So, define these Spring beans in the src/main/webapp/WEB-INF/cxf-servlet.xml:

```
<beans xmlns="http://www.springframework.org/schema/beans"
  xmlns:xsi="http://www.w3.org/2001/XMLSchema-instance"
  xmlns:jaxws="http://cxf.apache.org/jaxws"
  xsi:schemaLocation="
http://www.springframework.org/schema/beans
http://www.springframework.org/schema/beans/spring-beans-2.5.xsd
http://cxf.apache.org/jaxws http://cxf.apache.org/schemas/jaxws.xsd">
  <bean id="bs" class="com.ttdev.bs.BooksService">
  </bean>
  <bean id="br" class="com.ttdev.bs.BookResource">
    <property name="bs" ref="bs" />
  </bean>
</beans>
```

As you're using Spring beans as resource objects, you can't simply register the resource classes. Instead, define the resources in cxf-servlet.xml:

```
<beans ...>
  <bean id="bs" class="com.ttdev.bs.BooksService">
  </bean>
  <bean id="br" class="com.ttdev.bs.BookResource">
    <property name="bs" ref="bs" />
  </bean>
  <jaxws:server id="s1">
    <jaxws:serviceBean>
      <ref bean="br" />
    </jaxws:serviceBean>
    <jaxws:serviceBean>
      <ref bean="..." />
    </jaxws:serviceBean>
    ...
  </jaxws:server>
</beans>
```

Use this "br" bean as a resource.

List other resources.

To initialize Spring file, use CXFServlet which will load Spring automatically:

```
<web-app ...>
  <display-name>BookWebApp</display-name>
  <welcome-file-list>
    <welcome-file>index.html</welcome-file>
    <welcome-file>index.htm</welcome-file>
    <welcome-file>index.jsp</welcome-file>
    <welcome-file>default.html</welcome-file>
    <welcome-file>default.htm</welcome-file>
    <welcome-file>default.jsp</welcome-file>
  </welcome-file-list>
  <servlet>
    <servlet-name>s1</servlet-name>
    <servlet-class>org.apache.cxf.transport.servlet.CXFServlet</servlet-class>
    <init-param>
      <param-name>jaxrs.serviceClasses</param-name>
      <param-value>
      com.ttdev.bs.BooksResource ...BookResource ...BookSelectionsResource
      </param-value>
    </init-param>
  </servlet>
  <servlet-mapping>
    <servlet-name>s1</servlet-name>
    <url-pattern>/services/*</url-pattern>
  </servlet-mapping>
</web-app>
```

Now, package the project, deploy it again and restart Tomcat. Run the client and it should continue to work.

Deploying Axis2 web services

For Axis2, you can simply run the Axis2 server as a web application in Tomcat. To do that, go to http://ws.apache.org/axis2 to download the WAR (Web Archive) Distribution (e.g. axis2-1.5.1-war.zip). There are just a handful of files in the zip file. Unzip it and put the files into,say, axis2-war. The only important file there is the axis2-1.5.1.war file. To deploy into Tomcat, copy it into tomcat/webapps. Then start Tomcat by running startup.bat. To check that the Axis2 server is running, go to http://localhost:8080/axis2 in a browser. You should see:

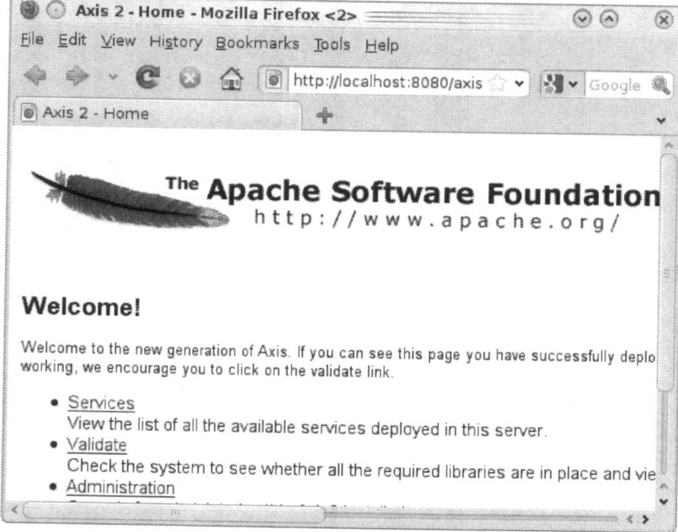

Check the tomcat/webapps folder, you should see that there is an axis2 folder created with the following structure:

```
tomcat
  webapps
    axis2
      WEB-INF
        conf
          axis2.xml
        services
          SimpleService.aar
          ???.aar
          ...
        modules
          addressing.mar
          rampart.mar
          ...
        lib
          *.jar
          ...
```

Configuration file for axis

To deploy your web services, just copy their .aar files into this folder as usual.

A .mar file for each module

jar files needed by Axis2 itself, the modules or your web services

To deploy the simple service, copy the SimpleService.aar file into the services folder as shown above. Restart Tomcat for the changes to take effect. Run the client and it should continue to work.

Using Spring with Axis2

To see how to invoke a Spring bean from the implementation object in Axis2, copy the Axis2SimpleService project and paste it as Axis2SpringService. Modify pom.xml to rename the jar file to be generated:

```
<project ...>
  <modelVersion>4.0.0</modelVersion>
  <groupId>SpringService</groupId>
  <artifactId>SpringService</artifactId>
  <version>0.0.1-SNAPSHOT</version>
  <dependencies>
    <dependency>
      <groupId>xerces</groupId>
      <artifactId>xercesImpl</artifactId>
      <version>2.9.1</version>
    </dependency>
    <dependency>
      <groupId>org.apache.axis2</groupId>
      <artifactId>axis2-codegen</artifactId>
      <version>1.5.1</version>
    </dependency>
    <dependency>
      <groupId>org.apache.axis2</groupId>
      <artifactId>axis2-adb-codegen</artifactId>
```

```
        <version>1.5.1</version>
      </dependency>
      <dependency>
        <groupId>org.springframework</groupId>
        <artifactId>spring</artifactId>
        <version>2.5.6.SEC01</version>
      </dependency>
    </dependencies>
    ...
  </project>
```

You have also changed the name of the artifact. Then create a SimpleBean class:

```
package com.ttdev.ss;

public class SimpleBean {
  public String concat(String s1, String s2) {
    return s1 + s2;
  }
}
```

Define the Spring bean in a file named beans.xml in src/main/resources folder:

```
<beans xmlns="http://www.springframework.org/schema/beans"
  xmlns:xsi="http://www.w3.org/2001/XMLSchema-instance"
  xsi:schemaLocation="
http://www.springframework.org/schema/beans
http://www.springframework.org/schema/beans/spring-beans-2.5.xsd">
  <bean id="simpleBean" class="com.ttdev.ss.SimpleBean">
  </bean>
</beans>
```

In order to let your implementation object (SimpleServiceSkeleton) access this simpleBean, the easiest way is to turn it into a Spring bean. So, modify the beans.xml file:

```
<beans ...>
  <bean id="simpleBean" class="com.ttdev.ss.SimpleBean">
  </bean>
  <bean id="simpleImpl" class="com.ttdev.ss.SimpleServiceSkeleton">
    <property name="simpleBean" ref="simpleBean" />
  </bean>
</beans>
```

Modify the SimpleServiceSkeleton class to have a property named "simpleBean" and use it to perform the business operation:

```
package com.ttdev.ss;

public class SimpleServiceSkeleton {
  private SimpleBean simpleBean;

  public void setSimpleBean(SimpleBean simpleBean) {
    this.simpleBean = simpleBean;
  }
  public com.ttdev.ss.ConcatResponse concat(
      com.ttdev.ss.ConcatRequest concatRequest) {
    String result = simpleBean.concat(
        concatRequest.getS1(), concatRequest.getS2());
    ConcatResponse response = new ConcatResponse();
    response.setConcatResponse(result);
    return response;
  }
}
```

Next, the most important step: You need to tell Axis2 to use this Spring bean as the service implementation object. To do that, modify the src/main/resources/META-INF/services.xml file:

Axis2 will ask this object supplier for the implementation object. This supplier will use the bean name specified here ("simpleImpl") to find and return the Spring bean.

```
<serviceGroup>
  <service name="SpringService">
    <messageReceivers>
      <messageReceiver mep="http://www.w3.org/ns/wsdl/in-out"
        class="com.ttdev.ss.SimpleServiceMessageReceiverInOut" />
    </messageReceivers>
    <parameter name="ServiceObjectSupplier">
      org.apache.axis2.extensions.spring.receivers.SpringServletContextObjectSupplier
    </parameter>
    <parameter name="SpringBeanName">simpleImpl</parameter>
    <parameter name="ServiceClass">com.ttdev.ss.SimpleServiceSkeleton</parameter>
    <parameter name="useOriginalwsdl">true</parameter>
    <parameter name="modifyUserWSDLPortAddress">true</parameter>
    <operation name="concat" mep="http://www.w3.org/ns/wsdl/in-out"
      namespace="http://ttdev.com/ss">
      <actionMapping>http://ttdev.com/ss/NewOperation
      </actionMapping>
      <outputActionMapping>
        http://ttdev.com/ss/SimpleService/concatResponse
      </outputActionMapping>
    </operation>
  </service>
</serviceGroup>
```

Don't need to specify this class anymore.

As this object supplier needs to use Spring, and it is Axis2 that calls this object supplier, you need to make the Spring jar files available to Axis2 itself. So, copy the <home>/.m2/repository/org/springframework/spring/2.5.6.SEC01/spring-2.5.6.SEC01.jar into tomcat/webapps/axis2/WEB-INF/lib.

Because when creating the simpleImpl bean, Spring will need access to your SimpleServiceSkeleton class. Therefore, it has to be available to Axis2 too. So, choose Run As | Maven package and then copy the jar file into tomcat/webapps/axis2/WEB-INF/lib.

Next, you need to tell Axis2 to initialize Spring and load your beans.xml file. So, modify tomcat/webapps/axis2/WEB-INF/web.xml:

```
<web-app>
  <display-name>Apache-Axis2</display-name>
  <listener>
    <listener-class>org.springframework.web.context.ContextLoaderListener
    </listener-class>
  </listener>
  <context-param>
    <param-name>contextConfigLocation</param-name>
    <param-value>classpath*:beans.xml</param-value>
  </context-param>
  <servlet>
    ...
  </servlet>
  ...
</web-app>
```

Now, restart Tomcat for the changes to take effect. Deploy the SpringService.jar file (copy it as an .aar file).

To test it, copy the Axis2SimpleClient and paste it as Axis2SpringClient project. The modify the SimpleClient class:

```
public class SimpleClient {
  public static void main(String[] args) throws RemoteException {
    SimpleServiceStub service = new SimpleServiceStub(
```

```
            "http://localhost:8080/axis2/services/SpringService");
        ConcatRequest request = new ConcatRequest();
        request.setS1("abc");
        request.setS2("123");
        ConcatResponse response = service.concat(request);
        System.out.println(response.getConcatResponse());
    }
}
```

Run it and it should print "abc123".

Summary

To deploy your web services with CXF in a web container, just turn your project into a web application and register the right servlet.

If you aren't using Spring, you need to load the CXF bus and set it as the default. Then publish the JAX-WS endpoints as usual. For REST resource classes, just list them in web.xml.

If you are using Spring, define your JAX-WS endpoints and REST resource beans as Spring beans and let the CXF servlet load the beans.

To deploy your web services with Axis2 in a web container, just deploy the Axis2 server as a web application. Then deploy the services as usual (as .aar files).

To use Spring with Axis2, you need to make all your classes available to Axis2 itself. Tell Axis2 to initialize Spring and point it to the location of your Spring bean definition XML file. For the service, specify to use a special object supplier in services.xml so that it will return a Spring bean as the implementation object.

Chapter 11

Unit testing your web services

What's in this chapter?

In this chapter you'll learn how to unit test your web services.

Difficulties in testing a web service in a container

If you're using Spring, usually you'll need to run your web services inside a web container such as Tomcat. If you make any changes, you'll need to restart your web application or even Tomcat in order to test them. This usually takes a lot of time.

In addition, if your implementation objects refer to Spring beans, you will ultimately invoke the real business logic and probably access the database. This will slow down the process and make it very difficult to test the web service in isolation: conversion between Java and XML, handling of WS-Security headers, given domain data is converted into the right response and etc.

Therefore, you need a way to test run your web service out of a web container and without invoking Spring beans.

Testing a web service out of container, in isolation

Let's do it. Copy the SimpleService project and paste it as a project named UnitTesting. Assuming that it uses Spring, so modify pom.xml:

```
<project ...>
  <modelVersion>4.0.0</modelVersion>
  <groupId>SimpleService</groupId>
  <artifactId>SimpleService</artifactId>
  <version>0.0.1-SNAPSHOT</version>
  <dependencies>
    <dependency>
      <groupId>org.apache.cxf</groupId>
      <artifactId>cxf-bundle</artifactId>
      <version>2.2.5</version>
    </dependency>
    <dependency>
      <groupId>xerces</groupId>
      <artifactId>xercesImpl</artifactId>
      <version>2.9.1</version>
    </dependency>
    <dependency>
      <groupId>org.springframework</groupId>
      <artifactId>spring-test</artifactId>
      <version>2.5.6.SEC01</version>
    </dependency>
  </dependencies>
  ...
</project>
```

Rename the WSDL as ComputeService.wsdl and modify it as shown below:

```
<?xml version="1.0" encoding="UTF-8" standalone="no"?>
<wsdl:definitions xmlns:soap="http://schemas.xmlsoap.org/wsdl/soap/"
  xmlns:tns="http://ttdev.com/cs" xmlns:wsdl="http://schemas.xmlsoap.org/wsdl/"
  xmlns:xsd="http://www.w3.org/2001/XMLSchema" name="ComputeService"
  targetNamespace="http://ttdev.com/cs">
```

```
<wsdl:types>
  <xsd:schema targetNamespace="http://ttdev.com/cs">
    <xsd:element name="compute" type="xsd:string">
    </xsd:element>
    <xsd:element name="computeResponse" type="xsd:string">
    </xsd:element>
  </xsd:schema>
</wsdl:types>
<wsdl:message name="computeRequest">
  <wsdl:part element="tns:compute" name="parameters" />
</wsdl:message>
<wsdl:message name="computeResponse">
  <wsdl:part element="tns:computeResponse" name="parameters" />
</wsdl:message>
<wsdl:portType name="ComputeService">
  <wsdl:operation name="compute">
    <wsdl:input message="tns:computeRequest" />
    <wsdl:output message="tns:computeResponse" />
  </wsdl:operation>
</wsdl:portType>
<wsdl:binding name="ComputeServiceSOAP" type="tns:ComputeService">
  <soap:binding style="document"
    transport="http://schemas.xmlsoap.org/soap/http" />
  <wsdl:operation name="compute">
    <soap:operation soapAction="http://ttdev.com/cs/compute" />
    <wsdl:input>
      <soap:body use="literal" />
    </wsdl:input>
    <wsdl:output>
      <soap:body use="literal" />
    </wsdl:output>
  </wsdl:operation>
</wsdl:binding>
<wsdl:service name="ComputeService">
  <wsdl:port binding="tns:ComputeServiceSOAP" name="p1">
    <soap:address location="http://localhost:8080/cs/p1" />
  </wsdl:port>
</wsdl:service>
</wsdl:definitions>
```

There is nothing special about it. Modify the CodeGenerator class:

```
public class CodeGenerator {
  public static void main(String[] args) {
    WSDLToJava.main(new String[] {
        "-server",
        "-d", "src/main/java",
        "src/main/resources/ComputeService.wsdl" });
    System.out.println("Done!");
  }
}
```

Delete the com.ttdev.ss package and run the CodeGenerator. Then create the ComputeServiceImpl class:

```
package com.ttdev.cs;

import javax.jws.WebService;

@WebService(endpointInterface = "com.ttdev.cs.ComputeService")
public class ComputeServiceImpl implements ComputeService {
  private ComplexLogic logic;

  public void setLogic(ComplexLogic logic) {
    this.logic = logic;
  }
  @Override
  public String compute(String parameters) {
    return logic.calc(parameters);
```

```
  }
}
```

The ComplexLogic interface represents some complex business logic. Create this interface as:

```
package com.ttdev.cs;

public interface ComplexLogic {
  String calc(String s);
}
```

Create the implementation which will be a Spring bean. As promised, you'll never be invoking this Spring bean during unit testing, so you can do whatever you like in the calc() method for this exercise because it will only be called in production:

```
package com.ttdev.cs;

public class ComplexLogicImpl implements ComplexLogic {

  @Override
  public String calc(String s) {
    throw new RuntimeException("not implemented");
  }
}
```

For deployment, create a beans.xml file in src/main/resources (if it is to be deployed as a web application, use it as the cxf-servlet.xml file):

```
<beans xmlns="http://www.springframework.org/schema/beans"
  xmlns:xsi="http://www.w3.org/2001/XMLSchema-instance"
xmlns:jaxws="http://cxf.apache.org/jaxws"
  xsi:schemaLocation="
http://www.springframework.org/schema/beans
http://www.springframework.org/schema/beans/spring-beans-2.5.xsd
http://cxf.apache.org/jaxws http://cxf.apache.org/schemas/jaxws.xsd">
  <bean id="logic" class="com.ttdev.cs.ComplexLogicImpl">
  </bean>
  <bean id="serviceImpl" class="com.ttdev.cs.ComputeServiceImpl">
    <property name="logic" ref="logic" />
  </bean>
  <jaxws:endpoint id="endPoint1" address="/p1"
    implementor="#serviceImpl">
  </jaxws:endpoint>
</beans>
```

To unit test the web service, create the src/test/java folder and src/test/resources folder. You will put Java files and resource files that are used for testing only (not for production) into those folders respectively. Then update the project configuration.

Next, create a ClientCodeGenerator class in the com.ttdev package in the src/test/java folder:

```
package com.ttdev;

import org.apache.cxf.tools.wsdlto.WSDLToJava;

public class ClientCodeGenerator {
  public static void main(String[] args) {
    WSDLToJava.main(new String[] {
        "-client",
        "-d", "src/test/java",
        "-p", "http://ttdev.com/cs=com.ttdev.cs.client",
        "src/main/resources/ComputeService.wsdl" });
    System.out.println("Done!");
```

```
    }
  }
```

Run it to generate code for the client that you'll use to test drive the web service. Then create a ComputeServiceTest class in the com.ttdev.cs package in the src/test/java folder:

```
package com.ttdev.cs;

import org.apache.cxf.Bus;
import org.apache.cxf.bus.spring.SpringBusFactory;
import org.springframework.test.context.ContextConfiguration;
import org.springframework.test.context.junit38.AbstractJUnit38SpringContextTests;
...
@ContextConfiguration(locations = { "/beans.xml" })
public class ComputeServiceTest extends AbstractJUnit38SpringContextTests {
  private Bus bus;

  @Override
  protected void setUp() throws Exception {
    initBus();
  }
  @Override
  protected void tearDown() throws Exception {
    bus.shutdown(false);
  }
  public void testCompute() {
    ComputeServiceImpl impl = (ComputeServiceImpl) applicationContext
        .getBean("serviceImpl");
    impl.setLogic(new ComplexLogic() {

      @Override
      public String calc(String s) {
        return s.toUpperCase();
      }
    });
    ComputeService_Service ss = new ComputeService_Service();
    ComputeService port = ss.getP1();
    assertEquals(port.compute("xyz"), "XYZ");
  }
  private void initBus() {
    bus = new SpringBusFactory(applicationContext).createBus();
  }
}
```

Tell Spring to load this beans.xml file.

This class is provided by Spring to allow you to test Spring beans easily.

This is the Spring application context created by the base class.

Load your service implementation object Spring bean.

Make the implementation object use a mock ComplexLogic object. Instead of doing complex calculation, its calc() method will only convert the argument to upper case.

Use the client to call the service. It should convert "xyz" to "XYZ".

This bus factory will look up the bus as a Spring bean when it needs to create one.

In order to provide the CXF bus out of a web container, create a Spring bean XML file, say, src/test/resources/beans-test.xml, to define the CXF-related beans (including the bus) as shown below. This file will define Spring beans used for unit testing only:

```
<beans xmlns="http://www.springframework.org/schema/beans"
  xmlns:xsi="http://www.w3.org/2001/XMLSchema-instance"
  xsi:schemaLocation="
http://www.springframework.org/schema/beans
http://www.springframework.org/schema/beans/spring-beans-2.5.xsd">
  <import resource="classpath:META-INF/cxf/cxf.xml" />
  <import resource="classpath:META-INF/cxf/cxf-extension-soap.xml" />
</beans>
```

This step is not needed in production because the CXFServlet will have done that automatically.

Tell the unit test base class to load this file after loading the beans.xml file (which is for production):

```
@ContextConfiguration(locations = { "/beans.xml", "/beans-test.xml" })
public class ComputeServiceTest extends AbstractJUnit38SpringContextTests {
  ...
}
```

However, your endpoint has been configured to listen on a path only, instead of a full URL:

```
<beans ...>
  <bean id="logic" class="com.ttdev.cs.ComplexLogicImpl">
  </bean>
  <bean id="serviceImpl" class="com.ttdev.cs.ComputeServiceImpl">
    <property name="logic" ref="logic" />
  </bean>
  <jaxws:endpoint id="endPoint1" address="/p1"
    implementor="#serviceImpl">
  </jaxws:endpoint>
</beans>
```

This will only work in a web application. For unit testing, you need to use a full URL. So, modify beans-test.xml to override this "endPoint1" bean:

```
<beans ...
  xmlns:jaxws="http://cxf.apache.org/jaxws"
  xsi:schemaLocation="
http://www.springframework.org/schema/beans
http://www.springframework.org/schema/beans/spring-beans-2.5.xsd
http://cxf.apache.org/jaxws http://cxf.apache.org/schemas/jaxws.xsd">
  <import resource="classpath:META-INF/cxf/cxf.xml" />
  <import resource="classpath:META-INF/cxf/cxf-extension-soap.xml" />
  <jaxws:endpoint id="endPoint1" address="local://ep1"
    implementor="#serviceImpl">
  </jaxws:endpoint>
</beans>
```

What is this local:// protocol? It is designed for testing. It is like the loopback network interface: the service can listen on, say, local://foo, then whatever the client sends to local://foo will be received by that service, without going through a web container. In order to use this local protocol, you need to define a factory for it:

```
<beans ...>
  <import resource="classpath:META-INF/cxf/cxf.xml" />
  <import resource="classpath:META-INF/cxf/cxf-extension-soap.xml" />
  <bean id="localTransportFactory"
class="org.apache.cxf.transport.local.LocalTransportFactory">
  </bean>
  <jaxws:endpoint id="endPoint1" address="local://ep1"
    implementor="#serviceImpl">
  </jaxws:endpoint>
</beans>
```

Modify the unit test to use the same local protocol factory on the client side and let the client connect to local://ep1:

```
import org.apache.cxf.transport.ConduitInitiatorManager;
import org.apache.cxf.transport.local.LocalTransportFactory;
..
@ContextConfiguration(locations = { "/beans.xml", "/beans-test.xml" })
public class ComputeServiceTest extends AbstractJUnit38SpringContextTests {
  private Bus bus;

  @Override
  protected void setUp() throws Exception {
    initBus();
  }
```

```
  @Override
  protected void tearDown() throws Exception {
    bus.shutdown(false);
  }
  public void testCompute() {
    ComputeServiceImpl impl = (ComputeServiceImpl) applicationContext
        .getBean("serviceImpl");
    impl.setLogic(new ComplexLogic() {

      @Override
      public String calc(String s) {
        return s.toUpperCase();
      }
    });
    ComputeService_Service ss = new ComputeService_Service();
    ComputeService port = ss.getP1();
    setAddress(port, "local://ep1");
    assertEquals(port.compute("xyz"), "XYZ");
  }
  private void setAddress(ComputeService port, String addr) {
    BindingProvider bp = (BindingProvider) port;
    bp.getRequestContext().put(BindingProvider.ENDPOINT_ADDRESS_PROPERTY,
        addr);
  }
  private void initBus() {
    bus = new SpringBusFactory(applicationContext).createBus();
    setupLocalTransport();
  }
  private void setupLocalTransport() {
    LocalTransportFactory localTransportFactory = (LocalTransportFactory)
applicationContext.getBean("localTransportFactory");
    ConduitInitiatorManager cim = bus
        .getExtension(ConduitInitiatorManager.class);
    cim.registerConduitInitiator("http://cxf.apache.org/transports/local",
        localTransportFactory);
    cim.registerConduitInitiator(
        "http://schemas.xmlsoap.org/wsdl/soap/http",
        localTransportFactory);
    cim.registerConduitInitiator("http://schemas.xmlsoap.org/soap/http",
        localTransportFactory);
    cim.registerConduitInitiator("http://cxf.apache.org/bindings/xformat",
        localTransportFactory);
  }
}
```

Now, right click the ComputeServiceTest class and choose Run As | JUnit Test. Then you should see some messages in the console. The JUnit window should say that the test has passed:

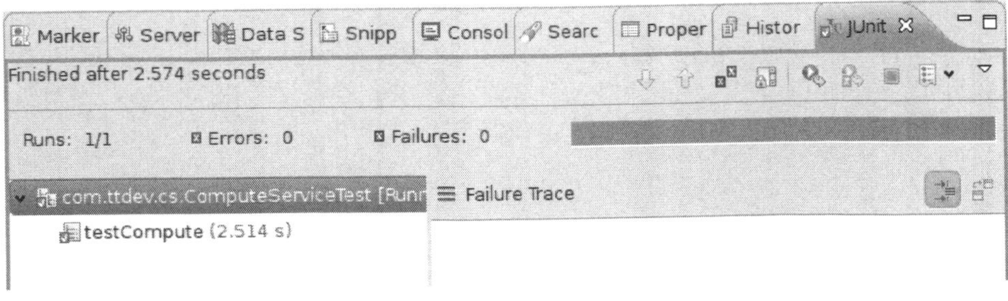

Summary

To unit test your web services, you should run them out of a web container and stop invoking Spring beans. To run CXF out of a web container, you can import the CXF Spring XML files. To stop your implementation objects from invoking Spring beans, just call their setters to put in mock objects.

For testing, you need to specify the full URL for your endpoints. A good way to do is to use the local:// protocol for faster speed. To set up the local protocol, you need to define the local transport factory as Spring bean on the server side and register it properly on the client side.

References

- Axis2 developers. Axis2 Documentation. http://ws.apache.org/axis2.
- CXF developers. CXF Documentation. http://cwiki.apache.org/CXF20DOC/index.html.
- IBM. Develop asynchronous Web services with Axis2. http://www.ibm.com/developerworks/webservices/library/ws-axis2.
- Nadana Mihindukulasooriya. WS - Security Policy. http://nandanasm.wordpress.com/2007/10/31/ws-security-policy/
- OASIS. Web Services Security: SOAP Message Security 1.1 (WS-Security 2004). http://docs.oasis-open.org/wss/v1.1.
- OASIS. WS-SecurityPolicy 1.3. http://docs.oasis-open.org/ws-sx/ws-securitypolicy/v1.3/os/ws-securitypolicy-1.3-spec-os.html.
- OASIS. Web Services Security UsernameToken Profile 1.0. http://docs.oasis-open.org/wss/2004/01/oasis-200401-wss-username-token-profile-1.0.
- OASIS. Web Services Security X.509 Certificate Token Profile. http://docs.oasis-open.org/wss/2004/01/oasis-200401-wss-x509-token-profile-1.0.
- Rampart developers. Rampart Documentation. http://ws.apache.org/rampart.
- Roy Thomas Fielding. Representational State Transfer (REST). http://www.ics.uci.edu/~fielding/pubs/dissertation/rest_arch_style.htm.
- Russell Butek. Which style of WSDL should I use? http://www-128.ibm.com/developerworks/webservices/library/ws-whichwsdl/?ca=dgr-devx-WebServicesMVP03.
- SpringSource. The Spring Framework 2.5 Reference Manual. http://static.springframework.org/spring/docs/2.5.x/reference/index.html.
- Sun Microsystems. JAX-WS specification. http://jcp.org/en/jsr/detail?id=224.
- Sun Microsystems. JAX-RS specification. https://jsr311.dev.java.net.
- Sun Microsystems. JAXB specification. https://jaxb.dev.java.net.
- Tomcat developers. Tomcat Documentation. http://jakarta.apache.org/tomcat.
- W3C. Decryption Transform for XML Signature. http://www.w3.org/TR/2002/CR-xmlenc-decrypt-20020304.
- W3C. Hypertext Transfer Protocol – HTTP/1.1. http://www.w3.org/Protocols/rfc2616/rfc2616.html.

- W3C. Namespaces in XML. http://www.w3.org/TR/1999/REC-xml-names-19990114.
- W3C. Simple Object Access Protocol (SOAP) 1.1. http://www.w3.org/TR/2000/NOTE-SOAP-20000508.
- W3C. SOAP Message Transmission Optimization Mechanism. http://www.w3.org/TR/soap12-mtom.
- W3C. URIs, URLs, and URNs: Clarifications and Recommendations 1.0. http://www.w3.org/TR/2001/NOTE-uri-clarification-20010921.
- W3C. Web Services Addressing 1.0 – Core. http://www.w3.org/TR/ws-addr-core.
- W3C. Web Services Addressing 1.0 - SOAP Binding. http://www.w3.org/TR/ws-addr-soap.
- W3C. Web Services Addressing 1.0 – Core. http://www.w3.org/TR/ws-addr-core.
- W3C. Web Services Addressing 1.0 - WSDL Binding. http://www.w3.org/TR/ws-addr-wsdl.
- W3C. Web Services Description Language (WSDL) 1.1. http://www.w3.org/TR/2001/NOTE-wsdl-20010315.
- W3C. Web Services Policy 1.5 - Framework. http://www.w3.org/TR/2006/WD-ws-policy-20061117.
- W3C. XML-binary Optimized Packaging. http://www.w3.org/TR/xop10.
- W3C. XML Encryption Syntax and Processing. http://www.w3.org/TR/2002/REC-xmlenc-core-20021210.
- W3C. XML Schema Part 0: Primer Second Edition. http://www.w3.org/TR/2004/REC-xmlschema-0-20041028.
- W3C. XML Schema Part 1: Structures Second Edition. http://www.w3.org/TR/2004/REC-xmlschema-1-20041028.
- W3C. XML Schema Part 2: Datatypes Second Edition. http://www.w3.org/TR/2004/REC-xmlschema-2-20041028.
- W3C. XML-Signature Syntax and Processing. http://www.w3.org/TR/2002/REC-xmldsig-core-20020212.
- W3C. XSL Transformations (XSLT). http://www.w3.org/TR/xslt.
- Will Provost. WSDL First. http://webservices.xml.com/pub/a/ws/2003/07/22/wsdlfirst.html.
- WS-I. WS-I Basic Profile Version 1.0. http://www.ws-i.org/Profiles/BasicProfile-1.0-2004-04-16.html.
- WSS4J developers. WSS4J Axis Deployment Tutorial.

http://ws.apache.org/wss4j/axis.html.

Alphabetical Index

Made in the USA
Middletown, DE
13 October 2015